THIRTEEN AMERICANS:

THEIR
SPIRITUAL AUTOBIOGRAPHIES

[Institute for Religious and Social Studies...]

RELIGION AND CIVILIZATION SERIES

THIRTEEN AMERICANS:

THEIR
SPIRITUAL AUTOBIOGRAPHIES

EDITED BY

Louis Finkelstein
CHANCELLOR, THE JEWISH THEOLOGICAL SEMINARY OF AMERICA

KENNIKAT PRESS, INC./PORT WASHINGTON, N. Y.

To

FRIEDA SCHIFF WARBURG

with affection and admiration
this book is dedicated

February 3, 1953

128531

THE INSTITUTE FOR RELIGIOUS AND SOCIAL STUDIES
THIRTEEN AMERICANS: THEIR SPIRITUAL AUTOBIOGRAPHIES

Copyright 1953 By The Institute For Religious And Social Studies
Reissued 1969 By Kennikat Press
By arrangement with Harper & Row, Publishers, Incorporated

Library of Congress Catalog Card No: 68-26190
Manufactured in the United States of America

ESSAY AND GENERAL LITERATURE INDEX REPRINT SERIES

This volume includes eleven lectures given at The Institute for Religious and Social Studies of The Jewish Theological Seminary of America during the winter of 1949–1950. Unfortunately Dr. Adolf A. Berle, Jr., could not write for publication his address in the series. The chapters by Mrs. Lieberman and Mr. Pickett were written solely for the book and were not delivered as addresses. Each chapter in this volume represents solely the individual opinion of the author.

CONTENTS

Preface by Louis Finkelstein	xi
Clarence E. Pickett	1
Ordway Tead	15
Henry Norris Russell	31
Edwin Grant Conklin	47
Richard McKeon	77
Erwin D. Canham	115
Elbert D. Thomas	129
Judith Berlin Lieberman	159
Channing H. Tobias	177
David de Sola Pool	201
Basil O'Connor	219
Willard L. Sperry	231
Julian Morgenstern	253
Biographical Sketches	275
Index	285

PREFACE

In the present volume of spiritual autobiographies, as in its predecessor, an effort has been made to bring before the public types of personality, which seem to be contributing to the preservation and advancement of civilization. Like all other human beings, those who have had the boldness and courage to reveal the secrets of their being, as they understand them, are limited and finite in outlook and in understanding. Yet unlike many others, they appear to be making a determined effort to transcend this finitude. Though they differ widely among themselves, they have this trait in common—they approach all other human beings with respect and affection. If it cannot be said that nothing human is alien to them, it may be said with precision that none of them regards any human being as alien to him.

It is impressive to note how this trait affects the action and thought of the people here described, and also how each of them interprets his outlook in terms of his particular tradition and background. It is also comforting to consider that the writers of these autobiographies differ from other people only in the extent of their dedication, and in the scope of causes they serve, but not in kind. If the trait common to all the participants in this series is regarded as "saintliness" or at least a degree of it, it may be said appropriately that this is a quality far more widespread among men than most of us suppose.

To me, one of the main joys in reading this volume has been to think of the manner in which character is moulded in the home. Through these pages we can trace the spiritual growth not only of the writers but of those who stimulated and encouraged them; namely, their parents.

I have found companionship and communion with the people

represented in this work an inspiration; and I part with it in the hope that this inspiration may in some degree also be shared by its readers.

As I write these words, I must record with sorrow that one of the writers, Professor Edwin G. Conklin, died on November 20, 1952. His passing is a personal loss to me, and it is a source of particularly poignant regret that he did not live to see this printed volume, in which he showed such real interest.

LOUIS FINKELSTEIN

January 14, 1953

THIRTEEN AMERICANS:

THEIR
SPIRITUAL AUTOBIOGRAPHIES

CLARENCE E. PICKETT

One day my mother, then well over eighty years old, told me in confidence a great secret. All my life, she had kept this tucked away in her innermost heart, biding the time when she felt it was appropriate to tell me. The secret was that when she found I was due to arrive in this world, the ninth child to whom she had given birth, seven of whom were still living, she was resentful. She was a little woman; she had little help in the house, except what the children could give to her; she was worn down and had supposed that she was beyond the age for child bearing. But the longed for rest from child bearing was not to be and for a time she was bitter. She told me of the spiritual struggle through which she went. But finally she came to the firm resolve to purge her spirit of all resentment, to look forward cheerfully to the arrival of a new child, and to pray that he might be a devoted and useful member of the Kingdom of Heaven on earth, in which she so profoundly believed. Although at times she was quite unwell, she was able to maintain this attitude of mind while I was in prenatal preparation for launching on an earthly career.

This explained to me the conversation that she had had with me when I was about ten years old. We lived on a Kansas farm, and as a growing boy one of my chores was to help with the vegetable garden. My mother and I were working in the garden together one day when she confided to me that she earnestly hoped I would be a missionary. My older sister, Minnie, had just gone to Japan, where she was to spend nearly fifty years of her life as a missionary. The current conception of the most complete devotion to one's religious faith was to become a missionary. Sharing that point of view, my mother had now expressed this vocational preference for me. And while in the technical sense her ambition has never been realized, I am sure that that first expression on her part, consistent as it was with her prenatal concern for me, has had no little influence on the direction which my life has taken.

The influence of my father, while in full sympathy with this point of view, was brought to bear upon me in a different way. I am sure he never thought of the incidents that I am about to relate as being of special importance to his growing son. Nevertheless, in retrospect I see them as having a genuine spiritual influence. I had been born in Illinois in a little Quaker community thirty miles south of Chicago. But the attractiveness of that rich land had drawn to our community a large number of German Lutherans. Many retained the practice of speaking the German language. They seemed strange to us, and my father with a growing family was somewhat apprehensive of the influence of these newcomers on his children. Other factors, however, were responsible for his decision to move farther to the West. An inner struggle within the Society of Friends had resulted in wide differences of opinion concerning matters of practice and belief, and the little Quaker Meeting to which our family belonged had its share of dissension. To my father this was very disconcerting. Then there was the depression of the late '8os, which had made the economic struggle most difficult. My father made a trip to Kansas and there found a little colony where Quakers had built an academy, where there was a thriving and united Quaker Meeting. But one thing deeply disturbed him, and to that he resolved to make a contribution. The disturbing factor was the scrawny nature of the work horses which Kansas farmers used. He sold his farm in Illinois, bought two Percheron mares and a stallion with the avowed purpose of improving the breed of Kansas horses, not only for himself, but in the community at large to which he was going. That ambition was abundantly realized, and in this unusual fashion he made perhaps his most significant contribution to the economic life of the new community to which he took his growing family. His sense of mission concerning good and useful horseflesh was, I am sure, of more significance to his growing son than he had any notion. It was his form of technical assistance!

The other story has to do with his deep and abiding sense of integrity. I was nine years younger than the brother next to me, and when all of them had left on their own, it was I who was looked to, to carry on the farm. During the later years of his life, my father was an invalid from rheumatism. We still owed $2,500 on the farm, a big debt in those days. My secret hope was to be able to get away to college when the debt was paid. We had grown a fine crop of hogs for the market, and together with other income, it looked as though at last we were going to be able to eliminate the mortgage. The hogs were almost ready for market, when one Sunday morning I went out to feed them and found one dead. Once cholera has started in a drove of hogs, it is likely that it will take the whole lot. A common practice, when the disease first appeared, was to rush all the well hogs to market hoping to get them to the packers without too much loss. Whether the contamination of hogflesh was transferable to humans who ate the diseased meat was an open question, but my father feared that it might jeopardize the health of the people who bought the meat. Without a moment's hesitation, therefore, he resolved not to run that risk and sent me to the nearby village where I routed out the railway station man (no trains ran on Sundays) and got him to telegraph to Kansas City for a new cure for hog cholera. The net result was that we saved a number of the hogs that were infected with the disease, but we had to fatten them all over again. With that additional expense all profits were gone. My plans for getting off to school had to be postponed. But the memory of that quick and accurate moral judgment of values on the part of my father always stayed with me as a contribution far more valuable than anything I would have gained by entering college one or two years earlier than I did.

Our home was a devout one; we were always at Meeting on Sunday; we had prayers and Bible reading at every breakfast time. When wheat harvest and threshing time came around, it was always a temptation to question whether we might not forego Bible reading and prayer during this special harvest season because we had so many hired hands about. But as far as my memory goes, no such accommodation was made. Nor was it simply my father offering a formal prayer on behalf of his family, but encouragement was given to any or all children or visitors to participate in the act of petition to a God Who was concerned with our welfare. Well do I remember times when, as a growing boy, I was anxious to get through with the ceremony and out into the more active pursuits of the day, but this performance was far more than a formal affair. Every attempt was made to make it a genuine moment of communion between the finite and the infinite. Whatever else may have come from that practice, I am sure there was built into my consciousness what still remains—namely, the closeness and intimacy of God with all of His children, even though He is unseen and often unrecognized. Religion was never forced upon members of our household, and I never knew of any of the family resenting the devotional practices which were carried on. And I am sure that the reason we escaped any sense of cynicism or complaint was that without ever putting it into words we recognized the deep integrity and consistency of our parents' lives.

As I see it now there was also a kind of holy restlessness which manifested itself from time to time in our family. My oldest brother had become a school teacher in the old community in Illinois. But partly because he did not think his little brood of growing boys ought to be brought up in town, and partly because of his yen for exploration, he decided to see what could be done to resettle his family on the land. He rode his bicycle from Illinois to our home in Kansas for a brief visit, and then on to Colorado where he found a setting as a market gardener to which he brought his family of four boys and a girl. My sister, Minnie, responding to this urge of the spirit, went East to Philadelphia to spend a year in study, and then was sent by Philadelphia Quakers as a teacher in the Friends' Girls School in Tokyo. I did not know then that Gilbert Bowles had asked for her hand in marriage and had been told that if after her five year term in Japan each of them still wanted to proceed with marriage it would be allowed. But that was really what happened.

I remember the day we hitched up two big work horses to a heavy lumber wagon and drove three and a half miles to the nearby town to put my sister on the train when she started on this long trip to the West Coast and then across the Pacific Ocean. She was a great letter writer. Letters came in rolls, yards in length. They were descriptive of Japan, of Japanese life, of her own work, of her interest in her family, and especially of her hope and aspirations for the growing, youngest member of the family. She did not like my writing, and sent me copies which I was to duplicate with my own efforts and return to her for criticism. But the mystery, and the glamor, and the buoyance of her life as revealed in these letters, I am sure, tended to turn my mind in the direction of some form of social-religious service, and toward new horizons.

Yes, my yen for exploration was caught by me partly from the intriguing experiences which my elder brothers and sisters were going through. One went off to Oklahoma to start life for himself; another married a Methodist minister, and the stories of their movings from one small parish to another almost yearly sounded to me like a wonderful life. I scarcely think it seemed so wonderful to my sister, who had to do the moving.

Anyway, from somewhere came not so much a specific decision but the assumption that of course I would go to college. None of my brothers or sisters had had this privilege, and I cannot tell where my assumption came from. Perhaps it was the suggestion of some of the older members of my family who had had some taste of higher learning and who wanted more of it.

Then there was by chance that precious year of high school when for some reason the village had invited a Quaker from Maine to be the superintendent of the school. He was a man of deep, religious spirit and of genuine literary culture. I had never met anyone quite like him. I think it was a hard year for him, because many of the students who came to high school had very inadequate preparation. But his wide knowledge of literature, of astronomy, of various parts of our own country, and his deep religious spirit I think unconsciously made me want to be like him.

One other factor in our community life which I am sure had its influence on me was the development of the Society of Friends. My earlier days were spent in a Meeting where we had no professional pastor; the ministry came from our neighbors, all of whom were farmers. James Pitts, our neighbor to the south, although a man of little formal education, had read widely, and as I think back now to the frequent and brief contributions that he made in our meetings for worship, I realize that they were profound, searching, and sometimes even eloquent. My family felt that he indulged in words that were not commonly understood sometimes; he certainly did have an unusual vocabulary, but he was a great spirit and of a very sound mind.

We were a little colony of Quakers, but we had some sense of responsibility for the people on the periphery of the community, whose habits sometimes showed up in objectionable ways. Now and again we would hear of drinking and dancing parties, quite unknown to our community. A professional minister came along imbued with the revivalist spirit of that time. He held a series of revival meetings in our community, and some of the people of whom we had been critical were "converted" and joined our Meeting. This expansion of interest and responsibility led to an important step. We employed the revival minister to be our pastor. I saw this process going on and welcomed it as a genuine progress. Perhaps it was. Over the years I have found myself welcoming the opportunity to return to the religious service where no professional leadership is required, but where the ministry arises out of the experience and the search of the members of the group itself.

We also took on more the color of general Protestantism when we organized the Christian Endeavor Society. This movement starting in the Congregational Church in Portland, Maine, swept throughout churches of the country as a great young people's movement. Each member who joined accepted the responsibility to participate in some way in each meeting that was held. While I was later to study in a theological seminary and take training in public speaking, no course I ever had in the art of public address did more to enable me to get on my feet and express myself than the experience in that little

Christian Endeavor Society. I am not sure how much it deepened my spiritual life, but it did have the effect of enabling one to give expression to his thoughts and experiences; sometimes I am afraid it was a bit perfunctory, but it was a good training ground.

The other and more searching influence which came from the nature of our community was the occasional traveling minister who came to our Meeting. Our house was the largest one in the community, and, therefore, the visiting minister usually stayed with us. I can recall at least a score of men and women who became members of our household for a few days or for as much as two months, who came from various parts of the country as concerned Quakers to nourish the growing life of the spirit in these scattered groups and colonies of Friends in the western prairies. Among all the visits, that of Henry Stanley Newman then editor of *The Friend,* an English Quaker magazine, stands out as of special significance. On Monday mornings we always did the family washing, and as a growing boy my job was to run the washing machine. Never shall I forget how surprised and gratified I was when this distinguished and somewhat austere Friend from England helped me run the washing machine on Monday morning after his speaking to us at our Meeting for Worship on the preceding day. As we alternated in turning the handle, he talked to me about life in England and of the orphanage that he had helped to establish, about the Quaker schools in England, and the Quaker Meetings. And when he went away, I am sure there was planted deep within me a feel for spiritual maturity which I had not known before.

I was twenty-two years old when I went to Penn College in Iowa. This struggling little institution, with the poorest of buildings and facilities, had a few great teachers. There was Dr. Stephen Hadley, who always seemed to me a paragon of learning, who through the instruments of calculus and astronomy instilled the concept of accuracy and precision in thinking, and who always left the impression with me that it was possible to develop the same accuracy in moral and spiritual judgments. Without being arrogant, he seemed to have endless assurance of the rightness of the decision which he reached, which was a good counterbalance to the age of relativity

I was soon to encounter. I have never known a better teacher anywhere than Rosa Lewis, who introduced me to Shakespeare, and Browning, and Wordsworth. Her beauty of appearance, her charm of manner, her effectiveness in speech, her personal interest in her students, at least illustrated what life might be. Then there was William Berry, teacher of the classical languages. He experimented with a class in Hebrew in my day. Alexander Purdy, a lifelong friend, and myself survived the year's course. But for me at least that innocent study of the language was really the beginning of understanding a critical study of the Bible and was an introduction to the thought and spirit of its authors. Professor Berry did not have to point out to us that there were two very different stories of the Creation in the book of Genesis. We discovered it ourselves and wondered how it could all happen. That day there was great fear on the part of many devoutly religious people that a critical study of the scriptural text would destroy faith. I have always been grateful that my approach to that problem was through the instrument of language. I cannot see how anyone can study the Hebrew text without coming away from it with a deepened sense that what we have is not a piece of literature mechanically produced, but one which grows out of the long hard struggle of a group of God's children to find the way to moral conduct and spiritual appreciation through many failures and some successes, and over thousands of years. To some, too, comes the sense of the rebel, the prophet who defies the customs, the mores, and the practices of his own time, who listens for the moral judgments of God Himself and not the evil which his neighbors practice. One saw the relative unimportance of the state, as compared with the central importance of the spirit of a dedicated life. One understood why Isaiah or why Amos had long outlived, in importance, any of the kings or states.

I was in college when the Student Volunteer Movement was at its height. Of all the extracurricular activities, none excepted, I believe it would be fair to say that the most highly respected group on the campus was this little band of students who anticipated being missionaries. The evangelization of the world in this generation was the great cry being sounded throughout the Christian world. There was a strong sentiment in our college for sharing in this great enter-prise. Little did we know, however, that the evangelization of the world was needed about as much at home as anywhere. But the inevitable happened. Those who belonged to our Student Volunteer Movement discovered this to be true. As I look back on it now, I cannot think of a single one who was in that band, who spent a life-time in the mission field outside of this country; a few had short terms teaching in foreign countries. But what the group really represented was a vocational fellowship of those who had tried to take seriously their religious life. Had the band in my college been centered around that motive, it would have more nearly represented what was to happen. There were three callings that we knew about: farming, school teaching, and some kind of definite religious activity. And although most of us came from the farm, the college turned out to be an orientation course for urban living for a great majority. One may regret that such a great migration was taking place from the farm to the city, but it was happening, and under those circumstances Penn College was for me about as good an introduction as I could have had to urban life. It talked not about adaptation, but attempted to cultivate the fundamental values of life, and put a high premium on the significance of men as God's children. While there was some feeling of being on the escalator going up and a kind of predestination of success, there was no illusion that success came without dedication and hard work. But I think we never could imagine the possibility of war happening again. Perhaps the phase of life which had least meaning for us was suffering. Many a time in later years, in dealing with individuals and groups of people who were hungry, and naked, and homeless, or in prison, mostly as a result of war, I have had to face in a way that I never could do in college, the significance of suffering in life.

Of course, during college days, one of necessity has his mind on what he is going to do in life. Three courses seemed available to me: teaching, farming, and the ministry. I cannot claim that a voice from heaven directed me, and I cannot say why, but I chose the ministry. It was partly because two ministers of great skill and of fine character crossed my path: Ellison R. Purdy, who was minister at the Quaker Meeting at Oskaloosa, Iowa, while I was in college there, and Charles M. Woodman, who visited our community during my college career and spoke very much to my condition. Both of these men were parish ministers, and the kind of men they were as well as their facility in expression, I am sure, affected my choice a good deal. In all honesty, it perhaps ought to be said that the fact that one could get a scholarship in a theological seminary, whereas such opportunities in other fields were not then as well known, may have had some influence. At any rate, I went to Hartford Theological Seminary for the next three years. I was just ripe for what Hartford had to offer. A warm fellowship of able, like minded men, who were much more sophisticated than I, and with whom I lived in the intimacy of dormitory life, stretched my spiritual horizon and expectations enormously. And the discipline of a scholarship centered with great rigor on church history, theology, and the text of the sacred scriptures, while difficult for me, was most rewarding. It was during my time in the seminary that Dr. William Douglas McKenzie, the president of the seminary, published his book, *The Final Faith*. In that volume, this huge, stalwart, Christian theologian sought to prove that Christianity was the one, only, and final faith. I had never been dealt with quite on that scholarly basis, and it was excellent discipline. Since then I have come to know many great spirits whose dogma was less emphatic but whose grasp of the reality of the spiritual life has led me further than any dogma, however clearly reasoned. I now find *The Final Faith* an inward experience much more than an outward confession. I find some of Dr. McKenzie's book very unsatisfying to me, but he did give me a good, strong anchor from which my mental and spiritual explorations could go forth.

I entered with zest into the parish ministry, first in Toronto in a Quaker Meeting and later at the Meeting which was attended by large numbers of the students at Penn College in Oskaloosa, Iowa. In both cases, my ambition was to work myself out of a job. It seemed to me that the recovery of a general sense of responsibility for the conduct of the Meeting by the total congregation was the goal that I ought to seek. I felt in Toronto that I made almost no progress in that direction, but I am happy to say that over the years which succeeded my service there, this transition has taken place in that group of worshipers. For the most part, it seemed to me that the congregation tended to become more dependent upon the minister rather than less the longer I stayed with it, and that therefore my ambition was one that could never be realized.

It was somewhat, perhaps, in this frame of mind that I welcomed the opportunity when I was invited to assume leadership in what was known then as the Young Friends' Movement across the country. For three years I worked with that organization, and then became professor of biblical literature at Earlham College. In both of these attempts, as well as in my parish ministry, viewing them in retrospect, the chief function that I served was to find out what were the yearnings in minds, in younger people especially, and to see if I could help in preparing them to fulfil their aspirations; also to help open channels of service where they could work at something to which they were dedicated and in which they were fully interested.

It was in 1929 that I came to the American Friends Service Committee, and if I have accomplished anything in more than twenty years of service with this Committee, I think it is chiefly in helping to find ways in which younger and older people can give of themselves to the need of humanity, renewing and revitalizing their own faith in the process, and perhaps adding some strength to the healing current of the life of the spirit in the world.

The life that I have led has been an active one which fits in with my own temperament. Life, however, tended to deny me the opportunity for continued study and pursuit of scholarship, the value of which I know and yearn for. As a consequence, especially during these past twenty-two years that I have been associated with the American Friends Service Committee as its Executive Secretary, a great deal of what has come into my life has come through meeting with people, often people in distress. I recall vividly trying to speak to a group of men and women in Vienna in 1934. Many of them had been so deceived by their experience with religion that the use of the term, "God," even more of "Christ," was the most effective way to shut their ears and hearts to anything of that kind one might have to say. And yet, one knew that they deeply yearned for the stability to endure persecution, which came from some sure, inner belief. I learned then how terminology may defeat one's most longed for purpose to be helpful, but to try to give a talk which comes out of the depths of one's religious life and not use the word, "God," or "Christ," or "Jesus," I found a real test.

Then there was that talk with Rabbi Leo Baeck, Chief Rabbi of Berlin, in 1934. I had asked him what persecution was doing to the spiritual life of the Jew. He reminded me that his congregation was approximately ten times what it had been before. He had to hold two services on Saturday and two on Sunday to accommodate those who wished to worship, when fifty was a good sized congregation in the old days. They would sit for two hours and listen contentedly to the reading of psalms of consolation and to the liturgy of the synagogue, knowing full well that as they left the synagogue they might be stoned by fanatics among the Nazis. Later, in this country, when he told me of his four years' experience in Buchenwald, his attempts to keep people from losing their sense of significance as individuals by reminding them that they were not simply numbers but that they were persons and God's children and precious in His sight; how they would assemble in the corridors at night when the lights were all out and listen for an hour and a half to a lecture on theology or to a sermon: all of this made me realize that I was sitting at the feet of a saint who had discovered that man's extremity was truly God's opportunity.

Many years later, talking in Jerusalem with Martin Buber, formerly of Frankfort, Germany, about the saints and scholars of Judaism, I was again in the presence of one who had discovered resources of life and spirit which resisted all external influence and made one radiant no matter what happened externally to his life.

It was experiences like this that made me realize that there was a "final faith," as Dr. McKenzie had insisted in my seminary days, but that that "final faith" was not confined to people who had found it by accepting a given theological concept concerning Christ.

There are people well versed in the art of theological thought and discussion who accuse the Society of Friends of ignoring evil. We, who are Quakers, often talk about "that of God in every man," a phrase used by our founder, George Fox. To some extent, the accusing finger of disregard of evil may be correct, but basically—no, it is not an informed judgment. George Fox said, "I saw, also, that there was an ocean of darkness and death; but an infinite ocean of light and love, which flowed over the ocean of darkness." The fact that one emphasizes the ocean of light does not mean that he disregards the ocean of death and darkness. It is the wisdom in the ancient Chinese proverb that "it is better to light a candle than to curse the darkness." This point of view is by no means inappropriate for consideration today; forced labor camps, displaced persons, restriction of liberties, all these are sadly characteristic of many parts of the world. But when one simply contents himself with crying out against them, so often the result is that he devises schemes similar to those used by his opponents to defeat them in their own ends. To be specific, many people feel we must have a better intelligence and counterintelligence system than those whom we dislike if we are to defeat them. Ours is not a denial that evil exists, it is asserting a triumphant confidence that evil can be overcome with good if one goes on a searching party to find that of God in men, even in those who may sanction, approve, and even enforce the machinery of torture. This viewpoint makes me tend in my own life, and in these more mature years, to respect but minimize the effectiveness of crusades to punish somebody for something; it deepens my confidence in the approach to any individual through whom evil is expressing itself, in an attempt to see whether the ocean of light may not overwhelm the ocean of darkness. To see this accomplished, one often has to wait many years, he may have to work alone, he may be so fully misunderstood that he will be thought a traitor to his country and to his religion; that has happened to Quakers over the years. But these things are incidental. The pathway to justice, right, and love leads often to a cross, suffering, and even death. The important question is, does one's life in some little extent redeem his fellows as well as himself from sin and failure? In this respect, it would be possible for me to feel I have been a failure. One might well ask whether such religious convictions, if valid, should not already have brought peace to the world. I have seen one world war produce the seeds for a second world war, and many people feel that the second has produced the seeds for a third. But I do not feel that way. Central to the whole problem of existence is the way in which the cycle of evil can be broken.

All too often a slight or hurt calls for retaliation which, in turn, must be met by doing injury to the one inflicting evil. Family feuds have been carried on in that way often for generations, and international ethics frequently are conducted on this basis, too. The Treaty of Versailles, to illustrate, was never accepted by Germans as other than a settlement of revenge, and it was not difficult to incite Germans to avenge this wicked document when Hitler came to power. Is there any escape from this prison of evil provoking evil? Parents often know what it is to suffer because of the sins of children, and when that suffering is undertaken deliberately and intelligently to redeem the wayward child, experience shows a reassuring percentage of success. Relief operations carried on where possible to friend and foe alike have often gone far toward breaking the vicious cycle of ongoing evil. The extreme illustration would be Jesus yielding up his life rather than "call down legions of angels" for protection. For myself to have had some part in the healing ministry of relief, and to have seen hardness of heart yield to the simple ministry to body and spirit, leads me to the clear conviction that the power to overcome evil lies in our hands. Our great difficulty is lack of confidence. Today we are assured that our security depends on force; but time, I feel sure, will show that true transformation will come only through the art of self-giving goodwill. This I believe to be not weak idealism but the only true realism.

ORDWAY TEAD

The justification for an autobiography of one's spiritual career is surely to try to be articulate about dominant motives, directions taken, and values one has sought to realize. Hopefully, such an account might throw light, not on success or failure, which no man can wisely gauge for himself, as on some central animating trend. For if there is any discernible trend, its meaning, its methods, and its outlook might conceivably help in being shared to hearten the efforts of others to chart a course and to set sail in hope and confidence and faith.

I propose to account for myself by some characterization of three periods—one a period of orientation and getting established, which ended shortly after World War I; two, a period of established directions which rather artificially I break at the time of my appointment to the Board of Higher Education; and, three, the subsequent period of recent efforts.

I

The major interests of my life were early and definitely set. My father was a Congregational minister who in theological matters was a thinly disguised Unitarian. In the whole latter part of his career, he worked professionally to promote the denominational colleges of the West, such as Carleton and Northland, and thus helped to extend Christian higher education. My mother was one of the early kindergartners who worked professionally in religious education at that age level. Throughout my childhood, she prepared the Bible lesson material widely used in "primary" Sunday schools; she was thus among the few women of that day who combined motherhood and a career, and took this as a matter of course. Since in later life my own wife has done the same, my outlook upon the woman problem in our society may be somewhat indicated.

Our childhood home in an industrial, lower middle class suburb of Boston was relatively a cosmopolitan one, not only because parish callers were from all walks of life, but because there were occasional visiting foreign missionaries, often exotic, and other lecturers who carried us in imagination beyond the Main Street of that day. Also, the family library was a good one and I early learned to supplement it in Sam Walter Foss's excellent city public library. The Bible was read and reread; as it was also in college; and from the outset it was viewed in the light of "the higher criticism." I had comparatively little baggage of mid-nineteenth century theology to throw overboard—a great help in the long look. It was never necessary for me to become so aggressively "anti" about much of religious doctrine, as it seems to me has been true of some of my generation who came out of more "fundamentalist" backgrounds, and reacted against everything "religious" in a crusading and sometimes in an almost obsessive spirit.

My father was a tolerant man and my mother was a devout woman. And it was natural that she would have been the one to try "to pray me into the ministry."

In the years just before going to Amherst College, I had already conducted boys' clubs in my own city and in a slum area of East Boston (where Albert Rhys Williams, later of national fame, was then ministering to an institutional church). I was aware at first hand of a "social" and of an "industrial" problem. I knew vividly the social separations between Catholic and Protestant, between Jew and Gentile, between rich and poor, between native and foreign. And I had been profoundly and permanently influenced to a heightened awareness in these matters by three books on my father's shelves. These were Walter Raushenbush's *Christianity and the Social Crisis;*

Francis Greenwood Peabody's *Jesus Christ and the Social Question;* and a volume by one Hudson, which I have since lost sight of, *The Law of Psychic Phenomena.* This last was important, not for where it arrived from a scholarly standpoint, but in its opening up of a psychological approach which supplied a point of view I have since pursued in wide ranging psychological study, which has yielded insights invaluable all along the way. My own first book, published in 1918, was, in fact, called *Instincts in Industry.* And it stemmed indirectly from Hudson, with additions from college study, from friendship with Carleton H. Parker out from the West (whose premature death was a great loss to the social thinking of our day), and finally from my first hand "labor audit" researches within business corporations.

The college years were incalculably rich in friendships with faculty and students, in eager and wide reading in and out of courses, fostered by direct access to the stacks of the college library, in long walks in the beautiful surrounding countryside. I had edited the high school magazine; I edited for two years the college literary journal; and I have, from 1921, edited ever since! Indicative of what the college thinking has added are the titles of my two "orations" prepared for the commencement platform in accordance with the then prevalent practice of senior "prize contests." They were "The New Education" and "The New Religion." And although I have not scanned them for a dozen years, I have a strong impression that most of what was there set forth has been the platform which a whole career has been spent in trying further to articulate, to implement, and to refine.

In the middle of senior year, I abandoned the idea of entering the ministry. And the reasons, however insufficient they may seem, were conclusive for me at that time. Nor have I ever felt the decision was unwise. The reasons were several. But most important, as I recall, was my sense of the "hypocrisy" of professing "Christians" in matters of race relations and economic relations. If their religion meant so little to them, surely it was a weak reed to lean upon! Notably, as I watched the relations of my "Christian" fellow students with the Jewish and Negro students on the campus, I was ashamed of their insensitive intolerance. And in the second place, as I studied the economic operations of our society, I was sure there was a great gulf between the "Christian" professions of industrial owners and managers and the conduct of their relations with the rank and file of workers. Problems of poverty, of unemployment, of exploitation, of severe inequalities of income—all this for me added up to an indictment of a society which seemed to practice quite other than it preached and professed.

I realize that other people's inadequacies offer no real excuse for not taking an even more vigorous stand for what one believes to be right. But there was further the sense that a paid ministry was in danger of being a kept ministry on issues in need of new and bold treatment. Finally, there was the theological aspect. For it seemed to me then, as it still does, that the church, except for the Society of Friends and a few other groups, carries an unnecessarily heavy super-cargo of doctrinal baggage which would to good advantage have been thrown overboard a couple of generations ago. In short, I was determined to be as free as possible to explore and advance the practice of the second great commandment, "Thou shalt love thy neighbor as thyself." I was clear that the world was *not* to be saved by "the foolishness of preaching." And I saw every reason why there might be a lay ministry consecrated to advancing fraternal regard among men, irrespective of creed, color, race, economic status, or social class. Indeed, it has been to the strengthening of that conviction and lay effort that increasingly over the years I have become committed.

Perhaps this thus becomes the appropriate point to include a conviction which the years have not shaken. It has always seemed to me that the danger of professional religionists is in too sublime a faith in good intentions and in avowals of goodwill; whereas to an important degree in our day, the difficulties of the world, personal and social, spring from ignorance as to *how* in specific fact one is to *act* as a good neighbor. Acknowledging as I do, the place of selfish wilfulness and of indifference in keeping people from being good neighbors in a statesmanlike way, I still find the churches as such not insistent enough that the necessary social engineering and personal moral behavior *both require profound, sustained, inventive, and ingenious thinking* by many individuals to guide neighborly sentiment into actual neighborliness. Good intentions on the part of unaroused and conforming members of the religious associations of all affiliations, are still accepted as moral behavior, to a degree that leaves little fighting edge required of the communicant.

It still seems to me true that too few members of our religious bodies are asking themselves with any persistent and anguished penetration: "How am I striving to apply my religious principles in my personal relations with others and in the multifarious relations of business and the community?" In short, the extent to which responsible good conduct has to be the fruit of reflective wisdom and scientific discovery, is still not widely enough appreciated. The controversy as to whether we are saved by "grace" or by "works" is old hat. We are saved by *both,* if they are properly defined. But also, and this is the emphatic moral mandate of the next half century, *we are saved by using our minds*—the best available intellectual resources that each and every person can mobilize. There is *a moral obligation to be intelligent.*

Nor is this emphasis on rational efforts, designed as it is to offset the saccharine sentimentality, the quiet desperation, or the smug complacency so rampant in our congregations, to be interpreted as any failure on my part to hold sin in view in its rightful place. I am clear that in any evolutionary or developmental view of human nature sin takes its place as a fact, along with the vestigial appendix and the impacted wisdom tooth, even though the remedies for these latter are of a somewhat different order from the remedy for the former! But I have never been one who needed Reinhold Niebuhr to remind me that sin is a reality; yet this is a view quite other than a belief in "original sin," which abstruse theological dogma I repudiate completely.

All this explains why I did not enter the professional ministry. And the explorations of the early postwar years were guided by a sense of the urgent need for understanding how to be friendly and loving in a great society, and for discovering the interdependencies between improved social environments and improved personalities. In the year 1912, just where to turn to help with the clarifying and focusing of goodwill, was not readily determined. I felt the need for new channels of approach and for a fresh probing of the alleviative efforts which social analysis was then suggesting. Fortunately, my approach had no doctrinaire, or what we now call "ideological" slants, although like many in that period I was being influenced by an omnivorous reading of H. G. Wells, John Galsworthy, G. B. Shaw, Henrik Ibsen, G. Lowes Dickinson, the Webbs, Graham Wallas, William James, John Dewey, and others too numerous to mention.

Hence when Robert A. Woods, an Amherst graduate who had in 1891 founded South End House, a settlement in Boston, and who had provided an Amherst fellowship, offered me this fellowship, I accepted. I held it for two years, with an additional year as assistant head resident of the "men's residence." This post provided an excellent opportunity to survey the urban social scene in relation to my own capacities. Mr. Woods was one of the early exponents of the "neighborhood idea"; his sociological grasp of the urban problem was both comprehensive and profound. The inventive implementing of goodwill was dominant in his truly religious outlook. His greatness as a social pioneer I have always felt was generally unappreciated; and I account for this in part by his independence of thought and his consequent insistence upon approaches of research, methods, and social prescription, which were wholly unacademic in terms of the formalized sociology of that day.

I like to believe that these three years laid a foundation for a *social realism* that has continued. No one can live in active participation in the life of an unskilled working class neighborhood for that length of time, and come away unmindful of the adverse conditioning effects of slum environments, and also of the resilient capacity of individuals to emerge out of them into a better way of life. Extremes of doctrine about social conditioning are still to be encountered. There are the social and economic determinists for whom environing influences account for all. And there are those for whom the Horatio Alger pattern of American life still proves the unalloyed power of something called "rugged individualism," to allow those who will to go onward and upward indefinitely. Surely the truth about the interrelations of personal and social influences lies somewhere in between.

It was in the period of mounting unemployment in the winter of 1914–1915 that a voluntary Massachusetts Committee on Unemployment was organized. Starting in a volunteer capacity, I presently become its paid secretary, a position held for about a year. This work led to close study into improved public employment offices and into the new English unemployment insurance, along with a publicizing of the practical efforts of a few advanced employers to "regularize" employment. But most importantly of all, the assignment led to a close working association with another formative and dynamic mind in the person of Robert G. Valentine, who was the chairman of this state body. He had in 1913 opened an office on State Street, bearing the novel designation, "Industrial Counsellor." The analogy to legal counsellor was intentional, in the sense that he held himself available to offer disinterested and objective advice to employers, labor unions, or whomever else, on matters of labor or industrial relations. This was, of course, a pioneering venture in a day when anything approaching a professional view of employer-employee dealings was unknown. Valentine brought to his newly created calling a healthy common sense, an analytical and inquisitive mind, a fund of humor, administrative experience as head of the United States Office of Indian Affairs under President Taft, and a wide acquaintance among his fellow Harvard graduates who were in influential positions in New England business.

It was into a personal association with this truly brilliant and beloved consultant that I had the good fortune to enter as the unemployment crisis lessened with the expansion of war production. Presently a partnership was formed and by virtue of being very much the junior, I gained invaluable grassroots experience in doing the factory field work and research interviewing, in order to make for a number of companies confidential reports on their plant labor conditions, to which studies Mr. Valentine had given the name, "labor audits."

This rich and rewarding first hand contact with labor conditions and issues of various kinds continued on through the war. It brought us to New York. It took me to Washington during much of the period of World War I. Valentine died prematurely in 1916, but the seed of an idea had already been well sown; and the technical advances in methods of study and in the kinds of proposals to be recommended, had been built up empirically into a total approach of increasing coherence, practical value, and social idealism.

It was with this background of experience in counselling with different kinds and sizes of corporations, that I undertook for the War Department in conjunction with Professor Henry C. Metcalf, then of the Department of Economics at Tufts College, the conduct of several War Emergency Employment Management Courses, under the auspices of Columbia University. We trained several hundred men and women for labor relations work in war plants. And it was the systematic and condensed lecture syllabi developed for this instruction which enabled Metcalf and myself to expand all this material, and issue in 1920 one of the first college texts in this field, *Personnel Administration: Its Principles and Practice.* This book has been twice brought up to date, and hopefully it has had a modicum of influence on the development of this new managerial function in the past twenty-five years.

II

With the business recession of 1920–1921, the opportunities for labor consultation service diminished to a vanishing point. And the invitation of Martin M. Foss, the vigorous and astute president of the McGraw-Hill Book Company, to join his staff as Editor of Business Books, seemed both a timely offer and a logical way to extend one's influence, at least by indirection, upon the then amoral conduct of American business.

Thus came a fairly well marked transition to the second period. I was now willing to work in and through corporate executive labors, as I had not previously elected to do. And from that day to this, I have played my part in that mythically important requirement of economic realism—namely, in proving my ability to "meet a payroll."

Even here, the claims of a more direct effort at spreading such understanding as might help to social and industrial melioration, were not to be denied. For a ten year period, I managed to find time in my publishing career to teach labor relations part time at the New York School of Social Work. And since 1921, I have each year valued the opportunity of conducting a two hour evening course at Columbia University on the subject of personnel administration. Additional intensive summer courses were included during World War II; and the total of those to whom in these and various other institutions as well, I have tried to elucidate a point of view of liberal democratic principles as illuminating good labor management, must add up to several thousands.

At the end of 1925, Harper & Brothers suggested a broadened editorial assignment, and early in 1926 I became "editor of social and economic books," a position which I still hold. And it is not irrelevant to this account to point out that in this capacity, and under the sympathetic and generous encouragement of my colleagues, I have had some small part in adding to the definitive American literature on race relations, the cooperative movement, public housing, small community developments, labor relations, group dynamics, and newer trends in higher education.

III

The year 1937, when I was appointed by Mayor La Guardia to the Board of Higher Education of New York City, may be used to demark the third and present period. And without further mention of other extracurricular activities in which I have indulged on a *pro bono publico* basis, I will only say that beyond my publishing activities, the major part of my spare time has in recent years been devoted in a trustee capacity to helping to guide the affairs of the four city colleges.

The chairmanship of this Board has been at once an extraordinary opportunity and a demanding responsibility. It has been possible to bring all my experience in personnel administration and in classroom instruction to bear upon the multifarious problems of the four free municipal colleges comprising the top layers of our city's public school system. My conclusion out of all this is that there are four major assignments to be covered in this trustee functioning for which diverse talents are ideally needed. The first is to try to use all possible influence to have politically disinterested but educationally interested new members appointed to such a Board as vacancies occur. The second is the selection and full support of able and high minded presidents. The third is the assurance to adequately paid faculties of a clear sense of freedom from political interference and encouragement to devoted teaching. And the fourth is success in securing adequate financial resources from the public treasury.

Combined with this responsibility for large scale education has been an equally fascinating task of trusteeship of a small, two year women's college, Briarcliff Junior College, of which my wife has been president. The high degree of personalized attention possible to give to each student in a college of two hundred students and the beneficial results which are so obvious and gratifying, supply a constant challenge to the contriving of new techniques to help enhance the personal influence of teachers under conditions of "mass education"—a corrective greatly needed, and one for which the public has still to be persuaded to pay the necessarily enlarged bill.

If thus far this autobiographical delineation has been more objective than subjective, that is partly because I would like to think that actions speak more loudly than would a philosophical or theological discourse to which I can bring only the resources of unsystematic study, albeit deep and continuing concern.

Also, retrospectively, it is difficult to bring vividly to mind the reasons for certain shifts of view. There was a period of at least fifteen years in which what is often referred to as "scientific humanism" or "anthropocentric humanism" seemed to me to account for all that needed to be accounted for about the whence and whither of man. I was content to let the rest of what William James called "overbeliefs" remain the luxury of others whom I then regarded as more tender minded.

But two specific influences can be named which carried me beyond a non-theistic to a theistic view, although my theism will no doubt seem to some a highly attenuated version. Nor am I too concerned if I cannot pronounce with professional adequacy upon that which is the ineffable and the unutterable in reality. W. MacNeill Dixon's poetic and noble utterance, *The Human Situation,* and the less technical writings of Alfred North Whitehead, are perhaps most responsible for my present basic faith and outlook.

It seems to me now that a truly religious view of life involves acceptance of the belief that in some deep sense this is God's world. A Creator still creating, a Judge always rendering inescapable and righteous judgments, a Redeemer in the sense of having made it possible for the individual to be restored and reinstated into a positive relation to life's becoming—these would seem to be profound and widely experienced realities. It is an unfinished world where the stake is preponderantly in human hands to play for, and the outcome is in doubt with an optimistic bias and "resonance" to hearten us as we strive.

I find profound illumination in the sentiment *that we do not ask God's help, we only ask that He be there.* As the unfinished creative process and organic unfolding of human destiny go on, we ask only assurance that the struggle does avail and does yield formative and beneficent influences in the world. Man can really build if he will. A natural orderliness, a human lovingkindness, magnanimity, and humility, a reverence before the unknown, a profound groping for whatever things are true and lovely and righteous—these attributes of nature and human nature represent the advancing and the unfolding phases of man's being. These qualities are ineradicable in man, and identify him as co-worker with the Source of all. The demonic and destructive phases are there, too, but the means to their sublimation and reduction are coming to be understood.

The paradoxes inherent in the human situation are seen to be tolerable, if we will humbly accept contradiction as of the essence of the world, even though the human mind can but dimly comprehend it; for we see through a glass darkly. There are goodness and evil at work; there are beauty and ugliness to be beheld; there are mercy and hideous cruelty to be encountered; there are inertia, complacency, stupidity, perversity—and there are vibrant strivings, divine discontents, noble tensions of mind and spirit, intimations of nobility, and saintliness of character. These all dwell together in the same world and in each human breast. I see no reason why our ambivalence of condition should lead us to cast reflection upon the Creator. We have enough of courage and determination, enough of knowledge of the ways to a kingdom of righteousness, to give us heart for the fray.

The hurdles placed in the path of our aspiring effort are surely of man's own making. Entry into the Promised Land is not precluded by some perverse malevolence, but by human inadequacy. Faith and hope and love; intelligence and science and rational power—these are the needful weapons, and they are human or they are nothing.

We have a right to believe that at the heart of things is a predisposition toward support of the human best. Our human characteristic to find, to cherish, to realize values of excellence in the realms of truth, beauty, and goodness, is deeply the *dominant* characteristic, given a reasonable chance.

But the necessary core of faith and hope is not the monopoly of any one institutionalized religious group. It is the monopoly of high religion. One is mindful of Schiller's statement that he believed in religion so much he could not believe in any of the different religions. Indeed, the institutionalizing of religious faith becomes so readily its undoing that "the scribes and the Pharisees" seem perennially to have overborne the prophets and the saviors. If the religion of tomorrow has any one doctrine which can be foreseen, it is this: whatever belief divides men of fraternal goodwill into different religious folds is supercargo; and there is no irreparable loss when it is thrown overboard. Whatever in faith and hope and love ties and binds man to man across the barriers of sectarianism, of religion, color of skin, nation, race, economic status, or social and educational level—*that* is the true. And no other is needed. We can and must adapt the words of the old hymn and say:

> Blessed be the ties that bind
> Our hearts in *human* love.

It is a hopeful sign of our turbulent yet dynamic times that I can readily draw upon two recent dramatic successes to give summary suggestion of the two great strands of that appealing belief which today gain widened acceptance. You remember the moving and exciting line of the Angel Gabriel in *The Green Pastures*—

"Gangway for the Lord God Jehovah!"[1]

And the last line of *Lost in the Stars,* the dramatization of the novel, *Cry, the Beloved Country,* said by the white man to the Negro clergyman whose son has murdered the white man's son, is:

"Let us be neighbors; let us be friends!"[2]

It seems to me additionally that the support which the insights of the heart get from those of the head increase in penetration and in volume almost daily. The warfare of science and religion has given way to reconciliation in which we recognize we are striving both to think God's thoughts after Him and to realize that those thoughts are of brotherliness, cooperation, and community among men, as the price of sheer survival. So fully is this true, that the ways to freedom and abundance, on the one hand, and to contemplative insight and the iron will of an ascetic, non-violent, eager cooperation, on the other, are seen to be the ways of scientific mastery. The ways of moral behavior, in short, are *marked* and they are *built* by scientific grasp— and that not by scientists alone, but by all of us as we become equipped to apply in action the knowledge required to act in God-like ways.

It is to this approach and outlook that the revelations of the religion of tomorrow are coming. It is in such humble striving that man will transcend himself, and share a divine life that is super-human but is *not* supernatural. And this is true for the good reason that at long last the natural is realized *to be divine,* even if not in complete fullness of disclosure.

Two final points should be made. The first is that in the transitional age which is ours the place of institutional religions, as I felt even in my youthful period, is critical and precarious. Do they attempt to be exclusive or inclusive? Do they cling to overbeliefs and not center heartily on essentials? Do they continue parochial, schismatic,

[1] Marc Connelly, *The Green Pastures,* Farrar & Rinehart, Inc., New York, 1930.
[2] Maxwell Anderson, *Lost in the Stars,* William Sloane Associates, New York, 1950.

and doctrinal? Or do they strive to use the universal, unifying, scientifically reinforced, supports of human fraternity?

In short, for what do the organized religions propose to *stand?*

The answer to this question is not in encyclicals, or the equivalent, from any official religious bodies. The answer is in the *conduct* and the *conviction* of the communicants. And the answer, let us confess, hangs in the balance. Progress here is possible; it is not inevitable.

The other point which is the summation of my span of experience, is that in the necessary, economic functionings of our society, morality and fraternity will have to become regnant by the efforts of men— or we will remain immoral, anarchistic, autocratic—which all mean irreligious, in the underpinnings of our common life. I know the pervasive role for good or ill of administration, management, and supervision in the organized institutional life of our day. Everyone who works has the moral quality of his living conditioned by the terms and relations of his employment. This is true in the kitchen and nursery as it is in a General Motors factory. We can redeem our working life from spiritual destruction, only as the work relations rise above the wage relations, and above the compulsions of monotonous, master-and-servant status. The scope for the creative impulse at work, the use of work as the medium of the productive and creative relation of the individual to his society, a status of cooperative partnership—these have to be clarified and restored, if salvation through living is to be a fact.

Organic to the creative expression of all people at work there have to be the occasions for autonomous, collective, *democratic* expression about work and its governance. Indigenous in social redemption is the use of administration as a fine democratic art, and of voluntary, organized, intergroup cooperative dealings as the way to productive group responsibility.

There are several words into which, if the proper overtones of connotation are read, we find the key to the moral responsibilities which modern life entails for mature persons. These words, into which as my career has proceeded, I have tried operationally to read significant moral and religious meanings, are—*administration* and management in all kinds of group organizations as expressions of moral responsibility; the social uses of *science* as guiding to a grasp and use of natural law and nature's resources; the wise applications of a law of *love* as the solvent of all human relations; the evocation of *democracy* to protect personal integrity and to invite the sharing of communal responsibility by every intelligent person; the assurance of enough general *education* to enable every individual to function socially at his most productive best, both in inner spiritual bounty and outer social creativity; the incitement of sufficient *high religion* to fortify more and more persons to commit themselves to lifelong projects of service to the Great Community which hopefully becomes the Kingdom of God.

My autobiography of the spirit is intertwined with the effort to bring practical and humane meanings to these words—"administration," "science," "love," "democracy," "education," and "high religion."

The projection of these essential human activities upon a level of performance where their common direction and divine intention are grasped—this seems to me to define a personal assignment one may be proud to share. And this kind of assignment can be shared with influences known and unknown in us all and about us. What more can we ask than some mysterious sense of fellowship with a Power that places us here and charges us "to press with vigor on"?

ADDENDUM

I ask the privilege of an ultimate word, because as I read this record the omissions seem so grave as somewhat to distort the portrait.

For I find I have made no reference to the importance of beauty through the arts and in nature. I have not stressed the value of non-violence and loving resistance as an aid to peace. Nor have I acknowledged the importance of creative silence and meditation. The problem of the role of women has always concerned me—as affecting men, as well as themselves. I have not elaborated upon the needful effort for the East and the West to come closer in understanding and integrated views.

There should be some further comment on the good and bad in the compulsions to activism as urban life requires it, and on the potency of pacifism when it is aggressively used. Gandhi is to be recognized as one of the greatest prophets of recent generations.

There should be something said about immortality; but I do not know what to say. The familiar phrase about "immortality of personal influence" accounts for all I can presently grasp on this theme.

As to the other spiritual concerns which I would mention, my comments run to the acknowledgment of opposites. Even absolute truths come into the arena of wise action, only as one realizes "that it is all a matter of degree." I believe, for example, in the value of a personal attitude which I may call *triumphant dedication*. The kind of *consecration* the scientist has toward truth seeking is needed by us all toward the good life. Yet I do not forget the wisdom of the Socratic injunction, "nothing in excess."

The dedicated life is the wise, happy, productive life. Yet I cannot ignore the thought which Christopher Morley once voiced, "It is all very well to wear a crown of thorns, indeed every sensitive person carries one in his heart. But there are times when it ought to be worn cocked over one ear."

I believe in the values of gracious living; but I believe, too, in holding to simplicity in one's demands upon life, in so far as possessions are concerned. The exception here is a good personal library which seems well nigh indispensable for intellectual and spiritual renewal.

I believe, too, in the virtue attainable only in living close to the soil (at least periodically); yet I am actually not competent on the land.

I believe in the virtue of families of several children; yet I have only one child.

I know the values possible in austere, reflective withdrawal; but I am plunged too fully into the maelstrom of events.

If all this adds up to the truth, there is a basic dialectic in striving to live creatively, that indeed seems to be of the essence of the Truth in which we have our being.

HENRY NORRIS RUSSELL

I

This story is no spiritual Odyssey. The case of a man half of Puritan and half of Lowland Scots stock, with a strong natural bent for mathematics, and thoroughly exposed to physics as it has advanced from the discovery of X-rays till now, is more likely to appear as an illustration of predestination.

But some description of the belief of so hardboiled an individual may be in order, especially as I am convinced that the general philosophy of modern physics may make valuable contributions toward the resolution of some old theological difficulties, and even more important ones toward the practical adjustment of our remaining differences, in effective cooperation.

Family tradition was strong, especially the Old Colony Puritan on my mother's side. A remote grandfather—schoolmaster in Salem—is on record as having "opposed the witchcraft delusion." Two ancestors of later date were ousted from the Society of Friends (quite properly) for participation in Arnold's expedition to Quebec in 1775. My great-grandfather, a Salem skipper, died of yellow fever on his own ship in the West Indies. His son declined an offer from a relative of a job in a distillery, and started on his own in New York. He became interested in the rubber business, married a descendant of the militant Quakers, spent ten years in Brazil (where my mother was born) and eight in Edinburgh (where she received much of her education).

He was a strong anti-slavery man and his wife's father a militant abolitionist.

My father's grandfather, according to family tradition was a weaver in the days of home industry, and an elder in the Kirk. Of older tradition on this side I know nothing—but there is no suggestion that it was Jacobite.

Steam machinery ruined him, and he died in debt. His children worked hard and paid it off. Then my grandfather married and emigrated to Nova Scotia, serving as a school teacher, and later as a Presbyterian minister. My father taught school, worked his way through college in Halifax, and studied for the ministry in Princeton, and met my mother there.

He settled down in a country village on Long Island and died as pastor of his first charge, thirty-three years later.

This is a highly homogeneous background, but it was not obscurantist. From Edinburgh comes a saying picked up by my uncle, a student of Lister's, "No one ever died a triumphant death of trouble below the diaphragm." My father was one of the small group of country parsons who started the movement which led to the revision of the Confession of Faith of the Presbyterian Church, which removed so much polemic sixteenth century phraseology; and Andrew White's *History of the Warfare of Science and Theology* was in his library. He spent most of his time in pastoral work, and his relations with the other village churches and their ministers were always cordial. My brothers and I did not have to memorize the Shorter Catechism; but my mother had a remarkable gift for connecting her rules for everyday behavior with the Ten Commandments by arguments which stand up very well as I recall them in later life. The emphasis was even more on moral principle than on religious obligation.

Reformation principles were postulated rather than argued: but later denominational controversies were rarely mentioned. Indeed, personal criticism of neighbors or acquaintances was definitely discouraged in the family circle. Abstract principle and the diplomacy necessary for a small town minister were both responsible.

I "joined" my father's church at fifteen, after some tribulation, (*vide Pilgrim's Progress*), which might have been spared except for Victorian reticence on my part.

School and college life in Princeton at the end of the past century fitted well with a simple evangelical belief. Most of the faculty were church members. One able chemist was sometimes described in private as "the agnostic." Neither he nor his orthodox colleagues attempted any proselytizing in connection with their teaching. That day had long passed. Chapel attendance was still compulsory by a century old tradition.

Undergraduate religious life expressed itself in class prayer meetings on Sunday evenings before church, and in Sunday school teaching in the town churches (I remember being taught, when a boy, by a prominent football player). I recall very little of that active participation in social work which is so important in these days, but lack of interest was far from being the only reason. Commonplaces of our time, such as operating a summer camp for city boys, or conducting a boys' club at the State Reformatory fifteen miles away, were physically impossible in those carless days; and social welfare work in the then small town was well taken care of by permanent residents.

College life was democratic. The man who earned his way suffered no social limitation. The rich man might perhaps have kept a riding horse (no one did).

Looking back, it seems the happiest of ivory towers. We knew that soon we must do our bit in the world outside, and most of us did. Meanwhile we had a good fellowship of our own, were happy, and knew it. *O fortunati nimium!*

The intellectual training was thorough and good, for those who worked. After receiving my bachelor's and doctor's degrees there I went to Cambridge in the great days of J. J. Thomson, and found myself adequately prepared.

I did not earn my own way, even in part. Legacies to my mother from her parents had made our economic position fairly comfortable, at least with the careful spending which came by tradition from the New England housewives who "feared dirt, debt, and the Devil, and nothing else."

In my case this was a boon. I have always been a bit like Lincoln's steamboat "with a four foot boiler and a six foot whistle." I spent all the strength I had on my work and in 1900, with my new Ph.D., I had to take two years off to rest. I shall never forget how my father said "Henry, remember that you have a home"—and I came home. The money accumulated from my postgraduate fellowships was kept intact to finance my study abroad—according to the original plan.

Had this breakdown come later, when I had given hostages to fortune, it would have meant disaster. At this time, it saved me, for it taught me to watch the boiler pressure as well as the whistle cord.

One more thing was fortunate. My father's country church happened to be in Oyster Bay, which at the turn of the century was far from being out of the world. Some of the city people who summered there were his parishioners, and many more our friends. Their friendships have been a major factor in my life—indeed, it was at the house of one of them that I first met my wife, more than fifty years ago.

Theodore Roosevelt was naturally my hero—and still is so, for he was the last Puritan. His power over the American people was based largely on arousing conviction of sin—not on inspiring hopes of a "brave new world," but on convincing them, by wholesale, that we ought to be ashamed of ourselves for having tolerated this or that specific evil so long, and must clean it up at once. As one of those who believe that our consciences, despite their limitations, are better guides than our hopes, I long for the next Puritan.

Yet it is tragic to recall how, between forty and fifty years ago, radical and conservative alike would have accepted Roosevelt's saying, "Our task in the future must be to shackle cunning as in the past we have shackled force." How blind we were!

Cambridge was my introduction to the greater world. Since I first settled down there, England has never been a foreign land to me. The unvarying courtesy and kindness which I received from everyone, in my college (King's), from my teachers, and from a growing circle of friends, made this automatic.

Professionally, my life was an expansion of previous experience; but I came to know, for the first time, people—Anglo-Catholics,

Agnostics, Tories, and so on—of a wide variety of beliefs with which I had previously had little acquaintance. They were obviously such fine people, in character as well as culture, that any sense of superior personal background would have been absurd.

The question, "how they did it," was gradually cleared up as friendship with them progressed and the foundation was laid for the convictions, clarified and strengthened by later developments in physical science, of which I shall speak in due time.

After a year at Cambridge I received a grant from the Carnegie Institution for some work on stellar parallax, which had been strongly supported by my friend Arthur Hinks, Chief Assistant at the Observatory. This demanded observations on every clear night, just after dark and before dawn. No lodgings were available within a mile of the observatory. Just at this juncture, my mother died—the severest personal blow which has yet befallen me.

The Hinkses promptly invited me to live with them for a year— nominally as a paying guest, actually as one of the family. If I made any return to them, it was by waking myself with an alarm clock every morning without ever once waking the baby!

As I review a longish life, I am overwhelmed with the number of deeds of pure goodness which have been done to me, and this was one of the chief.

Returning to America in 1905, I began my forty-two years' service at Princeton. The professional part of this is outside the present story: but some things should find place in a "spiritual autobiography."

I married in 1908 an Episcopalian of New England stock, with a Huguenot strain far back, and later Baptist and Unitarian forebears, and reared at St. George's in New York—a pioneer "institutional church." We found each other attached to our own churches, though with no convictions of the essential superiority of either, and followed the simple plan of attending both alternately, though not mechanically. Christmas and Easter found us at Trinity Church, and Thanksgiving at the Presbyterian. Our children later attended with us as a united family. For more than forty years we have been received in complete Christian fellowship in both churches, under five successive rectors in one and three ministers in the other, and each of us is entirely at home in both. Two of our children, on reaching "years of discretion," sought membership in one, and two in the other.

This practical experience of Christian unity has been a notable spiritual gain; not least is the advantage of acquaintance with the methods—and the benefits—of the various forms of religious services. There are, for example, three main traditions of Christian worship in this country—the liturgical, the reformed, and the evangelical. All, at their best, are noble approaches of the soul toward God, and I am convinced that one is a better Christian if he can join reverently, devoutly, and sympathetically in any one of them as he finds it, without too much distraction by genuflections, coldness of architecture, or the musical limitations of Gospel hymns.

I regret deeply that small town residence has deprived me of the privilege of equal acquaintance with Jewish worship.

Other experiences, too, have convinced us that, in the matter of religious fellowship "the best way to resume is to resume." We spent several happy summers in the 1920's on Clark's Island near Plymouth (where the Pilgrims "rested on the Sabbath day" before they landed on the Rock). There were thirty or forty people there in summer. We all went ashore in our own boats for supplies; but regular church going (with big tides in a shallow harbor) was out of the question. We started reading Morning Prayer for ourselves the first Sunday; some friends heard of it and asked to come—and in a few weeks our simple services were attended regularly by a dozen people, ranging in ecclesiastical connections from Unitarian to Roman Catholic. This continued for seven summers.

We always ended by singing Leonard Bacon's hymn,

> O God, beneath Thy guiding hand
> Our exiled fathers crossed the sea
> And when they trod the wintry strand
> With prayer and psalm they worshipped Thee.

Most of us were "descendants" and we were in the authentic place; but that was far from the whole story. People welcome a chance to share in simple worship if they can get it.

In the same decade, a group of faculty members at Princeton organized a series of Sunday evening talks upon various relations between religion and science or philosophy. These were held in university lecture rooms—we needed the larger ones—and, while definitely Christian in outlook, were deliberately kept on the intellectual side and clear of evangelistic appeal. I had a good deal to do with this, and was much impressed with the cooperation which we received from colleagues of greater or less unorthodoxy, and sometimes no church connection. I recall a conversation with one who met my first suggestion with, "My dear chap, I could no more do that than beat the big drum for the Salvation Army." I replied, "I haven't made clear what we are after. We want one of these talks to be a discussion from the intellectual side of the metaphysical aspect of religion, and nobody here can do that like you." It was a masterly talk. The last of these series was a discussion on "Evolution and the Bible," the speakers being the heads of the department of Old Testament literature in Princeton Theological Seminary and of the department of biology in the University. Both were eminent scholars in their fields—hence, naturally the two addresses showed practically complete agreement. There was no arrangement in advance to keep off contentious matters—the only stage management came when Dr. Davis asked me "Are you inviting me as a clergyman?" "No, as a Hebrew scholar." "Then I'll wear a colored tie." If we had only thought of having a stenographer, these admirable talks would have been available to far more than the eight hundred who heard them.

The most valuable comment on my own talk came from an old friend of approximately zero orthodoxy. "Then, at the end, you stuck your head down and said something that I suppose was a prayer; but I didn't hear it."

There is little more in the way of history. Some ten years ago I was asked to become an elder in my church and accepted when an old friend, professor in Princeton Seminary, told me after a long talk, "I couldn't conscientiously recommend you as a professor in this Seminary, but I see no objection to you becoming an elder." Incidentally, I told my pastor "I would wish to keep on going to

Trinity Church about half the time," and he answered "That's one of the reasons why we asked you."

II

More valuable than further details of a happy and rather sheltered life may be some account of the religious convictions to which fifty years' experience has led me.

First must come the effects of the radical changes in the conceptions of physical reality. It was fully recognized, long before 1900, that most of the familiar "physical" properties of matter, such as pressure, temperature, and elasticity, are highly simplified mathematical images which describe the behavior of exceedingly complex aggregates. There is "really" no such thing in nature as a continuous elastic solid or a pressure exerted uniformly over every minute area of a surface. But these "statistical properties" represent the behavior of the actual aggregates so closely, over a wide range, that our daily life can be based on them with complete security. When the number of particles involved diminishes—for example, when gas is exhausted from a tube—the accuracy of the statistical images *gradually* falls off—one part in a million, in a thousand—till they become useless.

Until some twenty years ago it was generally hoped that the properties of the ultimate units of which matter consists might in time be definitely determined. But this hope was shattered by the "uncertainty principle"—better named by Born the Principle of Limited Measurability. There is a vast mass of evidence indicating that all the fundamental physical quantities (such as electric charge and radiant energy) occur only in definite units, or *quanta*. All these quanta are, so to speak, of the same degree of fineness—they correspond to the same "level" of structure. We have a great and increasing store of knowledge as to what happens when a quantum of radiation is emitted or absorbed by an atom, when an electron is knocked out of it or returned, and even of the more complex changes which may occur in its nucleus. But what happens inside an atom while nothing enters it or leaves it, we cannot find out. Still less can we hope to discover whether the properties of electrons and other fundamental particles arise from some finer grained structure within them.

The hope that "something will turn up" to give an answer, is at present mere wishful thinking. We face the Veil of Isis, and cannot lift it. As Sir James Jeans puts it, "in physics we are not in touch with ultimate reality." His masterly argument[1] that the time has passed for supposing that the old mechanistic images represent reality, and his caution against assuming that our present abstract mathematical images do so, still hold good. But, nevertheless, physics is doing very well. Our present images and theories are not ultimate, but they are reliable, to a high and specifiable degree, over specifiable ranges of phenomena, and our continual efforts to make them still better are successful.

Here is the place to introduce an analogy with theology—and to begin with a caution. There has been a vast increase in our knowledge of physical phenomena during the past century. No one would maintain that there has been anything like as great an increase in our knowledge of the phenomena of religious experience. This is nothing against religion: it is the extraordinary advance in physics that is historically exceptional. Hence it is unreasonable to expect such rapid and radical changes in theological theory or religious practice. Moreover, we are dealing with a very different discipline, and must be on our guard against hasty translocation of conclusions, or even of methods. Nonetheless, I believe that physics can make useful contributions to theology.

Probably the most important contribution which physical science has made to the general progress of thought has been the repeated forcible expansion of the imagination. Time and again, we have found that ancient concepts which accounted satisfactorily for ordinary experience, and had come to be regarded as matters of common sense, if not as self-evident truths, were *too simple* to represent the phenomena of nature and had to be replaced by more complex concepts—sometimes bizarre at first sight. What bothered us most

[1] In the last chapter of *The Mysterious Universe,* The Cambridge University Press, New York, 1932.

the first few times was that the changes were made in what we had come to regard as the fundamental philosophy of the subject. (For example, relativity forced us to give up belief in absolute simultaneity.) Now we have learned to worry less about our preconceived philosophy.

I believe that there are cases in which the same principle may profitably be applied in the theory of religion. I may take an example from Christian theology—namely, certain details of the Trinitarian creeds adopted in the fifth and sixth centuries. It would be presumptuous of me to attempt to discuss the central issues. Suffice it for the present purpose that creeds were prepared by councils of devout men, formulating logically what they were convinced were the general beliefs of Christians. Now these were able men—indeed it is precisely of them that Walter Lippmann has said that it is a very poor policy to assume that the best minds of another generation were congenitally inferior to our own. In their solemn conclusions they affirm that the Persons of the Trinity are exactly equal in many expressly described characteristics, to an extent that not only raises questions by the human reason as to how the Babe of Bethlehem could be omnipresent, but is difficult to reconcile with sayings of Jesus reported in the Gospels—*e.g.,* "My Father is greater than I." These are elementary arguments, and must have been clearly realized by the Church Fathers. Are we justified in concluding that they were, after all, intellectually inferior? By no means. They were experts in the Greek philosophy of their age. I believe that their reasoning, put in my own words, ran something like this: "The Infinite is perfect. No part can be taken from it without introducing imperfection. Hence no one Person of the Trinity can lack any characteristic that another possesses."

Now this is a proposition not of religion, but of philosophy concerning infinity—and in this matter we can fairly claim to know more than our fathers—since the work of Cantor and others on transfinite numbers.

Putting the relevant results of a thoroughly tested theory as simply as possible:

1. Two assemblages of units are equal in number, if the elements

of which they are composed can be matched, one to one, both ways, leaving none over.

2. If, however the matching is done, some elements of A remain when those of B are exhausted, A is greater than B.

For finite assemblages it follows that the whole is greater than its part. But, for infinite, unending assemblages, this is not true.

The two sequences

1, 2, 3, 4, 5, ...

100, 200, 300, 400, 500, ...

both without end, are in an obvious "one-to-one correspondence" and the numbers in the two are equal by definition.[2] Yet the second is obtained by removing ninety-nine elements from the first for every one which is retained; and is a part of it! Hence, among infinite numbers the whole may be equal to its part.

Further precise study shows that this is, in fact, *the* distinctive property of an infinite number, by which it differs from all finite numbers.

The mathematical properties of infinite numbers do not prove anything regarding the nature of a transcendent God: but we may well be chary about applying a proposition of human philosophy in the greater case when it fails in the lesser; and so the apparent conflict between Christian doctrine and the text of the Gospels disappears.

The devout belief of many Christians that the authors of these creeds were divinely inspired to pronounce the truth, need not be affected, so far as I can see, by this view. The council was comprised of men; its conclusions were necessarily phrased in human language, and stated in terms of human philosophy. The belief that, within these inevitable limits, they were the best possible, is surely a belief in their inspiration.

My position is relativist rather than absolutist—a physicist can take no other. One who holds it must admit his certainty that the views to which he and his associates may come will, at most, have their day, short or long, and be replaced—probably by something more com-

2 *Ibid.*

plicated; and his uncertainty whether any particular view of his will survive impartial criticism at all.

But, to go deeper, one may believe—as I do—that man was created "to glorify God and to enjoy Him forever," whether he accepts or rejects the view that man was created capable of attaining an *absolute* knowledge of God—or of anything else. Such differences in the realm of abstract thought need not weaken our sympathy with other believers in God, nor interfere at all with our fellowship with them.

We meet with mysteries, too, on the physical side—if a mystery means a situation in which reasoning based on evidence in one part of the field leads to conclusions which appear to be irreconcilable with those derived from another part of it. These "incompletely understood phenomena"—as we call them—are often strange enough: for example, the behavior of an electron can usually be represented by the image of a charged particle, but under some circumstances it behaves like a train of waves.

By a *tour de force* of mathematical imagination a theory has been developed whose consequences include both: but only the elect few (of whom I am not one) would dare to try to explain this; and a completely satisfactory formal theory of the electron has not yet been attained. But we do not have to wait for such a theory to use effectively the knowledge that we have. Within a specifiable range, the particle-image represents the facts satisfactorily; within another range, the wave-image does so; and both images have been successfully applied to practical problems. The tubes in a radio set work on the first, the electron microscope on the second.

May not these things be an allegory? The theologian works in at least as difficult a field as the physicist. He has no laboratory, and no business whatever to conduct experiments upon human souls. If he has to acknowledge that he is faced with incompletely understood phenomena, and calls them by the classic name of mysteries, no one may think the less of him.

It is hard enough to form even a tolerable working image of God. Our relations with one another may be surprisingly well expressed in terms of the ancient image of persons, possessing at least some degree of intelligence, self-determination and purpose. And our relation with the Power behind the universe may reasonably be expressed by supposing Him to be a personal being—even though we

> must use a speech so poor
> It narrows the Supreme with sex.[3]

To confine our images of that Power to those which belong to the "lower" mechanistic or quantized levels, appears to me to be an arbitrary exclusion—certainly so long as we cannot successfully do the same thing for one another.

But, are God's relations to the universe as a whole, or even to that part of which we know something, expressible by the use of even the most august personal image that we can devise? This is quite another question, involving that most perplexing of mysteries, the problem of evil.

Personally, I find it very hard to use the word, "God," to describe a personal being Who is not in complete control of the universe. I am more willing to believe that a perfectly wise and good God, for reasons known to Himself (though to us unknown and possibly unknowable), has designed the universe in such a way that our race, on our planet, in our times, is in its present appalling situation, than to accept the alternative that these horrible things and people are outside His control. The first is a venture of faith; the second of despair.

The venture of faith must be bold. As Donald Hankey wrote from the trenches, "religion consists in betting your life that there is a God."[4] But the sharp theological antinomy that faced our fathers loses its edge if one admits, as I do, that our best intellectual images of God may not be, and probably are not, absolute and ultimate.

The vital thing is to use that image which is trustworthy and valid within the range with which we are dealing. So the old saying, "Every parson must be an Arminian when he preaches and a Calvinist when he prays," leaves him as consistent as any physicist.

But we should be on our guard against artificial mysteries. The

[3] William Watson, "The Unknown God," *The World's Great Religious Poetry*, edited by Caroline Miles Hill, The Macmillan Company, New York, 1938.

[4] Donald Hankey, *A Student in Arms*, E. P. Dutton & Company, New York, 1917, p. 190.

finest example I know comes from classical nineteenth century physics.

The differential equations which describe the propagation of waves of light in transparent media are identical in form with those defining the internal vibrations of a continuous, perfectly elastic, incompressible solid. The latter had been well worked out, and were very well known to the mathematicians of the day.

When a detailed theory of light-waves was developed, this analogy with the familiar was naturally greeted with joy. Light behaved just like vibrations of something. Hence it was assumed that there *was something real*—the Ether—whose vibrations constituted light. As the mathematical equations were the same, it was further assumed that the ether *was* an elastic solid. But the sun, planets, and stars move through space, leading to the conclusion: "All space is occupied by a continuous, incompressible, elastic solid, through which material bodies are moving with high velocities in all directions."

This is the famed Elastic Solid Ether. Was any hypothesis ever stated which better deserved the famous *"Credo quia absurdum"*? I am old enough to recall my own bemuddlement about it. We still speak of the ether, but might be inclined to define it now as "that property of actual space in virtue of which electro-magnetic radiation satisfies certain specified differential equations." This definition puts the facts as well as the old one—nay, much better, for with proper specification of the equations, it includes the effects of relativity. But the old almost unconscious *a priori* assumptions about what *must* be have vanished—and with them the absurdity and the mystery.

What theological propositions, if any, show elastic-solid characteristics, I do not presume to suggest. But I am convinced that consideration of these problems, with special attention to the elements of *a priori* philosophy involved in the reasoning, is likely at least to remove a good many minor difficulties. And, if we discuss these things with one another in the spirit that desires more to understand what the other man really believes than to prove him wrong, we will all be the wiser and better for it.

It is not to be expected—nor, as I see it, to be desired—that we will end in some generalized complete agreement. But we will at least understand what our friends of the various groups regard as matters of fundamental principle, and what as involving human logic and philosophy.

The former are of course far more difficult; but a great deal depends on the spirit in which they are met. Take, for example, the differences regarding the validity of ordination, etc., which complicate ecumenical conferences of Christians. Amid all the discussion of this, it is surprising that no reference has been made, so far as I have noticed, to a similar problem in the field of scholarship.

The Universities of Oxford and Cambridge form a closed group with respect to the "validity" of academic degrees. They recognize one another's degrees and no others. A visitor from overseas, who has the good fortune to be invited to one of the great festival dinners at some college, at which "Scarlet and decorations" are in order, attends in plain evening dress, though he may have received the highest earned or honorary degrees from Harvard or Goettingen, and be a foreign member of the Royal Society.

What effect does this discrimination have upon the relations of English and foreign scholars? Exactly none—and I know well whereof I speak. The fellowship of scholars is wholehearted, unbroken, and complete, and the forms are regarded only as parts of an ancient tradition which all alike would hate to lose.

The finest expression of the comprehensive spirit which I know is a century old, and the author was not a physicist, but a poet. If any one does not recall Browning's "Christmas Eve," I would earnestly recommend it for reading as near "this Christmas Eve of Forty-Nine" as may be.

The breadth of its sympathy is superb, and the illustrations of varying religious viewpoints seem amazingly modern. The crude but sincere congregation of Zion Chapel, the devout multitude at the Christmas Mass in Saint Peter's, and the earnest critical auditors of the professor at Goettingen are all still with us, and with us, too, is the climax of the poet's vision.

> Did He not say that, to the end
> He would be there with them, their friend?
> Certainly He was there with them.

EDWIN GRANT CONKLIN

Introduction

In attempting to trace the stages and factors in the development of my present philosophy of life, I am well aware of its fragmentary nature and the probable defects of a subjective report. But I have tried to pick out the high points in this development and to describe it in as objective a manner as possible, as is generally required in science, although subjective feelings and motives cannot be excluded from an autobiography as they are an important part of the record.

Throughout my professional life I have been a student of animal development, and, while most of my studies have been directed to the development of the body, I have not failed to observe that the development of physical, mental, and moral qualities in man follow essentially similar patterns. Indeed, a human being is a single person composed of many parts and functions, which are not divisible in real life. Physical, mental, and moral subdivisions of this *individual* do not represent separate personalities, but only different aspects of one non-divisible unity.

All development, whether physical, mental, or moral, involves growth and differentiation of an inherited germinal organization into the more complex and more highly differentiated organization of the adult, with the addition of particular nutritive and hormonal substances and under the influence of many kinds of stimuli—physical and social. In man and the higher animals physical development pre-

cedes mental and social, and is therefore more immediately dependent on initial heredity, whereas the later social and mental development is more subject to environmental influences. Heredity cannot
be changed except at its source, but environment can be modified or
controlled along the whole course of development. In the attempt to
influence or control development much more attention has been devoted to environment than to heredity, and this applies especially to
the control of mental and social characteristics by means of education.

From the biological point of view, education is in large part an
attempt to establish certain "conditioned reflexes" or habits and to
inhibit others. Such reflexes or habits are established by offering
rewards or satisfactions for desired responses, and punishments or
dissatisfactions for those that are not desired, until finally the desired response becomes habitual. Education is thus in essence the development of desired or good habits and the suppression of unde-
sired or bad ones. This is generally overlooked or obscured in most
educational procedures where lessons, lectures, laboratories, and examinations place almost all emphasis on the information acquired
and little or none on the habits developed in the process. Such information is usually soon forgotten, but habits are more enduring.
Indeed, it is my opinion, as a result of more than a half century of
teaching, that the most lasting and important effects of education are
the good habits that are established; and habitual methods of responding to conditions or stimuli constitute what is generally known
as character.[1]

With these preliminary statements of the teachings of science with
regard to the unitary nature of the individual and the principles of
development and education, I turn to my own spiritual development
and in so doing I shall interpret "spiritual" as including mental and
moral, philosophical and religious aspects of my personality. I cannot wholly isolate my spiritual development from the physical—
nature has not done that—but I shall try to emphasize the former.

[1] Edwin G. Conklin, *Heredity and Environment in the Development of Men,*
Princeton University Press, Princeton, 6th edition, 1939.

Earliest Years

My individual life began in the midst of the American Civil War and it is probable that the intellectual and social environment of those early years had some subconscious influence on my mental development. On the eightieth anniversary of my birth my older daughter wrote me: "Four score years ago—why Father, that sounds like the beginning of the Gettysburg Address." I had never thought of the date of my birth in relation to that address, but found on consulting history that Lincoln spoke at Gettysburg on the 19th of November, 1863, and I was born just five days later. Now that I have passed my eighty-seventh year the exact words of that address, *viz.* "Four score and seven years ago," coincide more fully with my present age, and they remind us how recent the history of our nation is when measured by human lives, for only two rather long lifetimes take us back to 1776 and the Declaration of Independence.

My earliest years were lived in two small villages in central Ohio— Woodbury, Morrow County, and Waldo, Marion County, and on a farm near Delaware, Ohio. My father was a country physician, "a horse and buggy doctor," and a leading man in his community. Woodbury was a Quaker settlement and reputed to be a "station on the underground road to Canada." I recall stories about the escape of slaves by this route, also humorous comments about the protestants against the continuance of the war, "the copperheads," and their proposed overground march to Canada, which never materialized. The hysteria of those reconstruction days was illustrated by my father's story of the "Yankee Doodle Preacher," who shouted in a sermon, "I will never be satisfied, no never, until Jeff Davis is hanged from the dome of the Capitol in Washington and the wind has played 'Yankee Doodle' through his bones a hundred years!"

A saving sense of humor helps to overcome such hysteria. Absurdities are more vulnerable to ridicule than to argument. In these days of hypertension in Congressional committees and elsewhere over atomic secrets, spy scares, Communist propaganda, and the general preparation for a coming war, we greatly need a sense of true proportions. Oh, for a Mark Twain or a Mr. Dooley to "shoot folly as it flies"! Oh, for statesmen who look beyond the goal of political or military victory to a just and peaceful world in which all nations may live together in harmony!

School and College

Between my sixth and thirteenth years I attended three public schools in the different places where we lived in central Ohio. These were one-room, one-teacher schools, of which I have many vivid memories, and which undoubtedly left many impressions upon me.

In the autumn of 1877, I entered the Delaware, Ohio, high school, from which I graduated three years later. I remember with gratitude the encouragement and inspiration of the woman principal of that school and my growing ambition to excel in scholarship, associated as it was with a sense of physical inferiority, for I was so nearsighted that in school I had to occupy a chair near the blackboard and could never take active part in sports; and a sense of social inferiority was at first forced upon me by the "town guys," who always called me "Hayseed" or "Seedy" because my home was two miles outside the town, made fun of my clothing or my shyness, and often challenged me to unequal combats. In this rough school of democracy I learned to defend myself, but soon realized that while I could not excel in strength, I could win respect by courage. No doubt this had its influence in turning my attention to activities in which I could excel. For more than seven years, while I attended high school and college, I lived at home in the country and walked or later rode a high bicycle every day to and from classes.

I entered the Ohio Wesleyan University in the fall of 1880 without any conditions in studies, but since I had never studied Greek I was classified in the scientific course, which permitted the substitution of extra courses in science and mathematics for Greek, but was otherwise almost identical with the classical course. However, I was advised to take up Greek in the summer school, and this I did for three summers, but since I had not finished all requirements for the A.B. degree before graduation I was graduated in 1885 with the degree B.S., but with the understanding that I might also take the

A.B. degree when I had finished all lacking requirements for that degree. After having taught Latin and Greek and other subjects after graduation, I was granted the A.B. degree in 1886.

In my third year in college I dropped out of classes from November to April to teach a district school in the country four miles from my home. After beginning college work that year I found that I lacked money for certain expenses which I felt were highly desirable, especially the purchase of many books in which I could make marginal notes, and as I did not wish to burden my parents with additional expenses I sought and obtained employment as teacher of a country school. Except for occasional jobs at day labor and the superintending of farm work for one summer, which my father turned over to me with the proposal that I could keep whatever I could make out of the farm, this was the first moneymaking employment which I had ever undertaken. It was not a great success financially for I undertook to teach the twenty to thirty pupils in that school, ranging in studies from the ABCs to high school subjects, and to serve as janitor, sweeping the room and building the fire each morning, for 100 days for $175. But while this experience in self-help was not a great success financially, it was one of the most valuable experiences of my whole life, for it taught me self-reliance and confidence in my ability to succeed. At the same time it served to review much that I had learned before, sharpened my sense of order and discipline, and gave me a real love of teaching.

When I entered college I had no particular predilection for any subject of study, but I enjoyed most my work in natural history, largely because of my admiration for the professor in that subject. He was a splendid teacher, and while he had no laboratory indoors he took his advanced students on occasional field trips where we collected many fossils from the Silurian limestone and the Devonian shale of that region, and many animals from the river and ponds, particularly mollusks. We classified these specimens but made no further study of them. Our course in botany was limited to the preparation of herbarium sheets and descriptions of fifty flowering plants. Zoology, anatomy, and physiology were studied from textbooks, with some illustrative material from the museum. In my senior year I served as assistant in the museum and thereby learned a good deal of zoology, especially about the classifications of mollusks.

Much attention was given in college at that time to elocution and public speaking and I took an active part in this. I joined a literary society, wrote short essays and verses, took part in debates and orations, and in general devoted more time to such extracurricular activities than to any one of my regular courses or to any form of athletics. Toward the end of my junior year I was chosen by my literary society to represent it in an oratorical contest between different societies which would be held near the middle of senior year and I spent much time during the intervening summer vacation in trying to find a suitable topic for my oration.

A study of John Brown's raid on the United States Arsenal at Harper's Ferry led me to believe that after his initial success in collecting slaves to be carried off to Canada, he changed his plan and decided that he could accomplish vastly more to arouse the nation against slavery by remaining and sacrificing himself and his band than by running off a few slaves to Canada—that he was in fact a self-sacrificed martyr. This was the theme of my rather perfervid oration and I think it marks a critical point in my mental and moral development, for I caught the spirit of self-sacrifice which it portrayed and resolved to devote my life to some great humane cause.

Choice of Profession of Teaching

Up to the middle of my last year in college I had not decided what I should do next. Almost all of my professors at that time were ordained ministers in the Methodist Church and one of these asked me why I did not consider entering the ministry. I replied that I had never felt a "call" to do so; he then said, "Any man with the proper qualities of head and heart has all the call that is needed." This deeply impressed me and a short time after, in company with several other students, I applied to a local examining board of ministers for what was known as a Local Preacher's license. We were put through a perfunctory examination on the Bible, and on our faith and practice, and were licensed to be local, or lay, preachers.

But upon my graduation, it was necessary for me to find some paying employment, for I had borrowed money to meet expenses in college and could not at that time go further into debt. My previous experience in teaching caused me to seek a position in some college or high school, but, in spite of many applications and letters of recommendation from my professors, I had no success. Finally, sometime in September, 1885, I had an interview with the Reverend R. S. Rust, D.D., Secretary of the Freedman's Aid and Southern Education Society of the Methodist Church, at which time he offered me a position as Professor of Latin and Greek in an institution that bore his name, Rust University, at Holly Springs, Mississippi. In spite of the fact that the salary offered was only $600 for the first year and $700 after that, with room and board furnished if I acted as proctor in the dormitory and dining hall, I gladly accepted the offer as it gave me the opportunity for which I longed, to take part in a most necessary and humane work—Negro education.

I found at once that Rust University was a university in name only; it included all grades of instruction from common school to college rank. For three years, 1885-1888, I held this position, teaching not only Latin and Greek, but all the sciences that were taught there, and in addition classes in English, elocution, and United States history. During these years I took an active part in the religious exercises of the institution, accompanied the white District Superintendent, or Presiding Elder of the Methodist Church (North) to some of his quarterly meetings in outlying Negro churches in various parts of the State, and thus became familiar with the general condition of the Negro, and with the relations between the races, in the "blackest State" in the Union.

During my first year at Rust University, where all the principal members of the faculty were white, I became engaged to Miss Belle Adkinson, head of the music department, and the daughter of the Reverend L. G. Adkinson, D.D., President of Moore's Hill College (now Evansville College) in Southern Indiana. A year later, in 1886, Dr. Adkinson became President of New Orleans University, a Freedman's Aid institution of the Methodist Church, and Miss Adkinson then went with her family to New Orleans and remained there until our marriage in 1889. For more than fifty years she was my constant helpmate, and the very personification of faith, hope and love as described by Paul (I Corinthians, 13).

With my engagement and expectation of marriage, my self-sacrificing idealism became tempered with some worldly realism, and my acquaintance with the enormous problems of the education and social welfare of Negroes caused me to realize that these problems could not be solved in one generation, and that the most effective leaders in this great work must be found among the Negroes themselves. There were no prospects of promotion at Rust University, and I came to feel that I might be able to do more important work in the future than I had been doing for the past three years; and when an unsolicited offer of a professorship in biology came to me from a college in Illinois, I declined the offer because I knew that I was not fitted for such a position and at once applied for admission to the department of biology in the graduate school of The Johns Hopkins University, and there my introduction to the critical habits of a scientific investigator began.

I was at Johns Hopkins for three years, 1888–1891, my principal subject of study being animal morphology under Professor W. K. Brooks, and my minors being physiology, under Professor H. Newell Martin, and geology and paleontology with Dr. W. B. Clark; and my associations with other instructors and graduate students were most enlightening.

I cannot begin to describe adequately the stimulus for scholarly work and research which I received at Johns Hopkins. It was as if I had entered a new world with new outlooks on nature, new respect for exact science, new determination to contribute to the best of my ability to "the increase and diffusion of knowledge among men." One of my early duties was to find a suitable subject for a doctoral thesis, and after a few preliminary studies of minor significance, but which led to my first scientific publication, I spent the summer of 1890 at the great biological center at Woods Hole, Massachusetts, and in that stimulating environment found almost ideal material for my thesis, in the study, cell by cell, of the development of an animal from the fertilization of its egg to its highly differentiated form. This study constituted my thesis and my first major contribution to science, and it has been the inspiration of much of my later research, just as this first summer at Woods Hole has been followed by more than sixty summers there, with the exception of two spent outside of this country and one on our West Coast. I cannot begin to name all the persons and events that have contributed greatly to my mental and moral development. Suffice it to say that "I am a part of all that I have met," and I have been most fortunate in my opportunities and associations.

Before I had finished my last year at Johns Hopkins I was invited by Dr. James W. Bashford, the new President of Ohio Wesleyan University, my *alma mater,* to become Professor of Biology there. I gladly accepted this offer, but on condition that I should be permitted to teach evolution, for I considered this the central theme of biology, the connecting thread on which all details of the science could be strung. President Bashford readily agreed to this and, to meet criticism which might be expected from certain quarters, he gave his first Sunday afternoon lecture, after I had joined the faculty, on the topic of theistic evolution, which he strongly supported. For three years, 1891–1894, I organized the biological laboratory there and taught all branches of that science, except physiology. I also gave a Sunday lecture course on evolution and religion which was largely attended. I also proposed a reorganization of the curriculum and a detailed system of elective courses, but as there were practically no elective courses and as I was the first full professor that had been added to the faculty in twenty years, I naturally created some disquiet on the part of some of the older members of the faculty, my former teachers.

᛫ Under these circumstances and amidst deep regret on the part of President Bashford, myself, and most of the faculty, I decided to accept a call from Northwestern University, Evanston, Illinois, to organize a Zoological Laboratory there and to be their first professor of Zoology. Again I specified that I should be permitted to teach evolution, because Northwestern had been founded by Methodists, some of whom were anti-evolutionists, President Henry Wade Rodgers jocosely said that whatever they could stand at Ohio

Wesleyan could be endured at Northwestern. Freedom in teaching and research I had in full measure and I heard of no criticisms on account of my evolution lectures until near the end of my stay there. Lyman Abbot had given the Commencement Address of 1894 at Northwestern on the subject of evolution, and this, together with my teaching of that subject, was used as a means of attacking the administration of the University by certain clerical members of the Rock River Methodist Conference.

However, at that time I eliminated myself as a cause of dissension by accepting a call from the University of Pennsylvania, where I was Professor of Embryology from 1896 to 1899 and Professor of Zoology from that date to 1908. There I had the utmost freedom at the University and in the learned societies of Philadelphia in advocating evolution and in exploring its causes, but on an early occasion, when I accepted an invitation to address the Philadelphia Methodist Preachers Meeting on evolution, I found that some of their members were as violently opposed to it as was William Jennings Bryan some twenty-five years later. Under these circumstances I did not transfer my church membership from Evanston to Philadelphia, but I still continued to speak occasionally on science and religion in churches and church congresses.

It would be amusing if it were not so pathetic to see how persistently some people hold on to traditional beliefs, especially in theology, long after they have been outgrown in advancing knowledge. And this is especially the case with regard to the warfare between theology and biology concerning the doctrine of evolution, a large part of which warfare has occurred in my lifetime. It was this unreasoning antagonism on the part of defenders of the traditional views of creation, whether they were clergymen, lawyers, politicians, legislators, or just plain men and women, that has led me to devote as much time as I could spare to writing and speaking in explanation and defense of evolution. I suppose I must have given outside of my classes a thousand public lectures on this subject. This was, indeed, one of the "causes" to which I pledged my best effort. I have in my files a large amount of correspondence, pamphlets, and books in denunciation of evolution, and of myself for defending it, and whenever any newspaper notice of a lecture of mine on this subject appears, it is almost certain to stir up antagonism. When my book on *The Direction of Human Evolution*[2] appeared some thirty years ago, President Hibben of Princeton University received letters from prominent churchmen demanding my removal from the faculty, and the editor of *The Presbyterian* fulminated against the book and its author. President Hibben replied that I was teaching what President McCosh had advocated fifty years earlier, and what the scientists of the world generally approved. In the course of centuries I suppose that such opposition to evolution will cease; I have seen no recent outbreak against the Copernican theory.

Religion and Church Relations

I have passed through several stages in my religious life and to many of my orthodox friends they will seem to be descending steps. My home life was normally and not excessively religious; my parents were leading members of the Methodist churches where we lived, and I went to church with my parents and my sister on Sundays and attended Sunday school where, because of my good memory, I received prizes for reciting whole chapters of the Gospel according to St. John, and various of the Psalms. Before I was seventeen years old I had read, perhaps as a stunt, the whole of the King James version of the Bible, and had committed to memory large portions of it.

When I was thirteen years old, a great revival meeting was being held and I determined "to go to the mourner's bench and experience religion." I had no proper idea of what I was seeking nor how to find it, but I knew I had many faults of which I repented, and in the puritanical atmosphere of *The Methodist Book of Discipline,* which had come down from John Wesley with few changes, such worldly amusements as card playing, dancing, and the theater, were condemned as sinful. I had not been guilty of any of these, but I had not avoided all Sunday amusements, and, in spite of the admonition, "I

[2] Edward G. Conklin, *The Direction of Human Evolution,* Charles Scribner's Sons, New York, 2nd edition, 1922.

must not work, I must not play, It is the holy Sabbath Day," I had frequently broken this interpretation of the Fourth Commandment. Also I had acquired the thought, from the "hush, hush" attitude of all my elders on that subject, that sex and sin were synonymous, and that all sex thoughts and feelings were sinful and must be suppressed.

Under these circumstances I went to the mourner's bench, repented of my sins, and sought forgiveness. I was told that if I clung to God and His promises I would feel the ecstasy of forgiveness and salvation, but I felt no ecstasy and therefore doubted whether I had been "converted." But I was baptized, joined the church and vowed to lead a religious life, and this I think I did as well as any other boys of my acquaintance. Indeed, I am sure that my public "profession of religion" kept me from yielding to many temptations. If "an open confession is good for the soul," an open profession is good for the spine, determination.

I presume that as a child I believed literally all that I was taught about God and the Bible, heaven and hell, sin and salvation, immortality of the soul and resurrection of the body, and I remember that as I began to question some of these orthodox beliefs I was warned that all such doubts were mortal sins that must not be allowed to arise. I was told that reason and learning were often false guides, and was advised, "Take your reason captive." But in spite of all this pious advice my gradual loss of faith in many orthodox beliefs came inevitably with increasing knowledge of nature and growth of a critical sense.

In college I took the required courses in Bible history, Evidences of Christianity, and especially Bishop Butler's *Analogy of Religion— to the Course and Constitution of Nature*, and later I read a multitude of books and sermons on the relations of science and religion, natural and revealed truth, nature and the supernatural, the foundations of faith, etc. On the other hand such books as J. W. Draper's *History of the Conflict between Religion and Science* (1874) and later Andrew D. White's *The Warfare of Science and Theology* (1905) showed the impossibility of harmonizing many traditional doctrines of theology with the demonstrations of modern science. But the possibility remained that these traditional beliefs were not essential articles of religious faith, or were not to be interpreted literally but rather poetically and figuratively. My early religious teachings and associations led me to adopt this view, and in several books and magazine articles I have attempted to show that science has revealed a grander universe than was ever dreamed of in prescientific times, and that while many former theological beliefs must now be abandoned, the fundamental articles of religious faith remain.

Evolution and Creation

While I was in college the bitter denunciations of evolution and of Darwin by our professor of mental and moral philosophy first turned my attention to that subject. I got a copy of Darwin's *Origin of Species* from the library, and, while I could not appreciate much of it, I was impressed with the fact that abundant evidence was offered for the general theory of evolution, and that the book ended on a quite idealistic note. The next time the professor indulged in one of his tirades against Darwin I asked him if he had ever read any of his books. He replied with emotion, "No, I wouldn't touch them with a ten foot pole!" I then asked permission to read to him and to the class the last sentence of the *Origin of Species:*

There is grandeur in this view of life, with its several powers, having been originally breathed by the Creator into a few forms or into one, and that, whilst this planet has gone cycling on according to the fixed law of gravity, from so simple a beginning endless forms most beautiful and most wonderful have been, and are being evolved.

When the professor heard this, he said in amazement, "Did Darwin write that?"

A general opinion of evolution among religious persons at that time was that it was an atheistic scheme by which it was hoped to get rid of a God. Thomas Carlyle wrote:

I have known three generations of Darwins, atheists all! Ah! it is a sad and terrible thing to see nigh a whole generation of men and women looking around in a purblind way, and finding no God in this universe.

And this is what we have got—all things from frog spawn; the gospel of dirt the order of the day!

This unreasoning attitude of anti-evolutionists, rather than the scientific evidences in its favor, first made me one of its advocates. Like Alfred Russell Wallace, co-discoverer with Darwin of the principle of Natural Selection, I tried at first to limit the natural evolution of man to his body, allowing a supernatural origin to the soul, and I endeavored to minimize theological objections by regarding evolution as a natural method of creation. Only slowly did I come to realize that evolution applies to the whole man, body, mind, and morals, just as individual development does. Indeed, individual development, or ontogeny, is the counterpart of evolution or phylogeny, and is at present the most fruitful means of studying species development. Most of the great course of evolution occurred in the distant past, and there is no present means of studying it experimentally, but development of the individual occurs daily before our eyes as one of the most common phenomena of nature, and if anything in the world is natural, all development, including that of man, is natural.

This conclusion like the Copernican, or heliocentric theory of the solar system, has proved to be devastating to many traditional ideas concerning man and the universe. What now has become of the idea that the earth is the center of the universe which was made for man; that he is the chief end and aim of all creation; that he was created perfect in body, mind, and morals; that by the sin of disobedience he "brought death into the world and all our woe"? These are some of the questions which modern science has raised concerning the governance of the universe and the origin of man, and the necessary scientific answers are so devastating that many devout and humane persons shrink from them and seek any possible way of escape.

From my first acquaintance with the theory of evolution, I have regarded it as the greatest and most inclusive theme of biology, and one of the most liberalizing doctrines in the long history of man's attempts to determine his place in nature. And yet I recognized its devastating effect on some traditional beliefs and tried to find ways of preserving the foundations of my faith. Many devout scientists suggested, and I agreed, that our present science deals only with one aspect of the universe and man, namely, that which is the object of our senses and is measurable; and they concluded that there may be other aspects not of this character, that there are indeed "more things in heaven and earth than are dreamed of in our philosophy." When one considers how recent all our scientific knowledge is, as compared with the millions of years of past evolution, it seems not unreasonable to suppose that there may be still other aspects of reality to be discovered and explored. This applies particularly, I think, to the subjective and personal aspects of our experience. Natural science deals chiefly with objective phenomena, and regards feelings, thought, consciousness, as the functions of certain parts or structures of the organism. But the precise relations between sense organs and sensations, between brain and thinking, body and consciousness, and in general between object and subject, the world and the ego, have not been satisfactorily explained. Some materialistic scientists have maintained that subjective phenomena that cannot be explained mechanistically as products of the vital machine, have no existence in reality. The material organism, they maintain, is the real thing, the cause of subjective feelings, desires, consciousness, which are mere "epiphenomena," or are not real. But nothing in the world is more real than feelings of sensation, identity, self; of purpose, thought, consciousness. If these are delusions, everything is delusion, including objective phenomena, for the latter can be recognized only by the subjective self.

I am always amazed at the self-satisfied confidence of some mechanists that all major problems of the universe have been solved by present-day science and that nothing more remains to be done but to fill in minor details. This was the attitude of physicists in general at the beginning of the present century regarding the phenomena of the world of physics. Albert Michelson, America's first Nobel prizeman, in physics said in an inaugural address at The University of Chicago in 1894 that future advances in the knowledge of light would be limited to changes in the sixth decimal place. And then came the discovery of radioactivity, the quantum theory and a new world of physics.

All principles and causes of evolution from bacteria to orchids, from amoeba to man, are now found by experimentalists in the chance mutations of genes and the natural elimination of the unfit— as if the almost infinite complexity, fitness, beauty, mentality, and moral qualities that have appeared in the course of evolution were all explained by these two relatively undefined factors—chance mutations and elimination of the unfit. It is natural for experimentalists to over-simplify their problems and solutions, but is it not the part of wisdom to look for new principles and new factors in the immense universe of life?

Purely materialistic conceptions of nature focus more attention upon the elements that enter into a process than upon the qualities that issue from it—upon analysis rather than synthesis—and this is especially evident when we consider the novel qualities that result from such syntheses. Throughout the whole of nature new qualities arise as a consequence of new combinations of elementary units which generally lack these qualities, that is, these new qualities are *created*— not out of nothing, to be sure, and not supernaturally, but nonetheless really. This universally present phenomenon is known as creation by synthesis or creative synthesis. It is present in all chemical processes, as for example in the synthesis of two atoms of hydrogen and one of oxygen to produce a substance, water, with entirely new qualities.

Similar creative syntheses occur throughout the whole of chemistry and physics giving rise to the innumerable properties of all the substances found in nature, and of many which man is now making for the first time. Among these are highly complex compounds of carbon, hydrogen, oxygen, and nitrogen, each with its own peculiar properties, the outcome of creative syntheses. It is highly probable, although not as yet demonstrated, that some of these syntheses produce different complex compounds that are specifically associated, that is, organized, and that this organization creates in such a system some of the elementary properties of life, such as (1) interstitial growth and division of constituent parts, or panmerism; (2) division of the entire system, or organism, and therefore asexual reproduction; (3) capacity to regulate or restore typical conditions when these are disturbed; (4) ability to respond to particular stimuli in specific ways and hence differential sensitivity. These are fundamental properties of life and there is evidence that they are the results of creative synthesis, and therefore that life has arisen by this process.

In the development of the egg of any animal or plant creative syntheses are taking place at every stage, and this joined with progressive segregation of different substances already present, leads to the differentiation of cells, tissues, organs, and systems with all of their different functions. This is the basis of the present theory of development known as epigenesis, as contrasted with a former theory known as preformation, which held that the complete animal or plant was present in miniature in the egg. According to epigenesis there is no homunculus, or little man, in the human egg, but only a system of compounds with their properties, a system of structures and functions which, by a series of creative syntheses among these and other units from the environment, give rise to all the structures and functions, instincts and behaviors of the developed man. The controversy between preformationists and epigenesists that occurred toward the end of the previous century concerned only the degree of complexity of the organization of the egg and not any proposed return to the impossible theory of preformation.

Whether this same process of creative synthesis can explain the origin of all the vast world of mental, moral, and spiritual phenomena seems to me less certain, and yet the unity of the entire individual as shown in the correlated development and decay of body and mind points in that direction. If we frankly accept the philosophy of monism, to which the scientific study of psychology, sociology, and philosophy are leading, must we not assign to the material and synthetic processes of development and evolution a more spiritual character than is granted in gross materialism? Indeed do not nature and natural law reflect many of the qualities usually ascribed to deity?

It is interesting to find that some of the world's foremost scientists and philosophers have recently expressed views of this character. The late Sir Arthur Eddington regarded his "qualitative principle," which in many respects resembles "creative synthesis," as a more complete conception of nature than any purely quantitative one. Alfred North Whitehead, late professor of philosophy at Harvard

University, regarded God and the world-process as in some way bound up with each other, and as co-eternal. Sir Edmund Whittaker concludes a recent lecture on "Eddington's Principle in the Philosophy of Science" with this inspiring thought:

The conception of a rule of law, in itself timeless, which is intelligible to our minds and which governs all the happenings of the material world, is the spiritual aspect of physical science. We stand in awe before the thought that the intellectual framework of nature is prior to nature herself—that it existed before the material universe began its history—that the cosmos revealed to us by science is only one fragment in the plan of the Eternal. . . ."[3]

Freedom and Responsibility

But while this more spiritual conception of creation by synthesis throughout all nature affords a basic philosophy which can find place for both objective and subjective, material and spiritual phenomena, it does not without further elaboration harmonize the apparent conflicts between the two. One of the first of these which at one time troubled me greatly, was the conflict between the determinism of nature and the freedom of the individual. This is a subject that is as old as civilization, perhaps much older, for, according to Milton, among the hosts of primeval hell there were philosophers who

> In thoughts more elevate, reasoned high
> Of providence, foreknowledge, will and fate;
> Fixed fate, free will, foreknowledge absolute,
> And found no end in wandering mazes lost.

Every effect must have its adequate cause, or rather causes, and if this relation of cause and effect is absolutely fixed, there can be no variation from it, and consequently no freedom. This position has been maintained by many philosophers since those of Milton's hell, and has been held generally by scientists. When the details of Mendelian heredity were being explored at the beginning of this century, it was found that the heredity of every individual is fixed

[3] Sir Edmund Whittaker, F. R. S., "Eddington's Principle in the Philosophy of Science," *American Scientist*, XL, 1, January, 1952.

at the time of the union of the germ cells, and while the environment may vary thereafter, the individual has little or no ability to control it in early stages of development. Consequently, it was held by many that man is never free, because he is the product of heredity and environment over which he has no control.

This conclusion was so contrary to general beliefs, practices, customs, laws, and especially to our own conscious experience, that I *felt* that something must be wrong in this reasoning. And yet some of my scientific and philosophic friends maintained it with conviction and attributed my defense of freedom to my religious background. In particular, my friend, Jacques Loeb, the physiologist, stoutly held that the sense of freedom which we have is a complete delusion, that in reality we are never free. As he said this to me, on one occasion, he saw his small son running down to the beach with an open clasp knife in his hand, and he shouted, "Bobby, close that knife. You might fall on it." I said, "Now, Loeb, live your philosophy." His only reply was to wink one eye at me.

Clarence Darrow, the distinguished criminal lawyer, maintained, in certain famous trials and in his book entitled *Crime,* that men do what they are compelled to do by their nature and therefore that they are not free nor responsible for their acts. He consulted me about this hoping to get my approval, but when I took the customary view on this matter, I could not shake him from his hypothetical but impractical position.

In 1912, I chose as the topic of my presidential address before the American Society of Naturalists the subject, "Heredity and Responsibility," and in it tried to show that the solution of this age old problem was to be found in avoiding extremes—the extreme of absolute determinism, on one side, and of absolute freedom, on the other. We know that we are neither absolutely free nor absolutely bound, but between those two extremes we do have a considerable degree of freedom and responsibility.

How this relaxation of complete determinism is made possible, has only relatively recently been clarified. We know that the "chain of cause and effect" is not a single straight chain connecting these two, but rather a complicated network. This is the principle of multiple causes of every effect, and it is nearer the truth to say that every effect is the result of everything that has gone before, than that it is the product of any single cause. Multiple causes increase the chances of variable results.

Another relaxation of absolute determinism is found in the fact that even exact science never reaches absolute certainty about anything. Science deals only with probabilities of a higher or lower order and must always allow for "the probability of error." The so-called "uncertainty principle" of Heisenberg, according to which it is not possible to determine at the same time both the position of an electron and its speed, might better have been called the principle of "limited measurability," which applies to all physical phenomena. In short, "the demon of the absolute" has wrought havoc in science as well as in philosophy and theology. The upshot of all this is the finding of a scientific basis for the common-sense view, widely held by people everywhere, that scientific determinism does not mean predeterminism or fixed fate, and that normal persons are left with a certain degree of freedom. Laws and customs of all civilized nations recognize this principle of *relative* responsibility; children and demented persons are not held equally responsible with others.

About the time of the famous trial in 1925 of the case of the State of Tennessee against John T. Scopes for teaching the evolution of man in his high school class in biology, which attracted worldwide interest, some enterprising students at Princeton University promoted a debate on the subject of the evolution of man between myself and Dr. John D. Davis, Professor of Oriental and Old Testament Literature in Princeton Theological Seminary. A large audience was present in Alexander Hall to witness what many hoped would be a conflict, like that staged at the Scopes trial between Clarence Darrow for the defense and William Jennings Bryan for the prosecution; but this hope was never realized. I spoke first, presenting the scientific evidence in favor of the evolution of man, in what I hope was a convincing but non-aggressive manner. Dr. Davis followed, beginning with a completely disarming statement: "I leave to the biologist," he said, "the scientific evidences of the biological origin of man. Theological interest begins when man first became a *free moral agent."* This definition of the proper areas of science and theology in this discussion completely avoided the provocation to a fight and admirably stated the basal claim of theology. Both science and theology can agree that man first became free when he learned to take advantage of the lack of absolute determinism, which lack human experience has always recognized, and science has only recently granted. He became moral when he first recognized the difference between right and wrong, when in the epic story of Genesis he ate fruit of the tree of the knowledge of good and evil. He became an agent, *i.e.,* an actor or doer, when he willed or chose to follow the right or the wrong, a capacity which he has always felt he had and which has only recently been confirmed by science.

Mechanism and Finalism

Rigid mechanists hold that science concerns itself only with means and causes, never with ends or purposes. They say it asks only the questions *What, How, When,* but never *Why.* But *Why* is the most important of all questions in dealing with the behavior of organisms and especially so with human behavior, and it is the most interesting question that can be asked regarding many phenomena of nature. Aristotle, "the master of those who know," was great in every field of knowledge, but perhaps greatest of all in zoology. He maintained that the essence of any animal is found not in *what* it is or *how* it acts, but in *why* it is and acts as it does. Some recent zoologists have barred this question *why* from their studies, largely because they have not been able to answer it in a purely objective and mechanistic manner, but nevertheless it remains as the most important question that can be asked about animal actions and reactions.

All structures and functions of living things serve particular uses or functions, and they appear to have developed for certain ends or purposes, *e.g.,* eyes for seeing, ears for hearing, noses for smelling, and so on with every organ and part of the body. There seems to be *purpose* in all these organs and functions. What is the source of this purpose? Formerly the theological answer was found in the design and purpose of God. But naturalists refused to abandon a natural explanation, and sought the answer in some power or principle of nature, but this remained relatively unknown and mysterious until less than one hundred years ago.

The most distinctive contribution of Charles Darwin to science and philosophy was not the theory of evolution, which had been proposed by several of his predecessors, but his theory of natural selection, which undertook to explain the origin of fitness in the living world, and consequently the "preservation of favored races in the struggle for life." He recognized the well known fact that different animals and plants vary in almost every respect and that some of these variations are more useful, others less beneficial. He also recognized what every careful observer knows, that in general many more young are born than can reach maturity, that there is an enormous death rate in nature, and that in general the weakest and worst fitted to live are first to die, while the better fitted are more likely to survive and leave offspring.

This almost self-evident principle he called "natural selection," and he marshalled a vast amount of evidence in its favor. It has now been tested for nearly a century in many thousands of animals and plants, and there is no doubt that it is a most important "perfecting principle." Many naturalists maintain that it is the only thing necessary to explain the wonderful fitness of organisms for survival in the places they occupy in nature. Time and space do not permit a further elaboration of natural selection in many fields, but there is no doubt that it is one of the most fundamental laws or principles in all nature.

A similar principle operates not only in the evolution of animals and plants, but also in their individual development and behavior. Not only are unfit individuals eliminated all along the course of development from germ cells to adults, but a similar elimination of unfit or injurious responses to stimuli leads to useful or beneficial behavior. For example, if the protozoon, paramecium, is placed in a glass trough of water one end of which is hot and the other cold, the animal continues to swim in all possible directions, but whenever it meets an obstacle or unfavorable condition it stops, swings into a new direction, and once more goes ahead. By this simple process endlessly repeated, it avoids obstacles, as well as the hot or cold ends of the trough, and finally comes to rest in the middle region, or in its food material. It has found favorable positions or conditions by eliminating in this way unfavorable ones.

This type of behavior is known as "trial and error," repeated until finally trial leads to success. It characterizes the initial behavior of all organisms, from the simplest to the most complex; and this manner of attaining useful behavior is found in all kinds of learning, as, for example, when cats learn to let themselves out of a box by lifting a latch, or horses learn to open a gate, or children learn to walk or talk or play games. In every such case many varied actions are tried at first, those that do not succeed or give satisfaction are not continued, those that do are continued. Animals that have associative memory remember past failures and successes, and thereafter learn to repeat only the latter. Trial and error is therefore a type of elimination of unfit responses in the realm of behavior. In higher animals it leads directly to intelligent behavior, for initial intelligence may be defined as the capacity to profit by past experience. This great principle of the survival of the fit and elimination of the unfit, is thus seen to be a guiding factor in the evolution of fitness in species and of intelligence in man and higher animals, and it offers a clue to the causal explanation of one of the most profound of all problems, namely, that of purpose.

Everywhere in the living world we see that ends or goals are involved; the universal goal is survival, as Darwinism recognizes. How is it possible in causal phenomena to have ends or effects serve as causes? This would seem to be a reversal of the usual order of cause and effect. But in the case of all animals that can learn anything, memory of past failures and successes acts as a cause in future responses. A similar principle is found even in non-living machines, for example, self-regulating devices such as governors, thermostats, etc., in which the effect of a previous reaction is "fed back" as a cause in a future reaction. Many phenomena in nature are repetitive, and in the living world almost all reactions are cyclical. In all such cases effects may in later cycles become causes, goals may generate new starts, ends influence means, ideals and purposes become causes.

This principle of the "feedback" of former effects into following causes has recently been exploited as a new brance of science, *viz., Cybernetics.*

In this way some of the most profound phenomena of life and mind are found capable of being classified as natural and causal. Indeed, there has recently been great activity in some branches of science in making calculating machines, differential calculators, even so-called "thinking machines," all of which demonstrate that important mental processes are synthesized from mechanical conditions; but of course such machines do not make themselves, back of every one of them is the mind and purpose of its inventor.

If any one should think that such mechanistic "explanations" of life and mind, of freedom and purpose, of ethics and conscience, are final and complete, he has not begun to appreciate the magnitude of the problems which these phenomena present. For example, consider again the proposed solution of the great problem of fitness or purpose in nature, which is generally regarded by biologists as having been solved by the single principle of the continual elimination of the unfit, until by mere chance the fit arrives and is preserved. Apply this principle to the many adaptations and co-adaptations of any one of a multitude of structures and functions, of needs and satisfactions, or crises and behaviors of any animal, and see what a strain is put upon this factor which is held to be purely mechanical and non-intentional. Consider, for example, the adaptations and co-adaptations that are found in the eyes of man or other vertebrates—the remarkable fitness of the retina, with its rods and cones for receiving and transmitting the stimuli of light of varying intensities and wave lengths; the beautiful dioptric apparatus of transparent cornea, lens, and humors; the elastic lens with the ciliary muscles for focusing the light coming from near and far objects; the iris with its intrinsic muscles for controlling the amount of light admitted; the eyeball and its accessory parts, tough outer coat, muscles, bony orbit, eyelids, eyelashes, eyebrows, lachrymal glands, and ducts, etc., etc.—when one considers such an assembly of remarkable adaptations and co-adaptations, it seems incredible, if not impossible, that all of these fitnesses, and multitudes of others which must be associated with them to bring about effective vision, should have been produced by individual chance mutations in each of these innumerable parts, followed by the elimination of those animals that lacked some of these fitnesses. Do we not load upon chance mutation an impossible burden in requiring it to provide all the functions and structures and correlations of such a series of remarkable fitnesses? Surely there must be other factors than those now recognized by biologists to bring about such wonderful adaptations! It is no wonder that Darwin is said to have confessed that he never thought of attempting to explain the evolution of the eye without a shudder!

Most of all when we consider the whole course of evolution from fire-mist to life and man and mind, does the mechanism of natural selection seem a useful but wholly inadequate explanation of the remarkable fitnesses that are everywhere evident. Even before life appeared on earth it was necessary that there should have developed a complicated fitness of the environment for life, as Lawrence J. Henderson has so ably demonstrated. And after life appeared the whole course of organic evolution "from amoeba to man"; from trial and error to intelligence and reason; from the relaxation of absolute determinism to relative freedom and voluntarism; from differential sensitivity, satiations and sufferances, satisfactions and dissatisfactions, to purposes, ideals, and aspirations; from instincts of mating, care of young, and mutual defense, to social cooperation, ethics, and conscience—when one considers this whole course of physical, intellectual, and moral evolution how incredible, or even impossible, it seems that all this should have come about by blind chance or mere accident! There must have been some directing cause, either outside of nature or in nature itself—a *deus ex machina* or a *deus in machina*.

One may discount or disregard excessive claims of universal fitness and purpose in nature, for there have been many misfits and mistakes; one may omit what Huxley has called "the frivolities of teleology," but there is left such a body of substantial facts in support of teleology in nature, as to convince Huxley himself and other serious students of evolution that *teleology is a principle of nature, correlative with causality*. On this Huxley wrote: "Perhaps the most remarkable service to the philosophy of biology rendered by Mr. Darwin is the reconciliation of teleology and morphology, and the explanation of the facts of both which his views offer." Darwin confessed the "extreme difficulty or rather impossibility of conceiving this immense and wonderful universe, including man with his capacity of looking far backward and far into the future, as the result of blind chance or necessity." On this subject Weismann said, "The most complete mechanism conceivable is likewise the most complete teleology conceivable. With this conception vanish all apprehensions that the new views of evolution would cause man to lose the best that he possesses—morality and purely human culture." And L. J. Henderson sums up his book on *The Order of Nature* with these thoughtful words: "Nothing more remains but . . . to conclude that the contrast of mechanism with teleology is the very foundation of the order of nature, which must ever be regarded from two complementary points of view as a vast assembly of changing systems and as an harmonious unity of changeless laws and qualities working together in the process of evolution."[4]

These opinions of distinguished naturalists could be indefinitely extended, and they give me courage in an age of scientific doubt concerning teleology to declare my conviction that science, no less than common sense, reveals to us a universe of ends as well as of means, of teleology as well as of mechanism. But such teleology is as much a part of nature as is causality.

Nature and the Supernatural

The conflict between science and the theology has centered largely in conflicting views regarding nature and the supernatural. In prescientific ages religion was usually associated with supernatural agencies and many devout persons today believe that supernatural beings and miraculous occurrences are fundamental to any and all religion. But with the progress of science the area of the supernatural and miraculous has gradually grown smaller, and the area of the

[4] Lawrence J. Henderson, *The Order of Nature,* Harvard University Press, Cambridge, 1917.

natural has increased, so that the latter now includes practically all of the universe that can be subjected to scientific investigation. Liberal theology now admits that "the age of miracles is past," but still maintains that miracles, that is, violations or suspensions of natural laws, occurred in former times. Indeed, supernatural agencies or occurrences constitute the very foundations of many religions. But gradually, under the impact of science, supernatural events have receded from everyday affairs to the misty mountain tops of origins and to inaccessible beginnings, or the dim recesses of mysticism, occultism, spiritism. Science has been exploring these mountain tops and caverns and finding that here also, as well as on the plains of everyday life, nature is supreme, in so far as it has been thoroughly explored. Therefore, it seems highly probable that everything in the universe is natural in origin and character, including all principles of causality and teleology, matter and energy, life and death, man and all his properties. In the words of Professor Brooks, my former teacher at The Johns Hopkins University, "The idea of the supernatural is due to a misunderstanding; nature is everything that is." Is not this misunderstanding the result of failure to recognize the infinite greatness and majesty of nature, which now includes all that was once ascribed to supernature, or deity, except the supposed lack of order, system, law in the latter?

It is interesting to find that this thought must have been in the mind of Darwin when he chose as significant texts for *The Origin of Species*, which texts are printed on the reverse of the title page of that book, quotations from Whewell's *Bridgewater Treatise,* Bishop Butler's *Analogy of Natural and Revealed Religion,* and Francis Bacon's *Advancement of Learning.* In abbreviated form the text from Whewell reads, "We can perceive that events are brought about not by insulated interpositions of Divine power, exerted in each particular case, but by the establishment of general laws." Butler's quotation runs, "The only distinct meaning of the word 'natural' is *stated, fixed,* or *settled,* since what is natural as much presupposes an intelligent agent to render it so . . . as what is supernatural or miraculous does to effect it for once." That is, there is no fundamental difference in the power and majesty of nature and that of postulated supernature; the only differences are in the assumption that the latter is not stated, fixed, settled, and that the former is not universal. These assumptions, like all universals or absolutes, lie beyond the reach of demonstration by methods of science, and must be regarded as probabilities of a higher or lower order. Regarded in this way, the universality of nature is highly probable, and the conclusion of Professor Brooks, "Nature is everything that is," will be accepted by most scientists. This conclusion carries with it modifications or cancellations of some common articles of religious faith; but there is neither time nor space here to deal in detail with these. If nature is universal, it is only necessary to inquire whether or not articles of faith are consistent with nature.

Confessio Fidei

All that I have tried to develop up to this point is a system of science and philosophy dealing with nature and man. Religion differs from this chiefly in that it is concerned in large part with the development of a system of right and duty. When I had felt compelled by increasing knowledge of nature to revise some of my traditional articles of religious faith, I was delighted to find that these changes had not modified in any essential respects my system of ethics. As I expressed it in my presidential address before the American Association for the Advancement of Science in 1937:

The ethics of science regards the search for truth as one of the highest duties of man; it regards noble human character as the finest product of evolution; it considers the service of all mankind as the universal good; it teaches that human nature and humane nurture may be improved, that reason may replace unreason, cooperation supplement competition, and the progress of the human race through future ages be promoted by intelligence and goodwill.

In all these respects the ethics of science does not differ from the ethics of enlightened religion. The religion of science leaves to us faith in the highest ideals of ethics and in the possibility of their realization among all nations and peoples. Whatever the ultimate basis of ethics may be, whether divine commandments or the decent social habits of mankind, the content is much the same. Whether written on tables of stone or on the tablets of our hearts, the "cardinal virtues" are still virtues, the "deadly sins" are still sins, and the commands of a God without are no more binding than those of a God within.

Scientists generally would agree, I think, that the faith and ideals of science include these articles: (1) Belief in the universality of that system of law and order known as nature. (2) Confidence that nature is intelligible and that by searching our knowledge of it may be increased. (3) Recognition of the fact that knowledge is relative, not absolute. (4) Realization that in unexplored fields we learn by trial and error, and finally trial and success. (5) The necessity of freedom, openmindedness, and sincerity in the search for truth. (6) Confidence that "truth is mighty and will prevail." (7) Realization that truth cannot be established by compulsion nor permanently overcome by force. (8) Belief that the long course of evolution, which has led to man, society, intelligence, and ethics, is not finished, and that man can now take an intelligent part in his future progress.[5]

The great system of nature calls forth feelings of admiration and awe in all who explore it, but, alas, it does not equally call forth feelings of love and devotion. Its appeal is to the head rather than to the heart, to the intellect rather than to the emotions, and in this respect the religion of science fails to meet some of the greatest needs of men, for it is in the realm of the emotions, rather than in that of the intellect, that religion has its greatest practical value. Indeed, religion is not so much a system of philosophy as an inspiration and guide to action. True religion breathes into the realism of science the spirit of lofty idealism. It cultivates among all classes, races, and nations of men, justice, peace, and mutual service, and if it does not do this it belies the teaching and example of its greatest prophets. It was Matthew Arnold, I think, who said that conduct is two-thirds of life; I think it could be said that right conduct is the greater part of religion; for "faith without works is dead," and "he that loveth not his brother whom he has seen, how can he love God whom he has not seen?"

[5] Edwin G. Conklin, *Man: Real and Ideal,* Charles Scribner's Sons, New York, 1943.

Ideal personal religion is one of love, which begins with the love of those persons nearest and dearest to us, and is then extended to abstractions and ideals such as truth, beauty, goodness, God. The pantheistic God of science may command our awe, but scarcely our love. It is difficult if not impossible to love "Evolution" or the "Order of Nature." Men need ideals more human and personal, and for this reason, no doubt, great religions have glorified and sanctified ideal persons—sages, heroes, martyrs, saints—and have personified their highest ideals as deities—Osiris, Ashur, Zeus, Brahma, Buddha. In the Christian religion these highest ideals are chiefly embodied in the persons of a Heavenly Father and a Divine Brother, Son of God and Son of Man, who bring into one family relation, so far as possible, the whole human race.[6]

These religious ideals go far beyond the teachings of science, but they are not for that reason to be rejected. Indeed, when one sees how such ideals are fitted to meet the desperate needs of men, one can only feel admiration and sympathy. No one can furnish scientific proof of the existence or nature of a divine plan in the fulfilment of which men may cooperate, but it is evident that such an ideal lends strength and courage to mortal men. Religious faith and ideals give the largest potential values to human life and the greatest stimulus to efforts for improvement. "By their fruits ye shall know them."

[6] *Ibid.*

RICHARD McKEON

The line which divides narrative from argument is tenuous and vaguely drawn, even when the account is of actions performed publicly and of matters of record attested by independent witnesses. Soldiers who have completed their campaigns or withdrawn from them and politicans who have put policies into effect or have seen them defeated have often set down some form of history in the conviction, expressed by Thucydides, that an exact knowledge of the past is an aid to the interpretation of the future.[1] The line is tenuous, however, because history is frequently transformed into fiction under the influence of arguments constructed to square actions with principles, and the arguments are twisted by the events into sophistry. Accounts of adventures among things of the spirit are still more esoteric than military and political myths. Incidents, dates, and even protagonists, are not easily determined by external witnesses to the evolution of ideas. The narrative therefore tends to reassemble the parts of an argument in the chronological sequence of their development, and the agents in the action tend to become ideas in dialectical opposition. Narratives of action reveal the interdependence of the careers and destinies of men; narratives of inquiry and speculation bring men together in common ideas encountered and in the common efforts to interpret them. In the treatment of intellectual and spiritual problems the individual mind is in contact with universal relations, and the grasp of a basic problem or the compre-

[1] Thucydides, i. 22.

hension of a true idea is not an individual possession to be explained adequately by personal traits or prior history. On the other hand, the order of experience takes on a significance, usually unsuspected until a problem is resolved, when the stages of the experience are rearranged as steps in the discovery or proof of what is later conceived to be valuable or true. In spiritual biographies the protagonist properly tends to lose his personal identity and his actions tend to be separated from the local conditions and temporal circumstances, for, as Spinoza proved, "insofar as men live under the guidance of reason, thus far only they always necessarily agree in nature."[2]

Habits of philosophic analysis and historical research, consequently, although they might seem useful instruments adapted to the effort of interpreting the memory of past problems with which one has worked and the sequence of the stages by which one has become aware of their implications and the requirements of their solution, in fact inhibit interpretation and reconstruction by suggesting prior questions. The account of one man's difficulties in speculation about principles, in deliberation about means, and in inquiry about consequences, is significant only if, on the one hand, the statement of his arguments has a bearing on ideas and aspirations as they are at once shared by other men of the time or tradition and involved in timeless principles or implications, and if, on the other hand, the account of the sequence of his efforts to clarify notions and achieve ideals contributes to the clarification of universal thoughts and common actions. Conversely, a slight knowledge of philosophy and historical method is enough to suggest suspicions concerning much that purports to be narrative accounts of thought or action: history is often made by equipping developments in theory or practice with subjective motivations which might justify but did not cause them, or by stringing events on significances later discerned but unexpressed and unknown at the time of occurrence.

The power and significance of autobiography and confession have their sources in these paradoxes, however much they may distress those who seek simple meanings of what is said and simple separations of the facts of narrative from the ideas of argument. The inter-

[2] Spinoza, *Ethics*, iv, 35.

dependence of actions and the interrelation of theory and fact tempt men to seek in the absolutes of independent empirical facts or eternal truths the significance of occurrences on which a life has touched and the developments which bind occurrences in a line of action or a growing insight. The actions of men are directed to satisfying like needs in like circumstances, and the thoughts of men encounter common matters and explore common patterns, yet the significance of the common and unchanged is rendered more intelligible by the circumstances and the changes that led to its expression in the particular manner of one person, one period, and one mingling of traditions. Doubtless motives may be manifest in any autobiographical account other than those recounted by the writer, and principles of selection operate in the determination of what occurrences should be chosen and emphasized, even in an account of speculation and inquiry other than the emergence of common problems and the clarification of universal ideas. The significance of the narrative can be sought in the delineation of a person and the circumstances of his times and culture, as well as in his approximations to ideas which influence many men and many times. Yet the reasons for writing about the circumstances which influenced one's thoughts and about the processes and events in which they were involved, can be only that the significance of thoughts, which is broader than the occurrences of one man's life, can be grasped concretely only in the particularities of expression and implication which are parts of biography, rather than of metaphysics or logic.

These considerations have determined the selection of autobiographical arguments which are presented in what follows. I have been concerned successively, for three rather long periods, with three problems which are problems of our times, or more nearly accurately, three approaches which our times have made to problems of universal scope and to truths of universal significance—problems of philosophic scholarship, of educational practice and administration, and of international and intercultural relations. Viewed in retrospect, these three problems seem so closely interrelated and interdependent that they may be described more nearly accurately as three approaches to the same problem. The same considerations, therefore, suggest that the narrative should run in the reverse of the chronological order, for the significances which I attach to events as I retell them were usually later additions, not recognized at the time. It is doubtless true that a man's characteristic attitudes are determined at an early age, long before the philosophic vocabulary which is later used to express them is available, but even if an autobiographer limited himself to such evidence as he could find concerning those first few years of his life and to the interpretations of his later life which his psychological or psychosomatic vocabulary permitted, those principles by which he arranges his narrative are themselves late acquisitions, grounded in philosophic presuppositions, as well as in psychological facts. The adjustments of the human organism are doubtless explained by basic principles, but those principles are discovered and tested by the human organism: the principles and attitudes that might be found in any such theory in what I have said would serve to characterize me, but I have been impressed by the recurrent conviction that the significant part of what I know in relation to what I do, always has been acquired during the past year, and my narrative is therefore of the process and not of the fixities by which it may have been conditioned. The story would, moreover, be better told backwards, if that were possible, for the beginning of an argument is its principles, and the principles emerge later in the evolution, but as it is impossible to present the narrative as argument, I shall try at least to distinguish the occurrences and later significances attached to them from the vantage point of some turning at which the two may be put in perspective.

I

The First World War was such a vantage point. I returned to my studies at Columbia University in 1919. The interruption of the war had been slight, for I had been assigned in the Naval Reserves to the Student Army Training Corps established at Columbia during the last months of the war. But I had been a "preprofessional" student before the war, engaged first on a program of studies designed to prepare for the law and later on a pre-engineering program; my further training in the Navy had been for engineering. Like many other returning students I found that my interests had shifted to humanistic studies, and for the next few years I read literature, history, philosophy, and the classics. In 1920, I wrote a thesis for the Master of Arts degree in which I studied Tolstoi, Croce, and Santayana, as expressions of three modern approaches to art and literature, and explored the relations and possible conciliation of esthetic phenomena conceived in terms of moral influences, esthetic experience, and scientific or psychological explanations. In retrospect I think the center of my interest was in the relation of esthetic values to science and to morality and in the methods appropriate to investigate in the art object the esthetic qualities of the object, the scientific foundations of the esthetic experience, and the moral and political implications of the creation of art and its influences. I was later to be impressed both by the need of new interpretations in art and morals because of developments in science and technology, and also by the danger of superficial and insubstantial analogies between the scientific method and the processes of moral deliberation and esthetic appreciation.

These purposes can be found in the thesis, but the recognition and statement of them is doubtless a later addition. The thesis also shows the marks of a more complete and systematic philosophy than I have been able to develop since 1920. The main outlines of the philosophy were determined (I thought), and it stood in need only of application to the varieties of problems of philosophy and related fields. The three chief ingredients of which it was composed were a scientific basis in behaviorism to account for how we think and how we act, a normative criterion in pragmatism to determine the meaningful problems of philosophy and the marks of truth and value by which to solve them, and a symbolic system by which to achieve precision in analysis and statement. It was a highly satisfactory philosophy, because it could be applied to a succession of subject matters and problems with little need of adjustment and with only a minimum of knowledge of the particular subject matter to which it was to be accommodated. I have never since been able to achieve comparable scope of system or convenience of method, but experience with later generations of students has kept me in contact with the later forms of that philosophy. In all its forms it combines a foundation borrowed from some science, a system of explanation couched in a technical vocabulary, and a ready applicability in the same form to all problems. Struggles with the simple distinctions of such philosophies usually raise doubts in their originators concerning the ideals to which they are directed. They led me by indirect ways to an interest in the vast diversity of problems which tends to be concealed in the simplifications, the unifications, and the analogies conceived in the name of philosophy and in the diversified adaptation of methods to materials and problems which tends to be forgotten in the hunt for formal precision and symbolic elegance.

The influence of science and of social and economic changes on philosophy and the determination of philosophic principles of scientific inquiry and social action seem in retrospect to have been the dominant interests during my graduate work in philosophy. The problems of scientific method and its metaphysical implications were prominent in the philosophic literature and in the philosophy courses of the early 1920s. These inquiries led me back to readings in the philosophers of the seventeenth century who had engaged in highly elaborated and diversified efforts to apply the scientific method to man and to human actions and to interpret what is entailed in the scientific approach. I was influenced in this exploration of present implications of science and past speculations concerning it chiefly by Frederick J. E. Woodbridge and John Dewey. Woodbridge helped and guided me in my study of Hobbes, Spinoza, and Locke, and was quizzically tolerant of the enthusiasms I discovered for Descartes, Leibnitz, and Boyle. I learned from Woodbridge to find philosophic problems, not in the massive oppositions of systems and in the rival propositions certified by technical analyses, but in the simple occurrences of everyday life from which the dilemmas of philosophic disputation are derived. The operations of the mind, so conceived, encounter the elements of order even in their most arbitrary decisions, and the intelligible structure of the universe is encountered in the exploration of ideas derived from experience. Most of all I learned from Woodbridge to respect the integrity of philosophic thought and to hold tenaciously to the assumption that what philosophers said made sense, even when I had difficulty grasping it, and that what philosophers meant might be comparable or even identical, despite differences in their modes of expression. Dewey had just returned from a long visit to the Far East and offered two courses in which he related the diversities of philosophic systems and methods to his own mode of philosophizing. From Dewey I learned to seek the significance of philosophic positions in the problems they were constructed to solve, to suspect distinctions and separations which remove the processes of thinking from the experience in which they originated, and to relate the formulation of problems and the discovery of solutions to the cultural influences which determined the manner of their occurrence.

My Ph. D. dissertation was a study of Spinoza which took its beginning in Spinoza's conception of scientific method in philosophy and of the use of reason in the resolution of moral problems. The arguments of Spinoza contained refutations of conceptions of the nature of science, and the application of scientific knowledge to moral and political problems which I had previously accepted without question. His analysis of scientific method is developed in a long correspondence in opposition to Boyle in which he argues against false empiricisms (as elsewhere he demolishes verbal scholasticisms) contending that experience alone can never refute a theory, because contrary evidence can lead either to the abandonment or the modification of the theory, and experimentation alone can never give knowledge of the fundamental nature of things or of basic scientific law. His use of method in moral problems can be studied in the massive attempt of his *Ethics* to treat the problems of action and passion *in more geometrico* and to provide precise mathematical proofs of moral theorems, but he argued that knowledge has no direct effect in the control of the passions and the motivations to knowledge. Irrationality can be controlled and the operations of nature can be understood, precisely because the universe is by nature intelligible.

Yet even when I had come to some understanding of this view of scientific method and its applications to morals, I was puzzled by its relation to the other parts of Spinoza's philosophic work. In his own time Spinoza was criticized as an atheist; during the eighteenth century Lessing, Jacobi, Herder, and Goethe found inspiration in his conception of God, nature, and human existence; in the nineteenth century, the great physiologist and comparative anatomist, Johannes Peter Mueller, thought it impossible to improve on Spinoza's analysis of the passions, and reprinted in his *Elements of Physiology* the aphorisms on the passions in the third book of the *Ethics*. It is an accurate rough description of the influence of Spinoza that its focus moved with the centuries down the sequence of the books of the *Ethics* centering "On God" in the seventeenth century, "On the Nature and Origin of the Mind" in the eighteenth century, and on "The Origin and Nature of the Emotions" in the nineteenth century. In the twentieth century the moral and political problems involved in "The Strength of the Emotions" came to new attention in interpretations which are not always consistent with the conception of God developed in the first book or the conception of "The Power of the Intellect" expounded in the fifth book of the *Ethics*.[3] I realized only later that the problems I encountered in Spinoza were twentieth century problems and that the Spinoza who influenced my thinking was neither the Spinoza criticized by Leibnitz nor the Spinoza admired by Goethe or Mueller. The application of scientific method to moral problems seemed to me to involve him in two difficulties, the first in relating the knowledge of man and his passions to nature and its processes by means of God and His attributes, and the second in separating the methods and controls of politics from those of ethics. My dissertation explored the unity of Spinoza's thought both in the natural bases which permitted the application of the geometric method to nature and to man, and in the differentiation of the purposes and methods of religion and politics from those of scientific analysis and morals.

[3] Cf. R. A. Duff, *Spinoza's Political and Ethical Philosophy,* Robert MacLehose & Co., Ltd., Glasgow, 1903, pp. 8–9 and C. D. Broad, *Five Types of Ethical Theory,* Harcourt, Brace & Co., Inc., New York, 1930, p. 15: "Before I begin to expound Spinoza's ethical theory I must state that I shall ignore -everything in his system which depends on what he calls *Scientia Intuitiva* or the *Third Kind of Knowledge;* i.e., I shall ignore his doctrines of the Intellectual Love of God, of Human Blessedness, and of the Eternity of the Human Mind."

From 1922 to 1925 I studied in Paris, spending the summers traveling in Europe and working in the libraries which determined in part the itinerary of the cities I visited. Much of what I have said about the direction of my earlier graduate studies should doubtless be dated during these three years, for they gave perspective to what I had done, both because I was able to place the traditions in thought of which I had become aware in the United States in the context of the European traditions from which they were derived, and because I was able to push further back my examination of the historical origins of the ideas and problems with which I had been concerned. Sensed differences in attitudes, purposes, and ideas encountered in different times, places, and formulations, are easily converted into myths, which have the kind of truth that is recognized in jokes about national characteristics. The student of philosophy can hardly avoid being impressed by tantalizing similarities of idea, expression, and purpose, even in philosophic discussions distantly removed, in space or time, from those with which he is familiar; but even in those which are close in origin and influence, the similar purposes are differently achieved, the similar expressions have different meanings, and the similar ideas appear in different uses and contexts.

My studies in French philosophy were inseparable from my discovery of America. I had learned that Francis Bacon was the first modern philosopher and that he had first inquired into the organization of the new sciences and formulated the methods by which they were acquired; I now learned that René Descartes was the first modern philosopher and that his inquiry into method and into the foundations of the sciences were the beginnings of modern philosophy. The philosophic movements which engaged the attention of students in the United States at that time were forms of realism and pragmatism constructed in revolt against idealism; philosophers like Henri Bergson and Léon Brunschvicg were engaged on like problems in revolt against absolute idealism but I found, to my amazement, that they were idealists notwithstanding their congenial approach to familiar problems. In that different climate of doctrines I became aware of characteristic American attitudes toward ideas—a tolerance of diversity of ideas, an absence of ideological marks of class differences, and an attachment to the method and application of the sciences. The tradition of liberalism in the United States was the expression not merely of a tolerance of differences'of doctrines, but of a confidence that truth is tested in the commerce of ideas and that values are derived from diversity; and when tolerance had been lacking in the growth of America there had been the physical space in which to move away from intolerance. Doctrinal differences had consequently become too numerous and complex to be organized into parties or to be made the mark of classes. When philosophies were constructed, they tended to claim relevance to present and actual conditions and to borrow examples and authority from scientific method. These attitudes gave a concrete pertinence to American philosophic speculation from the first, but they also exposed it to the dangers of that variety of intellectual and practical provincialism which results from employing principles insufficiently examined in relation to what other men have thought and done. Indifference to ideas may then pass as tolerance of diversity, and relativity of values may be substituted for the disposition to refuse to accept standards without further test merely because they are traditional. The absence of classes and parties based on differences or professed differences of ideas and ideals may invite the development of classes based on oligarchal differences and of parties based on economic differences. The cultivation of scientific method and real problems may be the excuse for the neglect of truths that have been discovered and of errors that have been exposed, and for the affectation of that spritely freshness of insight in which every philosopher recapitulates in his own person the whole history of thought.

Study in Paris provided the perspective not only of the approach characteristic of another culture to common philosophic ideas and problems, but also of the historical insight into the development of those ideas and the formation of those problems. The study of moral problems in their relation to scientific method and to social and political influences, had led me back to the first efforts of modern philosophers to treat those problems in the seventeenth century, and I had found in the study of those philosophers both the insight into later problems which comes from knowledge of their earlier forms and the insight into methods of analysis and resolution which comes from the rediscovery of alternative forgotten methods. But I also found much in their writings which was unintelligible and opaque without further historical study. I therefore worked with Brunschvicg on Spinoza and on the intellectual movements of which he was part. Brunschvicg had already published his study of the stages of development of mathematical philosophy, and he had begun to apply the same methods to the study of physical causality, moral conscience, and like concepts. I learned from Brunschvicg to use the historical development of concepts as part of the analysis of current problems in their interrelations in large departments of philosophy. I studied Descartes, Malebranche, and medieval philosophy with Étienne Gilson. My explorations of the background of Spinoza's philosophy had already brought me into contact with currents of medieval thought. My three years in Paris gave me the opportunity to study medieval philosophers more systematically—and to become interested in particular in the twelfth century background of Abelard and the fourteenth century context of Ockham—and I learned from Gilson to trace the basic patterns and unity of philosophic thought through the diversity of philosophic systems and expressions. Even before my medieval studies it had become apparent that Western thought is unintelligible without its Greek foundations. I therefore worked with Léon Robin on Plato and Aristotle, and learned from him philological and philosophical methods of interpreting the text and the structure of philosophic arguments. My indebtedness to these great teachers and the many others whose lectures I attended can hardly be summed up in a few sentences, and I suspect that I am unable to disentangle what I learned from the uses to which I put it, or to separate the ideas I was conscious of from the subtle modifications which the whole changed context of life worked in them. The interrelations of cultures must affect increasingly the developments of thought and its effective application, but life in Paris in the early 1920s cannot be rendered adequately in purely practical or intellectual terms.

I returned to New York in 1925 and taught philosophy at Columbia University for the next ten years. After the normal apprenticeship of teaching numerous courses in logic and introduction to philosophy, my teaching was divided between the history of philosophy and philosophic analysis. My historical courses concentrated on the Philosophy of the Middle Ages and the Renaissance, and my analytic courses, which were offered under the titles, "Metaphysics and Science" and "Metaphysics and Method," were devoted to the examination of the basic presuppositions and philosophic principles of the natural sciences, of the moral and social sciences, and of art and criticism. As I discussed these problems with my students and as I wrote about those portions of them in which the pattern of relations was clearest, I was brought to the conclusion that the startingpoint of philosophic discussion in our times must be the consideration of the vast diversity of analyses that have been made, and that are still being made, of problems which have a recognizable continuity, despite changes, revolutions, and new discoveries. There is a tendency in American philosophy to seek basic principles in operations or in linguistic forms of expression rather than in the nature of things or in the categories of thought. But the analysis tends to be of operations abstractly conceived, rather than of actual operations which define ideas in the context of associated ideas in cultures or systems and in relation to the subject matter to which they apply; or alternately it is an analysis of the forms of hypothetical pure languages, rather than the actual languages developed by men associated in cultures and engaged in the solution of practical and theoretic problems. The treatment of ideas and systems as functions of cultures and of intellectual methods and the exploration of the patterns of their expression in a kind of historical intellectual semantics have, therefore, seemed to me an important propaedeutic to the treatment of philosophic problems as such, and a defense against the shallow construction of patterns of culture which dispense with ideas, except as illustrative of cultural relations and of formal semantics which dispense with problems, except as consequent on the theory of language.

I have found that I returned often in these studies to the works of three philosophers whose speculations are explicit about the unity which they sought and about the distinctions which are important in the discovery of that unity. Aristotle found the basis of philosophy in experience, and sought to avoid the idealism of Plato and the materialism of Democritus; to that end he distinguished theoretic, practical, and productive sciences. Spinoza found the unity of knowledge and of things in Substance, God, or Nature, and sought to avoid the verbal explanations of Scholasticism (which he traced back to the tradition of Socrates, Plato, and Aristotle, as opposed to the tradition of Democritus, Epicurus, and Lucretius) and the constructions of "empirics and recent philosophers"; to that end he distinguished ethics, religion, and politics. Dewey found the unity of inquiry in experience, not as an epistemological beginning, but as the common cultural source of philosophic problems, and fought to avoid those abstractions from experience and nature which are embalmed in ideas constructed to solve problems of other cultures and times; to that end he distinguished problems, cultures, and forms of association. The problems which are presented in reconciling the truths of these three denials and assertions might as easily be approached from other beginnings, for the traditions of philosophy come to life in the debate concerning basic principles to order the whole range of philosophic problems in which each position is based on the denial of previous distinctions. The discovery of truth and the establishment of meaning are both dependent historically on the doctrines which become false or meaningless in the orientation of the new doctrine, and despite the impatience of practical men and dogmatists, there is fortunately no way to halt the eternal philosophic dialogue about things, knowledge, and systems.

II

During the early 1930s I met Robert Maynard Hutchins and discussed education in America with him, touching on both the problems of general education in the colleges and of the higher learning in the graduate schools. Among other questions, we talked about the relation of history to philosophy—the applications of history to the development of knowledge in the history of ideas and the application of philosophy to historical processes in the philosophy of history. I went to The University of Chicago as Visiting Professor of History in 1934–1935, to give a course in the intellectual history of Western

Europe and a seminar in the philosophy of history, and I stayed on as Dean of the Division of the Humanities and as Professor of Greek and Philosophy. During my twelve years as Dean, from 1935 to 1947, I was able to take part in the replanning of humanistic studies in general education in the College, as well as to cooperate with the departments in the reorganization of graduate work in the humanities.

The problem of the humanities in the present world is compounded of several dislocations which extend into many of the compartments of contemporary life—the readjustment of values to altered conditions and circumstances, the readjustment of methods of inquiry to the data and methods of science, and the readjustment of conceptions of the place of the humanities in education and life to changed philosophic presuppositions. During the period between the two World Wars there was widespread agreement concerning both the predicament of the humanities and the contribution which humanistic studies normally make to a well rounded education in a mature civilization; but there was little agreement concerning what the humanities are, or concerning what should be done to improve their condition and to put them to the uses of which they are capable. Yet it seemed probable that the predicament of the humanities could be traced to a circle of interrelated causes—the failure to recognize the contribution of the humanities to civilization and the consequent construction of a civilization in which the place of humanistic values is attenuated; when accomplishment is marked by accumulation and value by place, humanistic studies offer less obvious attractions to young students than the precisions and effects of scientific studies or the utilities and problems of social studies; and, as cause or consequence in such circumstances, methods of teaching and inquiry vacillate between the irrelevant technicalities of tested traditional methods and the irrelevant innovations borrowed from fashionable sciences and technologies.

At The University of Chicago, graduate studies are organized in four divisions under the Physical Sciences, the Biological Sciences, the Social Sciences, and the Humanities. This organization facilitates the assumption that the methods of the humanities are distinct from those of the natural and the social sciences in the treatment of subject matters and problems whose close interrelations are reflected in the affirmations and negations of philosophers concerning the separations and identities of the parts of our knowledge and behavior. During the early years of my work as Dean, members of the faculty of the Division of the Humanities met in committees, in small informal groups, and in divisional meetings to discuss the common disciplines which unite the various departments of languages, literatures, art, music, history, and philosophy in the Division. Out of those discussions there came an agreement that studies in the humanities should be conceived in relation to two bases—a material basis in the knowledge of a culture, a time, and a subject matter; and a disciplinary basis in the practice of methods of inquiry and criticism, and in the insights essential to their practice. The traditional separation of humanistic studies into departments such as English, Romance, Germanic, Oriental languages and literature, into Music, Art, History, Linguistics, and Philosophy, is token of the importance of command of the materials essential to humanistic studies in any given field of culture. The faculty decided that that organization was fundamentally sound, provided the methods and disciplinary approaches to the materials were broad and relevant to humanistic objectives. In order to maintain what is important in such specialized knowledge and yet prevent the fragmentation of the humanistic enterprise, they set up four interdepartmental committees—to operate in much the way departments operate in preparing programs of study and presenting students for higher degrees—in the four disciplines practiced in varying ways in all the departments: in language, history, criticism, and philosophy. These four disciplines cross the departmental lines, and the organization of the committees permits a student in Language and Communication, in History of Culture, in Comparative Studies in Art and Literature, and in the Analysis of Ideas and the Study of Methods to take work which involves several languages and symbolic systems, or a variety of cultures and times, or a variety of critical systems and literatures, or the bearing of philosophic analyses on a variety of subjects. Moreover, the interdepartmental work of the committees was calculated to bring greater breadth into the departmental work, while the cooperation of the departments in the work of the committees would serve the purpose of avoiding the vague and tenuous generalities which so frequently remain as the only mark that comparative studies in literature, history, and philosophy retain from the universal ambitions which motivate them.

The close relation of the humanities to the social sciences and to the natural sciences, as well as the characteristic differences of the methods employed in humanistic studies on materials which may fall also under the scrutiny of the sciences, become less difficult to discern when they are considered in respect to the disciplines of the humanities. Literature and the arts have their uses as data in the social sciences, and in those uses they are sources of information concerning cultures and peoples. Literature and art are also expressions of truths about nature, man, and the cosmos, and the continuity of human knowledge is marked in the inspiration Copernicus found in Cicero and Freud in Sophocles, no less than in the stimulation Lucretius derived from Epicurus, Hume from Newton, and Dewey from Darwin. But literature and the arts may be studied for the values which they embody, as well as for the light they may throw on the manners and ideas of men. Times and cultural circumstances facilitate the recovery of meanings expressed by men in other traditions and places, but the discovery and appreciation of values in the creations and expressions of men present problems other than solely the recovery of what they meant. The same times produce good and bad art and the same intentions are well and badly expressed. The study of the arts for the world-view they embody, or for information about the circumstances in which they were produced, and the study of art as embodiments of esthetic values, are supplementary inquiries into related aspects of human activities.

In like fashion, the study of language may be approached by inquiry into the physical and physiological bases of speech, or into the history of the development of languages and their uses in the communities and civilizations of men, or into the effectiveness of their employment for particular ends of expression. Anthropological linguistics has developed a technique for recording the modes of expression in different tribes and peoples and in different circumstances; humanistic linguistics adapts its techniques to the examination of the employment of language in rhetoric, literature, science, and other modes of expression. The diversity of linguistic patterns revealed in the one approach and the normative standards discovered in the other are not rival hypotheses between which the linguist must choose, but supplementary considerations to be brought to bear on the problems of languages. History, likewise, presents dimensions in the succession of geological ages, the evolution of animals, the marks which astronomical and meteorological phenomena have left on the planets and the surface of the earth and in the theoretic relations of time and space, which are properly treated in the natural sciences. The reconstruction and interpretation of social, political, economic, and cultural conditions and changes require techniques and theories which are devised in the social sciences. The history of art, music, literature, philosophy and the development of ideas, theories and values reflect the evolutions of nature and the circumstances of man, but the reconstruction and interpretation of the history of thought and expression depend on knowledge of those forms and ideas, and that history is the context in which theories about nature and man are developed. Philosophy, finally, is one form of knowledge, profoundly affected by the development of the sciences and by their methods; it reflects the interests of times, peoples, and cultures in which it develops; its proper domain is the principles and the systematic relations of explanations of things and their processes, men and their communities, and values and their expressions.

Concern with the predicament of the humanities in the world today is both part and consequence of reflection on the humanistic aspects of culture. The appreciation of art, literature, history, religion, and philosophy is one of the characteristic marks of a great civilization, and in the West the humanists have in various ages contributed to that appreciation by study of the tradition of art and learning. The humanists in Rome and in the Renaissance were able to adapt the knowledge of the past creatively to the formation of new cultures relative to new circumstances and new needs. The success of humanism depends on that double achievement—the perception of values as broad as humanity, and the expression of values in the living idiom of a people. Conversely, humanistic studies face two dangers in any period—the danger of debasement when the press of problems, the growth of tensions, and the confusion of education obscure common values, and the danger of obsolescence when the cultivation of traditional values and learned disciplines is removed from relevance to present situations and problems.

The problems of the humanities in scholarship and in the higher learning are closely related to the problems of the humanities in general education in the colleges. The problem of general education is basically the problem of establishing a common basis of understanding and communication which is the particular need of a democratic community. The determination of the contents of courses in the humanities in collegiate education, is part of the problem of constructing—with a view to the ideal that the opportunity will one day be open to all young people to continue their studies beyond the high school—an education for individual development, for citizenship, and for the utilities and amenities of common life. The solution to that problem determines, in turn, the preparation which students will have if they choose to go on to further studies in the humanities, and consequently the form which higher studies and research will take. At the College of The University of Chicago, work was in progress to revise the content of education for the new four year degree of Bachelor of Arts, which had been constructed on the basis of a division of education into six years of elementary education, four years of secondary education, and four years of collegiate education, instead of the customary division into eight, four, and four years. In the new scheme a student normally receives the A.B. at the age of eighteen or nineteen, and the program of more specialized work in one of the departments for the degree of Master of Arts becomes a three year program, instead of the nominal one year allotted to such training under older schemes. Having participated in the Division of the Humanities in the planning for that enlarged M.A. training, I was glad to accept the invitation of the College to take an active part in planning and teaching in the new program of the College. The program for the A.B. was conceived as a common program for all students in the College, divided into courses according to the major divisions of subject matters and disciplines, and tested by objective comprehensive examinations based on the field rather than the peculiarities of courses or instructors. My own work on the program was in two courses, the general Humanities course and the Integration course.

The committee which planned the course of studies in the humanities approached its problem by discussing the general question of the place which humanistic studies should occupy in contemporary education. The functions and uses of the humanities, in turn, involved the committee in searching considerations of the nature of the humanities and the methods proper to study and teaching of the humanities. A one year general course in the humanities was required of all students of the College, as part of the "New Plan" which had been put into effect in the early 1930s. This was a pioneering course, and it is widely influential in American education—and indeed it is still frequently the basis of what is said, in criticism and in praise, about the Chicago course in the humanities, in spite of the radical changes of the 1940s. It was a good course, but it raised many problems, among which one had a recurrent and fundamental character. The course followed the historical sequence of artistic, cultural, and intellectual developments in the Western world, and the humanistic disciplines required for the appreciation and interpretation of arts, letters, and philosophy, tended to be lost in the story, while the story tended to be accepted uncritically. It could be argued that education should provide a training in the humanistic disciplines, as well as in the disciplines required for the understanding of the historical developments by which values and their environing circumstances evolved. The committee therefore recommended that two courses be planned—one in history and one in the humanities— and that a close relation be maintained between the history course and the general courses in the humanities, as well as the social sciences, and the natural sciences, by referring the materials and methods treated in those courses to their historical contexts and to the conditioning influences of historical times and movements. The problem of constructing a humanities course, when it is separated from questions of "covering" the history of art, literature, and philosophy, is the problem of determining the contribution which the humanities might make to contemporary life, and, therefore, the problem of making available to students and to the times such benefits as might come from knowledge of men's great achievements.

It would be dubious history—even beyond the autobiographical license of reading theories later conceived into the development of earlier actions—to attribute to the group that discussed the plans for the humanities course any large consensus concerning the nature and the present purposes of the humanities. In the course of discussion I urged three objectives: the development in the student of taste and broad acquaintance with the arts, literature, history, and philosophy, sufficient to direct his interests and afford guidance into the rich satisfactions and improvements which exploration in these fields might afford; the formation of the abilities which are necessary to the recognition and appreciation of artistic, cultural, and intellectual values, as opposed to the random associated reflections which frequently accompany the attentive attitude and proper remarks that pass for appreciation; and, finally, the analytical abilities needed to integrate taste and interest, on the one hand, and critical judgment and discrimination, on the other hand, into the context of the principles—philosophic and social, theoretic and practical—which are particularized in the character and attitudes of a man, and universalized in the philosophies and cultural communities men share.

In my opinion those three purposes have served to signalize objectives that might be attributed to the parts of the three year course in the humanities which grew out of the planning started in that early committee. The first year of the course was devoted to bringing the student to a broad acquaintance with literature, music, and the visual arts, and with the basic problems involved in their interpretation. The second year concentrated on the problems of literature, in the broad sense in which it includes, not only *belles-lettres* but history, philosophy, rhetoric, and like forms of expression, and undertook to explore, not the historical sequences or the spirit of ages, peoples, or writers, but the questions which the critical reader should learn to ask concerning particular kinds of works or concerning particular aspects of all works: in respect to history, questions

concerning the adequacy of the narrative, representation, or argument
to particular facts; in respect to rhetoric, questions concerning the
adjustment of forms of statement and argument to particular audi-
ences, and their effectiveness, and value; in respect to philosophy,
questions concerning the principles and the development of arguments; and in respect to appreciation and criticism, questions bearing
on the forms of dramas, novels, lyric poems, the utilization and
expression in them of the tensions and aspirations of men, and the
communication they afford and effect to the spirit of men. These
questions were raised in a succession of readings in works of history,
rhetoric, philosophy, drama, novels, and lyric poetry, and the student
was trained, not in reciting a dogmatic humanism or philosophy of
culture, but in framing and considering the questions which are
presented to a critical mind by the varieties of forms, contents, and
proposed values. Once he had learned to consider historical questions
relative to works of history, philosophic questions relative to works
of philosophy, and esthetic questions relative to poetry, drama, and
fiction, he was expected to venture also into the tangled intermingling
of questions which constitutes much of the literature of criticism
and appreciation, by treating philosophy as poetry or history, exploring poetry as metaphor, argument, or ritual, and transforming
history into a metaphysics of cultures, an appendage to scientific
theories borrowed from thermodynamics or evolution, or a dialectic
with poetic, scientific, or religious overtones. During the third year
the student returned to the study of musical and visual, as well as
literary arts, to treat them in the light of critical principles as they
apply to individual works, as they relate works to men and times,
fashions and tastes, or enjoyments and uses, and as they integrate
life, expression, and community in basic philosophic forms.

The program of general education in the College was developed in
the various fields by planning and discussion similar to that which
led to the formation of the three year course in the humanities, and
the program consisted, therefore, of courses which the student would
normally take in preparation for the comprehensive examinations,
constructed to test whether he had the abilities and information
which are the marks of the possession of a general education. The

interrelations of the parts of such an education seemed to the faculty to deserve particular attention, and an "integration" course, to be taken in the last year of work, was therefore included in the plans of the program. I was a member of the committee which worked out the curriculum of this integration course. The objectives of the course are briefly adumbrated in the title "Observation, Interpretation, and Integration," which was attached to it in the early stages of faculty discussion. The committee began by considering the various ways in which the parts of knowledge might be integrated: they might be fitted together in an inclusive and neutral frame in an encyclopedic manner; their interrelations might be found in the fashion in which they could be put to applications in life in a practical manner; or their integration might take the form of the development of a systematic view of the organic unity of experience and the world in a philosophic manner. A general education, however, does not depend on encyclopedic knowledge, but on a framework of information and acquaintance with the uses and checks of available sources of information. The practical applications of general education, moreover, are not something separate from education, to be simulated in classroom reconstruction of cases or in field tours of regions, and the philosophy required for a general education should take the form of insight into relations among the parts of experience and knowledge, rather than of deductions from doctrines or dogmas. The committee concluded that integration in a general education must come from critical awareness applied to what had been acquired as knowledge and belief, and from the will and ability to explore the grounds and interrelations of what is known or thought to be known, to estimate intellectual and practical consequences, and to judge the criteria used in such inquiries. Such an integration would also provide the skills by which to accomplish and test encyclopedic, practical, and philosophic integrations.

The student comes to the end of his four years of collegiate education—even in the new programs of colleges in which "general" courses are constructed to facilitate his contact with large areas of experience and knowledge—with a number of large subject matters and the variety of methods related to them adjusted somewhat haphazardly in his habitual attitudes and modes of explanation. The adjustment of these parts of knowledge, habit, and attitude is the problem of "interpretation" in the large sense in which personal attitudes and knowledge are arranged, often unconsciously, according to fundamental preferences and basic sciences and ultimately referred for explanation to precepts of psychology, sociology, or economics, to theology, physics, folklore, or literary taste. The student is made aware of the problems of interpretation and their ramifications by studying the ways in which such adjustments have been made and have been justified in the "Organization of the Sciences" in the first term of the course. The unity of the sciences, the diversity of the sciences, the relations of theory and practice, the metaphysical examination of the principles of sciences, the reduction of sciences to their physical elements, to their logical, psychological, and epistemological forms, to their social and political conditions, the influence of the natural sciences on logic and ethics, of ethics on politics, and of politics on logic and science, form part of the patterns in which the sciences have fallen.

This formal interplay among the parts of knowledge and the varieties of unity which have been found in the sciences or imposed on them, is usually established or rejected by appeal to the facts. What is known and what is believed are tested by experience and by the consequences of action in accordance with the tenets of knowledge and belief. The problems of "observation," conceived in a large sense, turn on the relation of knowledge to facts, and on the variety of methods employed to relate what passes for knowledge to what passes for facts, and to achieve in statements of fact precision, generality, and relevance. The student is brought to the problems of the discovery of facts and their adjustments to theory, in the study of the "Methods of the Sciences" in the second term of the course. The methods and data of mathematics, physics, biology, the social sciences, and the humanities, are studied in the formulation and resolution of problems proper to their respective fields, as well as in the transfer of methods by which mathematics is made a physical science, or the subject matter of physics becomes organic and that of biology, some form of physical forces, or chemical processes, while the social sciences debate the validity of analogies to the physical and biological sciences, and the humanities accept or resist the methods of sociology, physiology, or linguistics. Finally, the constructions of our habits and knowledge, of their interrelations and their references to facts and experience, are organized according to principles, casual and unobserved in the processes of action, or precise and tested in the demonstrations of the sciences. Principles are often signalized in the inquiries and discoveries of individual men; they are often acknowledged in the common acceptance of an age or a people; their impact or alteration is often the mark of revolutions in science and society. The systematization of knowledge, values, and the relations of men, is the problem of "integration," in the broad sense in which principles are found underlying the interrelations of habits and emotions, of actions, knowledge, and communication, of individuals, groups, and nations, which are in turn referred to the regularities and laws of nature by principles which determine the interrelations and systems of the sciences. The student encounters the problems of integration in the study of "Principles in the Sciences" in the third term of the course, and he examines concepts like "pleasure," which many moralists reject as an ethical principle, but which hedonists and utilitarians make the principle of all human actions, and "cause," which was long the basis of all scientific explanation until philosophers and physicists questioned the meaning and the very existence of causes.

The exploration of the problems of the humanities in general education and in graduate studies was reflected in my program of teaching during these years. I taught sections in the Humanities and Observation, Interpretation and Integration courses in the college; I taught in the various interdepartmental committees and in the two departments in which I held my professorship, Greek and Philosophy. Departmental distinctions have led to the separation of the Plato and the Aristotle taught in Philosophy Departments from the Plato and the Aristotle taught in Departments of the Classics: the former frequently held doctrines which would be expressed with difficulty in Greek, while the latter wrote works full of philological problems but relatively free of philosophy. I adapted the methods I had learned from Robin to read Plato and Aristotle with mixed classes in which philosophers learned some Greek, and Greek students learned to discuss philosophy. I read Cicero and Aquinas with combined groups of philosophy and Latin students. I gave courses in which literary and art criticism was related to the discussion of philosophy and esthetics, courses in which scientific methods and the varieties of logical theories were related to their metaphysical assumptions, courses in which political and moral theories were examined in their bearing on the relations of cultures and on the political disputes of our times, courses in the philosophy of education, the philosophy of law, the philosophy of language, and the philosophy of history. I came into contact in this curriculum of teaching with a more diversified group of students than could have afforded the adventure into philosophy in the older schemes of study. A generation of students is only a few years, and I can look back at several generations at The University of Chicago who have been able to move more widely in their studies than could their predecessors, both in the range of related interests and in the application of knowledge to present problems and things; who have conceived from the humanities a love for things human, for arts, letters, and sciences; who have learned to use languages, to apply methods of analysis and criticism, and to judge principles; who have acquired some sense of the histories and interrelations of peoples and cultures; and who can resort to reason without the suspicion that its cold light is destructive of humanistic values or irreconcilable with democratic processes. The educational practices which we established and the philosophic meanings which we explored, are already involved in the processes of change and misinterpretation, but the contacts with languages, with arts, with history, and with philosophy afford the student points of reference and support by which to judge their education and philosophy amid the changes; and the students who have made those skills and disciplines their own are a better expression of the ideals we set in education than any statement of our new plans or of the philosophies which animate them.

III

Planning for new forms of general education is grounded in present problems and in the relevance and efficacy of training in the major fields of human knowledge—in scientific method and knowledge of the results of scientific advance, in the background and problems of democratic life and man's attachment to the guiding principles of freedom, and in appreciation of humanistic values and powers of communication and expression. Teaching and research in the humanities consists in the exploration of the great achievements of man in the study of their continuity in history and universality in values, at the point where tradition affects the present in the use of languages, the appreciation of art, the interpretation of history, and the construction of philosophies. In modern times general education and humanistic studies have both been influenced increasingly by the interrelations of cultures and the broadening of interest beyond the limits of the traditions of Western European and American culture. The coming of the Second World War accentuated that process and gave it a practical turn. During the early 1940s, planning for the effective use of educational institutions in contributing to the military success of the United States in the war took many forms, in respect both to research and to teaching. I participated in the planning of the Army Specialized Training Program, particularly the Area and Language Studies, and I became Director of the unit of that program established at The University of Chicago. The purpose of the Area and Language course was to give Army personnel a speaking ability in the language and a knowledge of the geography, and of the social, economic, political, and cultural conditions of the country in which they might serve liaison and similar functions. The University of Chicago unit undertook training in German, French, Italian, Russian, Chinese, and Japanese, and the planning of the course included the choice of methods of teaching language and the determination of what kind of knowledge of the region, the people, their ideas, values, and institutions would be most useful to enlisted men and officers in the discharge of their duties. There are impressive indications that the courses served a useful purpose in achieving the practical ends set for them during the war, and the influence of the experiences of the units set up at the various universities of the country, have continued in the postwar period, particularly in the methods of language teaching and in the planning of studies concerned with areas and peoples which had not been treated conspicuously in prewar education.

The teaching of languages in the Area and Language Courses profited by the intensive training which was possible and by the motivation which was supplied by the circumstances. The student was under Army discipline and his continuance in the course depended on his progress in acquiring fluency in the language he was studying. A large portion of his day was devoted to classroom training, guided study, and practice with language records and reproducing apparatus. Some of the schools made use of the methods of teaching language developed in the teaching of "non-literary" languages for which few "informants" or speakers, and no experienced teachers, could be found, and extended it also to languages with extensive literatures, well known grammars, and tested techniques of teaching. Publicity in popular magazines during the war was calculated to give the impression that it was a method used in all units sponsored by the Army, and that the techniques of language training had been revolutionized by a "scientific linguistics" which used the example of "informants" to induce proficiency in foreign languages as one had acquired one's native language without the formalities of grammar. The linguists and language teachers at The University of Chicago concluded that the argument was based on a fallacy, for the analogy between acquisition of language in youth and in maturity neglected the devices which the mature mind might employ to facilitate learning, and on a misconception of the fashion in which grammar was used in recent language teaching. They found the linguistic method of language teaching wasteful: it dispersed the student's efforts by requiring some acquaintance with the distinctions and terminology of a linguistic theory which was not particularly pertinent to his problems, as well as with the language he was learning, and the peculiar objectives to which the method was directed extended little beyond acquiring phonetic accuracy in the production of sounds. In languages possessed of literatures and related to cultures for which information is available other than that assembled by the question techniques of anthropology, richer and more efficient teaching resources are available. The teachers at Chicago were convinced that they could achieve phonetic accuracy more effectively by other devices perfected in recent experiments in language teaching and that they could also give proper attention to other related objectives, such as use of a larger vocabulary, fluency of idiomatic and grammatical speech, and development of ease and ingenuity in solving problems of expression in new subject matters. Tests were devised in which these various objectives were distinguished and the student's ability was examined with respect to each. Any generalization concerning the effectiveness of methods of language teaching would depend on the systematic construction and administration of such tests, but more important than the decision among the rival methods which were tried during the war has been the continued development of methods and teaching materials along the directions indicated by those experiments. The importance of strong motivation and intensive training, however, is one of the undisputed lessons of wartime language training.

The problem of what to teach concerning the "area" in the short time available in the course, was more difficult than the problem of how to teach the language of the area, and the nature of the difficulty is indicated in the choice of the word, "area," to indicate what was at least a geographical expanse in each case, and in addition, in varying degrees, a social, economic, political, cultural, and intellectual region, as well. The criteria of selection of what to teach were set in a general way by the range of possible duties that might be assigned to a soldier in the territory of a friendly or an occupied enemy country; but the possible duties were too variegated to determine categories of facts that might be useful, and area courses were constructed in the various units on the basis of indispensable minima of geographic, economic, industrial, social, historical, and cultural information integrated by a variety of accidents and schemes. At The University of Chicago the emphasis tended to be more cultural and humanistic than at some other units, on the ground that the problems encountered in any assignment would be in part problems of information and in part problems of contacts with people; and whereas it would be difficult, if not impossible, to anticipate the details of information that might be required, familiarity with the culture and the values of the people would facilitate cooperation, and in most cases provide the means of securing the needed information as well. Some knowledge of the literature, the philosophy, and the institutional, cultural, and intellectual history of the area was therefore woven into the information concerning rainfall, industry, transportation, and ethnic groups.

The area and language courses doubtless served a useful and urgent purpose in attacking a practical problem of liaison and contact during the war. That problem was the simpler form of complex problems of cultural contacts which were to have increasing attention in education and in political negotiations after the war. The history of the relations of the peoples of the world has been written in the past largely in terms of political, military, dynastic, and commercial contacts. Conquerors have swept across Asia Minor, Europe, and the Far East, frequently proclaiming the motive of "world dominion" to unite all mankind; explorers have skirted Africa and crossed the Atlantic from Europe in the interests of trade and as the precursors of settlers and missionaries; and it would seem, at first glance, that instruments, arts, and ideas traveled the pilgrim roads, the trade routes, and the paths of crusade and conquest, frequently unobserved in their immediate effects, following in the wake of these movements of power, profit, and salvation. The contacts of cultures are, however, older and more intricate than the tales of foreign lands which soldiers might bring back from their campaigns or sailors from their voyages: they are part of a texture woven into the folksongs which continued a living tradition after entering the Homeric epics; into the successive translation of Aristotle and Galen from Greek into Syriac, Arabic, Hebrew, and Latin; into the influence of the Bible in Judaism, Christianity, and Islam; into the spread of Buddhism, the migration of symbols, and the development of tools and technology. Since the war the contact of cultures has forced itself into prominence in the discovery that the economic, political, and social problems of the world are inextricably interrelated, and that knowledge and common values are indispensable instruments in the construction of a world community within which political institutions can operate on a worldwide basis.

The educational aspects of the problem of the relations of cultures had become apparent even before the outbreak of the Second World War. Education in the United States had been based largely on the tradition of "Western Europe," or even on efforts to concentrate on the American experience and what was peculiar to it: large regions of the world—the Far East, India, Austronesia, the Near East, Russia, Africa, and even neighboring Latin America—were touched on only glancingly as they impinged on that local interest. Important advances had been made before the war in the improvement of Far Eastern and Russian studies on the graduate level, and it became increasingly clear as the war drew to a close that general education and the higher learning would have to reflect the broad scope of common problems revealed by the contacts of peoples which resulted from, and the common aspirations which were made practicable by, the advances of technology. The temptation to carry over the techniques of the area and language courses as a means to solve this problem was strong and widespread, and the regional "institutes" specializing in Russia, Latin America, the Far East, or Europe which have proliferated so rapidly since the war are often mere rearrangements of information and of traditional courses of study in new boxes, presented as novel results of the reexamination of problems and of the use of new methods for their solution.

The organization of knowledge and the planning of education are not simply questions of arranging collections of data and information in patterns of time, space, and culture; they depend on involved relations of the problems of times, the methods of sciences, and the aspirations of peoples. In our times they reflect common practical and material problems of war devastations, of food, disease, and security, and of the effects of technology on the lives and cultures of peoples on whom the impact of the advances of industry and science has been sudden and late; they are instruments in the attack on the political and social problems of vast numbers of people who have recently acquired the right to self-government, in the extension of fundamental education and human rights, and in the development of the interrelations of the nations of the world; and they are the structures which determine approaches to problems of comprehension and achievement of shared values and of understanding and advancement of common knowledge. In our discussions of these problems in their bearing on studies in the humanities at The University of Chicago it was decided to subordinate new regional arrangements of the program to new considerations of problems and methods for their treatment. In the Division of the Humanities the interdepartmental committees afford a frame for treating problems of cultural relations in terms of their reflection in problems of language and communication, of the cultural significances of art and literature, of the broadened frame of cultural history, and of the prominent intrusion of ideas and methods into modern discussions and ideological conflicts.

The political aspects of the relations of cultures and of educational devices became apparent in the preparations for the peace. As early as 1942, the Conference of Allied Ministers of Education (CAME) met to plan for the reconstruction of educational facilities and means of communication destroyed during the war. The Charter of the United Nations, signed in 1945, provides for the promotion of "international cultural and educational cooperation." From these beginnings plans for the United Nations Educational, Scientific and Cultural Organization (Unesco) grew, in the conviction, stated in the Preamble to Unesco's Constitution that a peace based exclusively upon the political and economic arrangements of governments could not secure the lasting and sincere support of the peoples of the world and that peace must therefore be founded upon the intellectual and moral solidarity of mankind. Unesco is an experiment in the relations of peoples; it is an effort to use education, scientific, and cultural instruments for a political end, the achievement and safeguarding of peace. I participated in some of the early meetings called in the United States to discuss the form which Unesco's program and operation might take, and I was Adviser to the United States Delegations at the first three sessions of the General Conference of

Unesco, in Paris in 1946, in Mexico City in 1947, and in Beirut in 1948. I returned to Paris in 1947, after the establishment of Unesco, to serve as the first Acting Counsellor on Unesco affairs attached to the United States Embassy in Paris, and on my return to the United States I served as a member of the United States National Commission on Unesco.

In September, 1947, a Committee of Experts was assembled in Paris to advise the Director General concerning the program of Unesco in philosophy and the humanities. I attended the meeting as one of the United States experts, and as Rapporteur I drew up the basic document prepared at the meeting. The Committee differentiated three levels of activities in the field of philosophy and the humanities: the continuing service activities, such as the exchange of persons, information, bibliographical compilations and the like, in which philosophy and the humanities should share with the other disciplines; the activities related to its program which Unesco would stimulate and encourage international organizations in philosophy and the humanities to undertake; and, finally, projects bearing directly on the purposes of Unesco to be carried out under Unesco's direct supervision. The Committee recommended two such projects, one in philosophy and one in the humanities. Both projects were conceived, not as scholarly enterprises undertaken in their respective fields, but as efforts to formulate the direct and immediate contribution which philosophy and the humanities might make to the peace of the world. The Committee decided that, if one asked what place philosophy has in the search for means to avoid conflict and to establish that dynamic order among the nations of the world which is the definition of peace, the answer must be found in the fact that philosophic issues were involved in the so-called "ideological conflict" which affects the discussion of diplomats, the reports and editorials of newspapers, and the ideas and formulations of men everywhere. The ideological conflict is basically an extension of philosophic problems to the discussion of problems of ordinary life, of national policy, and international relations, and a project was therefore planned to examine certain fundamental terms, such as human rights, democracy, freedom, law, and equality, as they enter into contemporary practical problems and statements about them. In like manner, if one were to ask how the humanities might contribute to mitigating the confusions and reducing the conflicts of our time, and how they might give emphasis to the elements of understanding and community which are beginning to emerge, the answer must be found in the study of humanistic aspects of cultures, in the communication which arts and letters establish, not in doctrines, but in basic values underlying differences of expression, tradition, and times, and in the community of traditions in their mutual influences and their common values. The Committee recommended, therefore, that a second project be set up to treat the hierarchies of values characteristic of cultures and expressed in artistic and intellectual productions as they bear on the relations of peoples and the problems which peoples face in common.

I continued work on both projects. The first form which the examination of ideological conflicts took was the study of human rights undertaken by Unesco early in 1947, in cooperation with the Commission on Human Rights of the Economic and Social Council which had just started on the task of drawing up the Universal Declaration of Human Rights. Unesco was to examine the intellectual bases of the rights of man, first, in their historical development from the philosophic principles on which they were formulated in the classical statements of human rights in the eighteenth century to the principles invoked in their definition and defense today, and second, in the present day opposition of principles which leads to diverse interpretations of human rights and in particular to the opposition of traditional political and civil rights to more recently asserted social and economic rights. The Unesco Committee on Human Rights issued its report in July, 1947, and the collection of essays made in the course of its inquiry was published under the title, *Human Rights: Comments and Interpretations,* in 1949. The project was continued in an inquiry into the ambiguities which surround the word, "democracy," in recent discussions and manifest themselves in opposed institutions and practices, as well as in propaganda maneuvers and accusations. A volume entitled, *Democracy in a World of Tensions,* appeared in 1951, published by The University of Chicago; the study of the diversities and shades of meaning attached to the term, "democracy," is addressed both to clarifying differences of meaning and to exploring means of reducing differences of action.

The study of the humanistic aspects of cultures has meanwhile been directed to two related aspects of the relations of cultures—the study of the effects of new technologies on the customs and values of peoples who have been little affected by technological and scientific advances, and the structures of values in cultures that have adjusted themselves or are in process of adjustment to industrialization and political independence. The pattern of basic philosophic attitudes and values embodied in the institutions and in the ways of life of people or assumed in their statements about their institutions and actions, cannot be abstracted from the conditions or the relations of peoples; and with proper cautions against ambiguity and conscious deception, the relations of peoples can be better understood by reference to that pattern of ideas and values. Even the political and economic relations of the various parts of the world are affected by what men believe and by what their beliefs mean, and the promulgation of a universal declaration of human rights will be translated by the peoples of the world into comparable actions in recognition of those rights only after the different meanings of "rights" and the different hierarchies of values which give effect to rights in different cultures have been transformed into motivations to comparable common ends.

The three problems which I have presented in the guise of an autobiographical account of my activities during the past thirty years —the philosophic, the educational, and the political problems of our times—have close interconnections both in the logical interrelations they would assume in any philosophy and in the historical interdependences they would reveal in any time. They have only an accidental relation in the career of any one man, and the irrationalities and paradoxes which he encounters are frequently the marks by which to reconstruct a version of the relations which they have in logic or in culture. The form according to which I have arranged this account makes the events it treats fall into the sequence of a consecutive search for a truth which is unified, and the sequence of the narrative is easily restated in an argument which proceeds in sorites from basic premises. It could as easily be recounted as a sequence in which I backed at each stage into the interests and basic convictions of the next, and it could then be restated in an argument that proceeds by paradoxes in which the contraries of each stage are reconciled into one of the contraries in the paradox of the next.

I backed into philosophy as a means of securing insight into the conflicts of theory and practice, of values and actions, which became increasingly prominent at the time of the First World War. I moved down the history of philosophy in my study of the antecedents of contemporary intellectual and moral attitudes, and I have backed into the broadening of my philosophic position in an effort to understand what would be implied in the positions denied by a series of philosophers. Dewey denied the distinction between art and science, practice and theory, and I found that the significance and power of what he taught depended on understanding the differences which separated the pairs of terms he collapsed. Spinoza denied the separation of the order and sequence of things from the order and sequence of ideas by scholastics engaged with words and by empirics engaged with manipulations of things, and I first appreciated the value and validity of his denials when I understood that proof might be distinguished wholly from process or be reduced to operations which can be controlled and repeated. Aristotle denied the idealism of Plato and the materialism of Democritus, and I began to have some insight into the peculiarities of his scientific and philosophic method and into his influence on the later history of thought, when I learned the opposed contributions of the ideas of Plato and the atoms of Democritus to the inquiry of men into the nature of things and of change. The denials seemed to me at first encounter so plausible that I found it difficult to understand how any one could ever have held the positions so readily and so persuasively refuted, but in each case a return in history or a reconstruction in theory made the refutation one more example of how men turn easily away from the theories they criticize but seldom because they have discovered error and destroyed its grounds. The importance and use of denying the distinction between art and science and between theory and practice are indeed directly proportional to the force and validity of the distinction and the length of time during which a tradition and a culture have acquiesced in it.

The relation of scholarship to teaching and of both to the social and political relations of our time, may be stated in terms of the same dialectical processes which are forced unobtrusively or reluctantly on scholarly inquiry. It is not merely that the pursuit of philosophy is itself both a process of education and a consequence of problems encountered in or induced by the educational process, but the education of a time and a people is a philosophy stated in genetic form and it serves to organize available knowledge and cogent beliefs in a kind of metaphysics of habitually accepted principles of action. When knowledge has been vastly increased, when the actions, productions, and relations of people have in consequence been altered, and when communications among men have been facilitated but obscured, then values that have been recognized to be common to all men are increasingly difficult of access to any man and the problem of reviewing and reorganizing education becomes in a fundamental sense philosophic. Yet philosophy, in our times, has become an academic pursuit and the philosopher backs from speculation to teaching as a career which permits leisure for scholarship and thought. Moreover, teaching has become a middle term, in our times as it has frequently before, to connect knowledge and scholarship to the status and operations of citizenship. Propaganda, communication, and education were seen to be powerful political instrumentalities during the war, and the political relevance of education and philosophy, which were doubtless apparent long before Plato constructed a perfect state by educating philosopher-kings, must continue to be recognized increasingly during the peace because of the dangers, as well as the opportunities, presented by new media of communication, new subjects of knowledge, and new recipients of education.

The logical relations among these three problems must be inferred from the accidental relations in which they fall in the life of a man or the intercourse of a group. I have talked about myself, therefore, by recalling the ideas I have encountered in a manner which would be justified by Aristotle's argument that the mind which is actively thinking is the objects which it thinks, or by Spinoza's conclusion that men agree in nature and are united by the common possession of the true ideas which they share. Either account of their interrelations—the metaphysical account of their essential interdependences or the autobiographical account of the accidental sequence in which their intermingling is discovered—is an index to the nature of our times. We face a *philosophic* problem of formulating the organization and interrelations of our knowledge and our values, the interplay of our ideas and our ideals, the influence of our new sciences in providing means for the solution of old problems and in laying the beginnings of new problems, and the distortions and misapplications of what is called scientific method and of what is claimed as democratic practice. That philosophic problem is inseparable from the *educational* problem of equipping men with abilities and insights to face the new problems of our times and to use the new instrumentalities with wisdom and freedom. The philosophic and educational problems are both implicated in the *political* problem of achieving common understanding among the peoples of the world who might, if ideas continue to become opaque in the oppositions of interests, be divided into parties determined by classes, the wealthy and the dispossessed, rather than by ideas and purposes. Understanding of common ideas and common ideals is the one means to combat and discredit the assumption that values and ideas are simple reflections of class interests and ideologies, that philosophy, art, and education are simple badges of privilege or instruments of revolution, and that the differences which threaten to divide the world are impervious to methods devised for the peaceful resolution of differences and for agreement and cooperation on common courses of action, but can be resolved only by subterfuge, violence, and suppression.

The philosophic problem is not one for the speculation of the isolated scholar engaged in the construction of a personal doctrine. It depends for its statement and examination on participation by a broadly educated public and on testing of basic doctrines and values against the fundamental presuppositions of other philosophies, religions, systems of values, and modes of life. Philosophic universality is easy to achieve by reducing all other views to the requirements and limits of one preferred creed and system, but it distorts the doctrines it refutes; and a similar easy and violent victory in imposing uniformity in political practices, with its consequences in suppression and hostility, is the only alternative to a political universality based on common understanding and on common values. True universality in intellectual, as well as in practical relations, depends on insight into the diversities of cultures, philosophies, and religions, and on acquaintance with the methods and consequences of science. The educational problem is not a simple choice between preserving the old and denominating anything new as good, but requires an integration of a new kind to be achieved both by applying new knowledge to values and by according new recognition to the claims of peoples and the values of cultures. International understanding, finally, will not be achieved either by programs of propaganda and information, or by setting forth the patterns of cultures and laboriously trying to think and feel as other people do. Values are based on the peculiarities of cultures, but they are understood and appreciated, even by those who share the culture in which they originated, because of their universality, and international understanding is based on the recognition of common values in the vast diversity of their forms and idioms. Understanding has a practical bearing both on action (because education and knowledge can build a foundation for international cooperation and world institutions) and on theory (because understanding and the preservation of peace are indispensable conditions for the progress of science, the construction of values, and the cultivation of the good life). These three— the understanding of order in nature, in the relations of men, and in knowledge, the education of men sensitive to the marks and uses of that order, and the appreciation of differences in the modes in which peoples express that order and seek their fulfilment in accordance with it—are the three related aspects of a problem which we all face in our individual lives, our communities, and in the world relations in which all communities have been placed.

ERWIN D. CANHAM

As I write these words, our plane has just risen above a 3,000 foot
overcast which has kept the Atlantic seaboard in a dull and oppressive
gloom for several days. In just seventy seconds from the time our
wheels left the runway, we have risen into the most brilliant sun-
shine which is painting with soft pastel colors the clouds far beneath.
This familiar experience vividly enacts the transition many of us have
lived as we emerged from the mists of dependence on materialism
into the reality of God's spiritual universe and our place in it. This
was precisely what happened to me and to my family when we found
Christian Science and began to live a spiritually aware life.

I was born into a strong religious and moral tradition. It was
formal and stern, there was much that was good in it, but it had
failed to give my parents and me what we needed most in life:
awakening and health, progress and the demonstrability of spiritual
truth. The virtues of our old religious tradition were mainly negative.
It had failed altogether to open the vistas of illimitable spiritual
dynamics.

Nevertheless, it was an immensely wholesome and sturdy environment into which I was born, and I am very grateful for it. Had I
not seen something of its ultimate sterility, I should not have been
so aware of the significance of spiritual awakening. Its positive values
laid a good foundation for further progress.

My father and mother were earnest and scrupulously practicing
Methodists. I remember church sermons and suppers, Sunday school

sessions and Sunday school picnics, from earliest childhood. But I must confess that I recall no spiritual lessons at all from these early days. My most precise memory of the Methodist Church, I must admit with apologies, is of marching around the Sunday school room while the collection was being taken, singing (to the tune of *Onward Christian Soldiers*):

> Hear the pennies dropping,
> Count them as they fall.
> Every one for Jesus,
> He will get them all.

But this is unfair. Of course I have a precious heritage, within its limitations, of our Methodist days, although it is inseparably blended with the standards and precepts of the community and the time. I was born in the small city of Auburn, Maine, in 1904. My father was a reporter—and sometimes a printer—on a small daily newspaper. His father and grandfather had come to Maine from the eastern counties of England. My grandfather, who was a weaver in a woollen mill, was also a Methodist lay preacher. He was a true and earnest exponent of the tenets of John Wesley. In England, he and all his relatives had always been "chapel folk."

My grandfather and grandmother were sweet and gentle people. Indeed, there has run a strain of contentment and love—of simple goodwill—through all the Canhams of our branch that I have ever known. Nearly all of them have been poor and humble people, but they have always been gracious and contented, and their family circles have been warm and intimate. I do not know of a single broken marriage out of my scores of uncles and aunts and cousins. The family has had a great sense of kinship and affection. My grandfather, whose household began to swell steadily in the 'seventies and 'eighties of the past century, wanted keenly to save enough money so that he and his wife could travel back to England to see the haunts and friends of their childhood. The only way he could contrive to do this was to give up the one nonessential item of his household, his pipe tobacco. This he did. The resultant savings took him and his wife on two trips back to England in their ripe years, and started a family tradition. My father never smoked, and I do not, although our abstinence also stems from the teachings of Christian Science. My grandfather and father and all the members of the family that I know were also total abstainers from alcoholic drink.

We were, you may say, a dour and spartan lot. But that is far from the fact. My grandfather and grandmother Canham were beaming, rosy cheeked little people (I do not resemble them physically) and their legacy to me was a deeply felt sense of sweetness and good in the home, a profound devotion to organized religion, and a loving family circle. This is, indeed, no mean heritage, and I am grateful for it and for my gracious kinfolk.

My mother had been a school teacher in her teens, in the one room district schools of rural Maine. Neither she nor my father had the possibility of earning their way in college, and although both were studious, they also felt upon graduation from high school—which was a great event in their lives—the need of going right to work to help their families. They had been sweethearts in school, and their marriage came four years after graduation.

My mother's people had been in Maine since Colonial days. Her father was a farmer who eked out the inadequate fruits of a hardscrabble rock strewn Maine farm by working off and on all his life as a bricklayer and mason. He was a craftsman of the best folk tradition, and the tops of his chimneys avoided Victorian ostentation and swelled with simple Grecian lines. I can still see many of his chimneys as I drive the country roads of Androscoggin County, Maine, and they make me proud of his untutored, graceful work. He, too, was studious and thoughtful, an avid reader. He loved to have me as a small boy read to him, and some of the facility to read aloud which stands me in useful stead nowadays before a microphone stems from the practice I had in reading to my grandfather in the country kitchen, during the long winters when he could not work as a mason and the chores were all done.

His wife, my grandmother, was another simple soul whose loving, gentle goodness had also something of the fierce protectiveness of a mother hen. Let any external influence try to harm or tempt her brood! She would dispose of that! She was also a fine craftswoman, but in the making of rugs, and quilts, and rich, golden, beautifully molded butter which she sold to townsfolk to add a little of the badly needed cash income.

From these two grandparents came three daughters—my mother and her two sisters—who are among the most remarkable women I have ever known. They have all become Christian Scientists, and they have long shown—as I suppose many women have—the kind of tireless energy and effectiveness which is typical on another stage of Eleanor Roosevelt. One of these aunts, now widowed, is the Treasurer of a Maine county. She is likewise a craftswoman of surpassing capability and a lady of magnanimous heart. I know of no particular craft that my Aunt Millward cannot do well. She rises early and labors late, and she expresses love and unselfishness in everything she does. My second aunt never married. To support herself she first worked as a milliner, and then took up the making of fine chocolates. Her sweets are much sought in Maine, and are sent by the hundreds of pounds to all parts of the country, although she does all the work herself and refuses to expand the business. She, too, is markedly unselfish and kind, a keen student and an active participant in intellectual and religious activities.

The third sister, my mother, has been a striver after spiritual truth all her life. She, too, was brought up a devout Methodist, and she and my father were active in the church during their young married life. I am an only child. Before I was born, my mother began to have serious and debilitating physical difficulties. Her continued ill health explains my parents' decision not to have more children. I, too, was a very sickly child during the first few years of my life. So sternly was I dosed in my first year or two, that something—attributed to over-medication—affected my baby teeth, and I lost many of them prematurely.

To help make both ends meet, my mother worked whenever she was able to in the newspaper office where my father was employed. When I was about two, the family moved to a farm outside the small city, and my father tried to make his living by combining farming with newspaper work, with selling insurance, and with various other devices. For a number of years, he and my mother were itinerant country correspondents for the newspaper. They would travel to surrounding towns by street car, by train, or often by horse and buggy, to gather the news and write it up for the paper. Often I would be taken along. My earliest recollection of newspaper work is of my father gathering news by telephone and then typing it into copy on his ancient typewriter. I would stand beside his typewriter, which I could barely reach, and let my hand ride back and forth on the carriage as he typed. But I remember with the most warmth the trips to country towns in search of news—and what news!—of daughters back from the city for Sunday with the folks, of the entertainment and speaking at Grange meetings, of good crops and calves and colts.

But I must curb the free flow of these memories. Let me summarize them by saying that my youth was spent—familywise and otherwise—in a happy, peaceful, serious, hard working environment. It was part of the tradition to work hard—children, too. We had very little money, but we never felt poor. Until I was in high school, I doubt if our family income ever averaged as much as thirty dollars a week. My toys were often second hand, my clothing strictly utilitarian, and our diet very plain. But our little family was well knit, we shared our thoughts and pleasures. I had few play fellows, for nobody with children lived near our farm. Our very sharing, however, meant also sharing the inadequacies and uncertainties of our life. Life was tolerable, life was sometimes fine, but we were still living under the overcast.

Moreover, my mother's frequent illnesses cast a constant shadow over our relative well-being. I was continuously subject to more than my share of ailments and resultant dosings. My father was restless and insecure. There was no focal point in our lives. Despite all the fine and lovely things I recall, we were still in an atmosphere of spiritual gloom and low visibility. In every sense, we were earth-bound.

Then disaster tried to strike. My mother was taken seriously ill with constricting tumors or other growths in her throat, and the medical diagnosis was foreboding. No hope of healing lay along the line of medical or surgical treatment, as our good friend and neighbor, the village physician, frankly advised us. My mother had once or twice heard of Christian Science in the year or two preceding this crisis. So, in her extremity, she asked us to obtain the services of a Christian Science practitioner. Such a person was located at a distance of over one hundred miles, and she was asked by telephone to give my mother an absent treatment. Overnight, during the first treatment, the growths in my mother's throat broke and passed harmlessly away, and she was completely healed. From that time to this, my mother has enjoyed the most radiant of good health, as have I, and our lives have been illumined by a spiritual light and focus which comes only by awakening.

We began at once the eager study of Christian Science. Within a few years, my mother became a Christian Science practitioner herself. My father was equally imbued with the truth of this new insight into the Bible and this new possibility of spiritual healing—daily and hourly, and not only of physical troubles, but of all the problems that faced us. His life was steadily thereafter given direction and purpose. Ultimately, he became the agricultural editor of two daily newspapers in Maine. For some thirty years he spent happy and fruitful days traveling among his farmer friends, recording their progress toward better ways of farming and stimulating them to better methods, constantly spreading among them the friendly glow of his cheerful, enlightened character.

From the time we entered into the study of Christian Science, lives which had been wholesome but earthbound became empowered with purpose and demonstrability. My mother, whose integral reliance on the power of the word of God is transcendent, has helped bring healing into the consciousness of thousands of eager or tortured seekers for truth. Our horizons lifted. The way was opened for me to go to a city high school, rather than the poor country school where I had begun. It took me some time to catch up with the others in school. Indeed, I did not do so during high school. It may encourage some laggard boy or girl to know that I had to take four entrance examinations to get into Bates College—a virtual disgrace, for only a B mark would qualify for entrance without examination. But in college, so swiftly were my horizons widening, I was on the honors list during the first semester and never looked back. My Bates years were very fruitful. I was chosen—while yet a freshman—to debate against the first group of debaters the Oxford Union Society ever sent to the United States. Later I took part in many intercollegiate debates, edited the college newspaper, was president of the college Outing Club, and led a debating team on a tour of seven British universities. Later I was chosen as a Rhodes Scholar and spent three priceless years at Oxford.

Throughout all this time, Christian Science was the central element of my life. First, of course, came its influence in the home. When a small boy of ten sees his mother turn from a semi-invalid of many years standing into a blooming picture of health and fruitful activity, he is naturally happy and grateful—and curious about what has worked the change. When he sees his father turn from a restless, in-confident, troubled, and aimless man into a person of purpose and conviction, he knows that something big has happened. When he, himself, manifests health and freedom which he had never known before, he knows there must be some mighty cause.

The cause, of course, was the tremendous spiritual direction that had come into all our lives, and was henceforth to engross them for the rest of our human experience. My first steps in Christian Science were not only at home, where my mother taught me its fundamentals as she learned them herself, but in Sunday school. Our Christian Science Sunday school is a simple but direct institution. We have no picnics and no games. We take pupils only up to the age of twenty, for there are other modes of adult instruction and study. In the Church Manual, written by Mary Baker Eddy, it is stipulated that children shall be taught as fundamental first lessons the Ten Commandments and the Sermon on the Mount. A study of these elemental bases for spiritual living, coupled with illustration by many simple Bible stories readily understood by children, takes up the first ten years or so of Sunday school. It does not become monotonous, for there is always new richness and meaning to be discovered in the Law and the Beatitudes. Nothing is more deeply engrained in the Christian Scientist's thinking than the universal validity of these two texts, and their applicability to all human problems. This applicability is illustrated by the way the Prophets, as well as Christ Jesus and His Disciples, carried out these truths in their daily lives and work.

In addition, the beginning student of Christian Science—young or old—learns the meaning of God by studying the synonyms of God given in the Bible. These, as summarized by Mrs. Eddy in *Science and Health with Key to the Scriptures,* the Christian Science textbook, are Mind, Spirit, Soul, Principle, Life, Truth, Love. All these are to be found in the Bible except Principle, which, however, is one of the best ways of conveying the meaning of God to modern man.

It is easy to see how the study of these synonyms opens great vistas of spiritual insight. They provide fruitful periods of Sunday school discussion, always oriented toward proving the truth of precept by actual demonstration. Thus a good deal of Christian Science Sunday school activity will be devoted to the sharing of experiences in which children and young people have worked out in their own daily lives better ways of living and thinking in accordance with God's law, and of proving their birthright of health and harmony in tune with the Infinite.

As children grow older, the Sunday school teaching turns to a study of the Christian Science Bible Lessons. These are citations from the Bible and *Science and Health,* varied each week, on a series of basic subjects which repeat themselves twice a year, but always with fresh citations and insights. These Bible lessons are again directed toward two objectives: better understanding of God's Law, and ways of proving it in daily living. These are all simple lessons, but they can be exceedingly fundamental and impelling. In his personal life, the Christian Scientist—if he lives up to his faith—is a total abstainer, a non-smoker, and deeply devoted to sexual morality and the sanctity of the home. These things, too, are embedded into the thinking and action of the Sunday school pupils by discussion and the sharing of experience and standards.

All of this came to me in my formative years. In addition, I attended Christian Science Sunday morning services, and Wednesday evening testimony meetings. At the latter, after readings from the Bible and *Science and Health,* members of the congregation as they are moved to do so, tell of experiences of healing or of spiritual benefit. There again, the emphasis is all on a demonstrable, dynamic, applicable faith. And in our own family, I saw the stream of patients who came to my mother and found spiritual healing as she was able to awaken their thinking to a reliance on God and an understanding of His Law. In my own household, after marriage to a young lady who had found her own way to Christian Science after a careful investigation of many other faiths, I have experienced the great joy of fruitfully unfolding family experiences and the opening of spiritual doors to our own children. They, too, are learning and applying the infinite power of God's love. I have also had the privilege of Christian Science class instruction, which is simply a two week period in which a very experienced Christian Scientist teaches fully and penetratingly the elements of its work to a group of thirty students. Annually, these students meet for a day with the teacher for spiritual refreshment and reclarification of their teaching.

All of this represents a religious conviction which is also a profound and pervasive way of life. I am deeply persuaded of God's allness and goodness. Thinking of God as Mind or Principle, for example, I can also understand Him in terms of modern cosmological theory in physics or mathematics. I have watched and studied with engrossing interest the falling away of materialistic theories of man and the universe. I have observed the swiftly mounting acknowledgment of mental causation among the natural scientists, the physicians, and, indeed, among thoughtful men in all disciplines. I am impressed when men like Dr. Edmund W. Sinnott, Dean of Sheffield Scientific School at Yale University, say: "The good old days of billiard ball atoms, Euclidean geometry, and the indestructibility of matter are now gone . . . Matter in the old sense indeed has ceased to be . . . The universe in which our fathers felt so comfortably at home has vanished . . . Great things are in the air, exciting new ideas in the sciences which may still further modify our understanding of the universe. This is no time to be dogmatic or complacent, for almost anything can happen now. The idealist who follows the ancient highway of the spirit toward reality has gained a more respectful audience than was his a half century ago . . . Man, not matter, is the chief problem of the world today."[1]

I am likewise impressed by such summaries as those of Lincoln Barnett, in his book, *The Universe and Dr. Einstein,* when, after referring to "sense-imprisoned man," he says:

Physicists have been forced to abandon the ordinary world of sense perceptions, the world of our experience. Even time and space are forms of intuition, which can be no more divorced from consciousness than can our concepts of color, shape, or size. Space has no objective reality except as an order or arrangement of the objects we perceive in it, and time has no independent existence apart from the order of events by which we measure it.[2]

Naturally I have also studied as much as I could in the swiftly expanding field of psychosomatic medicine, wherein mental causation is now recognized by physicians as being impelling in a vast proportion of either organic or functional disease. Out of a great multitude of cases proving mental causation, let me mention but one, in Dunbar's *Emotions and Bodily Changes,* published by the Columbia University Press, and quoted in *Psychodynamics and the Allergic Patient,* by Dr. Harold A. Abramson. The experiment is recorded of two groups of patients who were hypnotized. I quote:

One group was told that they were going to be given, after the hypnosis, a laxative medicine, and the other group was told that they were going to be given medicine which had a constipating effect; but actually the medicine was reversed. The gastrointestinal tract proceeded to obey the suggestion given by the hypnotists and not the pharmaco-dynamic action of the drug.[3]

This experiment—and its like is recorded many times in the medical texts—seems to me to leave little basis for faith in drugs. Nor does it encourage me in the direction of hypnosis, which must inevitably degrade the integrity of the individual's thinking. It is so much more

[1] Edmund W. Sinnott, in a Yale University press release, October, 1947.

[2] Lincoln Barnett, *The Universe and Dr. Einstein,* William Sloane Associates, New York, 1948.

[3] Helen Flanders Dunbar, *Emotions and Bodily Changes,* Columbia University Press, New York, 1935.

pertinent and efficacious to turn in the direction of spiritual healing, in accordance with the noble exemplifications of the Prophets of old, Christ Jesus, His Disciples, and all those who have turned receptively to God down through the years.

I do not wish unduly to stress the element of physical healing, which is the least of the awakenings Christian Science brings to the individual. Far more significant is an awareness of spiritual reality in an hour of such grave and foreboding crisis to our materialistic society as is this hour. All the world, as we all know, needs an awakening to spiritual reality. This can come only, I am confident, as organized religion turns to the spiritual dynamics of which healing is a part, but the re-making of individual lives into God-awareness is the whole.

It is the belief of reality in matter—now being spurned by the more thoughtful natural scientists—which blocks our way into the new society that must be. And in our own time, we have had powerful proof that matter cannot save us now. The atomic bomb, possibly the hydrogen bomb, are merely the latest in a series of proofs that our only salvation lies in an awakening from the materialism which has encrusted human thinking. The key to that awakening is an understanding of spiritual reality, as contrasted to the falsehood that matter ever has or ever could save civilization. Mary Baker Eddy, in *Science and Health,* has written a passage which has vivid applicability to this very hour in history. She wrote:

The more destructive matter becomes, the more its nothingness will appear, until matter reaches its mortal zenith in illusion and forever disappears.[4]

It seems to me that right now, matter has reached a zenith of destructiveness so overwhelming as to be able to awaken human thinking to its nothingness—its total lack of ability to save us or to order society. It is the acceptance in human thinking of the claims of matter which gives it destructiveness. When once we refuse to let ourselves be dominated by an acceptance of materialism, and found our lives instead on spiritual truth, the nothingness of matter will become a

[4] Mary Baker Eddy, *Science and Health with Key to the Scriptures,* Christian Science Monitor, Boston.

reality in our experience. This is not far from what the physicists are saying when they renounce the world of sense-impressions and of billiard ball atoms. Again discussing the claims of matter, Mrs. Eddy wrote that they would disappear when "the radiation of Spirit destroys forever all belief in intelligent matter."[5] It is interesting and moving that she uses the word, "radiation"—the word which today so grimly suggests the peril of our materialistic world. Surely there can be wide agreement on the thesis that the radiation of Spirit can, indeed, solve our problems and lift us out of the lethal clouds of matter. It is this radiation of Spirit, I am sure, which must imbue our national thinking and our statecraft, in order to cut through the present hate and fear.

It has been my ineffable experience to work with many noble colleagues on *The Christian Science Monitor,* and in the organization which supports it, in a continuous effort to awaken human thinking to spiritual reality. It is further evidence of her practical wisdom and foresight that Mrs. Eddy founded a daily newspaper, against the advice of those about her and in the face of the cynical and patronizing judgment of the journalistic world. She saw that a newspaper would be a mighty channel for good to the world in the years to come. *The Christian Science Monitor* is not published for a denominational audience, and its spiritual mission is not always overt. But that mission is invariably implicit, as best we can practically apply awakened thinking to the affairs of the day.

I believe that all mankind, whether it knows it or not, is ready for spiritual dawn. Many men today are saying, sometimes with a voice of anguish, that peace can be found only in the minds of men. With us here and now is the Truth on which that peace can be demonstrated. It is the Truth which is the spiritual heritage of mankind, which is enshrined in the One Law so many of us have inherited, which is exemplified in the doctrines of Christianity, and which is to be found gleaming at all times and in varying measure in the spiritual experiences of all races and peoples when they turn to God with understanding hearts. The Truth is with man. The awakening must come. Yours is the responsibility and opportunity, as it is

[5] *Ibid.*

mine, to sound the call of alarm and to affirm the blessed assurance of the power and goodness of God. When enough of us awaken to that power, and demonstrate it in our lives, we will have set to work in human society the illimitable and infinite force of the "radiation of Spirit." That power can itself be a chain reaction. But undoubtedly we need to apply to its organization and mobilization the same immense common effort we are putting into the development of atomic fission and fusion. Let us realize this in our own thinking, and let us apply ourselves to its fulfilment. We have at hand the wellsprings of God's power. What we need to do is to understand and apply the truth which has brought human society through many wildernesses and will ultimately lead it into the promised land of God's governing—when understood and demonstrated.

ELBERT D. THOMAS

We see America from our windows. We are cliffdwellers who know few neighbors. But we are not alone. In our building live Catholics, Protestants, Jews, a Moslem, a Hindu, and Mormons. From our window one way are the roofs of the Catholic University of America where men and women break a tradition and attend school together. The other way is the Episcopal Cathedral, growing slowly as cathedrals did in old Europe, and housing the remains of Dewey, who carried our flag so far, and Wilson, who made America universal, a Protestant holdover of a Catholic Europe.

Across is a playground and a recreation center where health through play and leisuretime guidance are directed. At our right is a library and across the street a public school. From the same window we see Cardinal Gibbons and Marconi in bronze. Science and religion—no conflict from our window, but what memories rush through my mind. Disturbed as my associates were over this conflict, my mother's words saved me when she said there could be no conflict because the basis of God's power is knowledge. To God there are no miracles. He just knows how. I remembered my mother when I saw a Buddhist prayer wheel being turned by a water wheel. No conflict there between science and religion! Without moving our chairs and within a stone's throw we see five churches and the most beautiful Catholic edifice in Washington, with its sixteen-petal-chrysanthemum window. Sixteen-petal-chrysanthemum—a Buddhist symbol and the Japanese imperial crest. I found a sixteen-petal chrysanthemum on a chariot of a Pharaoh in the Cairo museum. It is on the Damascus gate in the wall of Jerusalem. To me it is most significant, but when talking about it to the greatest Near Eastern archeologist I ever met, he said it was just a decorative symbol! On Sundays the streets are crowded with worshipers, but none unhappy because all go to the church they wish—for this is America.

We like our apartment, because a glance out brings to us every day the meaning of America, for there is the dome of the Capitol under which was worked out for man the first, just, classless tax system ever developed by a government of men. A fair tax is the foundation of American dollar democracy. We see the Washington Monument, representing the character of the man it honors, whose "honesty is the best policy" makes Washington, as a founder of a nation, without a peer. Back of the Monument the Jefferson Memorial appears. In the Memorial are words of Jefferson which give to man the dignity of gods: "God created the mind free, no man shall be compelled to support any religious ministry nor suffer on account of his beliefs. All men have liberty of religious opinion. Their morality is part of their nature. I know but one code of morality for men whether acting singly or collectively."

To the south shines Moroni, typifying the "Restored Gospel." Moroni to us represents America's religious gift to all men, augmenting and making more clear the eternal truth concerning God and His purposes. From the Capitol, Washington, Jefferson, and Moroni, America's great symbols of liberty, has come Elbert Thomas, American and Mormon.

American and Mormon, yes, but in his own mind, one often implies the other, but never to the extent of confusing the two. Without America his religion could never have been. Without his religion American political fundamentals would not represent divine truth. The activities of his church are broader than the teaching of theology, for they do have economic, social, educational complexities which cause individual and group controls, but there is no intermingling or confusion, and the individual's free agency is never questioned. Through cooperation, so essential around an irrigation ditch where water is the life blood of the community and belongs to all but is controlled by each, both public and private, church and non-church interests are understood and do not conflict.

It is of more than passing interest that the Mormon Pioneers developed the equivalent of the Chinese longest lived private property land system in history, which recognized the public or community interest along with the individual or private. The Chinese divided their land into squares which in turn were divided into nine smaller squares, eight private and one public. The center one being the public one where the community well was, and to this day the Chinese character for well represents this division $\#$. The Mormon Ward in the beginning of Salt Lake City was divided the same way. The middle square belonged to all. There the Meeting House stood. The other eight squares were privately owned. There was this difference between the Chinese and Mormon division, while both reflected an aspect of our democracy, private and public property, the Chinese forgot roads, which led to confusion and a breakdown of the system. But the Mormons divided each square by public roadways. The Church is a large property owner. Therefore, in a Utah community there is public property belonging to all the people, the Church property which may be both taxable and non-taxable, according to its use, and private property.

The Mormon Meeting House is an institution whose character is all its own. Its use is religious, social, recreational, civic, and political, where there are no other halls. The Mormon Meeting House reflects American frontier life. The simple building is generally puritanic in design. But it is more than a church. It is a theater; it is a dance hall, a workshop, and a community center, as well as a chapel.

American and Mormon influences have jointly and separately contributed toward the making of Elbert Thomas and they are related. As the Mormon missionary moved into foreign lands, his appeal would be accepted only by those who were converted to the meaning of America as well as the Gospel. The combined appeal, until restrictions were put on immigration, was always "Come, Gather up to Zion."

Thus the spiritual autobiography of Elbert Thomas must reflect activities of a complex life: student; Main Street merchant; teacher and University administrative officer; politician, who has dealt with problems incident to foreign relations, treaties, world organization, military policy, education, labor, public welfare, pensions, aid for veterans, and mining; a writer; and a man whose faith in God is as childlike as his love for his mother and father, whose life is a prayer, whose religion has never been questioned by himself, and who has never argued with himself or with others about it. His God and his religion have been taken for granted, and he has never experienced any dissatisfaction with either, although he has seen hundreds of gods and studied a score of religions. This is prologue.

I am a product of the public schools. I went to kindergarten and I finished with a Ph.D. It took a long time, but during every minute I was exposed to American ideals. If there is a history guide to which I can turn it is the 174-year struggle of my country to make a political concept work and become universal.

My father was born in Cornwall, England. His father was a property holder, referred to as "squire." Father, after finishing his apprenticeship, met Mormon missionaries in London. He was baptized, confirmed, "ordained an elder," and "set apart" as a missionary on the same day. He was very young, only nineteen when he arrived in Salt Lake City in 1863. He crossed the plains without relatives with a body of "Saints." His duties on the plains were those of a scout who rode ahead alone to look out for unfriendly Indians and to select camp sites near water and grass for animals. Later, he brought several members of his family to America but none ever became Mormons. His first job was copying parts for actors in the Salt Lake Theatre. Established in business in the northern part of the Territory, he married in 1865. My mother was from Devonshire, England. As a girl of fifteen, she had walked from the Missouri River to Utah.

In 1869, my father returned to Salt Lake as manager of Walker Brothers, an institution out of which have come many institutions. In 1869, the Walkers supplied food for workers who were building the Union and Central Pacific Railways. The Walkers were non-Mormons. Our home was in a part of Salt Lake where non-Mormons were predominant. Father spent weeks in the East every year.

His friendships were broad and our home was visited by persons from almost everywhere.

My mother's and father's interest in the theater never lagged. They built for us children one of America's well known "little" theaters, "The Barnacle"—a made-over barn. Its novelty attracted many and some of America's outstanding players visited it and trod its boards. The Barnacle was responsible for developing many interests in us children. Through The Barnacle and the Salt Lake Theatre, which became a national institution, the theater became part of me. In The Barnacle, I made my first political speech and did my first acting.

Our home was good. I remember the candle chandeliers being piped for gas, then made over into electric fixtures. We had candles, lamps, gas, and electric lights at the same time, and, to her dying day, my mother always kept a candle on her dressing table. Pioneers take no chances.

Our library was full. Our interests were as broad as I have known them anytime.

A Mormon child is blessed and given a name as a baby, and while his name is kept on the Church rolls he is not "born in the Church." He must wait until "the age of accountability." When he is eight he is baptized and confirmed a member of the Church. I was baptized at eight and taught its meaning so positively that my responsibilities seemed great. The impressions gained have never left me.

In Chicago, before I was ten, I was taken by my mother to International Women's meetings and to the International Congress of Religions. There I was impressed by the speech of Kinza Hirai, who represented Shinto. I met Mr. Hirai later in Japan. To this day I remember a Hokku poem he quoted:

> There are many roads that lead to the top of the mountain
> But when once the summit is gained the same moon is seen.

The World Columbian Exposition, with its midway, was an education for any boy. Since meeting Sol Bloom my midway experiences are renewed. Was he responsible for all the good shows? Well, I have met no other.

Already disciplined in my religion—and its children are not neglected—I listened to many representatives of the world's religions. I knew that I would be a missionary because that is expected of every Mormon boy. When the call came it was with a happy significance, for it read, "When you have married Edna Harker you and she may proceed to Japan." Then began one of life's ventures, and before it was completed Edna Harker Thomas had become the first lady Mormon missionary to circle the globe.

In June, 1893, I turned ten. While in Chicago the Panic broke. I had learned that nations as well as individuals suffered for their acts—Jefferson and Lincoln both said that and my Sunday school teacher taught it. We left home well to do. We returned, as the books showed when I studied them after my father's death, thousands of dollars in debt. It was not a case of from riches to rags, for credits kept things going, but I heard and learned of gold, silver, interest, and international exchanges, and, above all, the meaning of money. Japan, China, and Europe taught more. Textbooks never taught as clearly as I learned those lessons first hand. From that day to this I have been certain that the nation that invented the gold standard, in order to exploit backward peoples, and doubled investments in the Americas by cutting in half the value of the American dollar, would someday suffer for this act. World events have not caused me either to belittle or reject what Jefferson and Lincoln said and what my boyhood teachers taught.

1893 was my first panic. I was to see more. With each I have sought the reason for its beginning and studied for its cure. The getting of the nations of the world to accept the Declaration of Philadelphia in 1944, seemed a natural culmination of a life of thought. When I convinced my own nation to accept the Declaration, I did it with a firm conviction that depressions can be avoided, if nations will throw their whole energy to the task, as we do so well to win a war.

1893 taught me to be thoughtful about what my future college instructors called the Industrial Revolution. Coal-energy and machinery to work for man has seemed to me to be one of the great spiritual aspects of the promises incident to the restoration of the Gospel. God's purposes for the ultimate redemption of man and the making of the earth a better place, were all parts of my thinking in regard to "a great and marvelous work about to come forth."

In college the two greatest nineteenth century concepts, Darwinism and Marxism, did not attract. Marxism meant clash and ultimately single-willed dictatorship. Therefore it would destroy the freedom. Darwinism, when united with the concept of progress, might have had some attraction, but I never became interested.

When the Second World War started, as I look back on my feelings in regard to it and what I did, I discover that I reacted wholly and completely to form. America must win, so that American theories could be spread throughout the world. The American Revolution seemed to have meaning in thinking of the two world wars, and the dignity of man could only become worldwide under American auspices. While most of my work as Chairman of the Military Affairs Committee had to do with the war activities, I could never rid myself of the idea that ultimate victory can come only through a change in men's hearts and ideas. More with that zeal than the idea to destroy, I supported the experimentation which resulted in the atom bomb. Therefore, I also gave myself over wholeheartedly to psychological warfare. I had studied in Italy, Germany, and Japan. The Office of War Information used my name almost everywhere, but I, in a sense, concentrated my own efforts on my messages to the Japanese people, which I started in December, 1941, right after Pearl Harbor, and continued up until 1946. In those messages I had but one theme, and that was that Japan was ruining herself, because she had turned apostate to the best ideals that Japanese civilization had developed. I knew how the Japanese constitution worked. I knew that the generals in the field were absolute. They could not be controlled by the home government. I knew, therefore, that we had to have a constitutional surrender under the auspices of the Emperor, or we would turn loose on the world millions of guerrillas who had learned how to live on the land, and that our soldier boys would be chasing those guerrillas over half the world. That my judgment was not bad is proved by events in Greece. That I knew what I was talking about is proved by the surrender itself. The opposition to my ideas by those who wanted to destroy and bring anarchy in Japan, hurt me in much the same way all prejudicial opposition has hurt me. But in this activity, as in my religious activity, I was sustained by a sense of knowing that I was right. The world, of course, will never be interested in what was accomplished, but the world some day will know that order comes from order, that chaos comes from chaos, and that stability must be built upon stability. But it will be a long time before a world which has accepted contrary philosophy throughout its history, will see the point. That does not make me feel that those who support what might be called the spiritual and intellectual approach, are wrong. We cannot build world organization without morals, even if we do follow bright young men who learned much in German gymnasiums and became fascinated by Bismarck's theories of "national self-interest." Of course, Bismarck was not the creator of a foreign policy built upon "national self-interest," but from Bismarck's time to the fall of Hitler the world has seen the rise and the fall of an empire which at no time accepted any fundamental national doctrine but that. America's mission is not based upon a "national self-interest." This nation which accepts a higher law than a national one, also recognizes responsibilities and objectives larger than national ones. Our history proves it. America's place in the world of tomorrow will be where it has been since 1776, when Jefferson, Franklin, Adams, Livingston, and Sherman wrote eternal principles into our Declaration of Independence.

Besides the Chicago World's Fair and the great panic, 1893 also brought the dedication of the Salt Lake Temple. To a ten year old boy, this was a monumental experience which could not help but affect his future spiritual life. As kiddies in primary and Sunday school we sang "We Want To See The Temple." Every Fast Day I took my donation for it. It was indeed a symbol of sacrifice for the whole Mormon people.

My father was appointed one of a committee of two to furnish the temple. My mother's father was one of its chief stonecutters, and, therefore, a builder. The temple was only a block from our store in the center of the city. It was near our home. Mormon people will always be a temple-building people, because the temple reflects so much of the deep meaning of their religion. It could not help but give me an interest in temples as I wandered over the earth.

There are many things in a person's life too sacred to talk about. The temple, to the Latter-Day Saint, is one of those things. The temple, more than any other institution, is the symbol of unity between man's earth life and his eternal existence. It is the place for marriage, and it is the place that all Mormon missionaries go before they depart for their missions. In the case of marriage and in the case of a mission, it is the starting of a new life. To one who has observed marriages the world over, temple marriage is beautiful and simple, but full of the deepest of religious meanings, and gives to love between husband and wife a sacredness which to the thoughtful and the prayerful influences the whole of life. The temple tempers the parting, when death separates for a time a life's companionship, and when a new relationship is gained, it is entered into with such deep understanding that the sacrament of marriage influences all acts and thoughts of life.

I have and I will mention the temple many times in this little spiritual life story. The Mormon temple is to the understanding Mormon boy all and even more than the ancient temple at Jerusalem meant to the Jews. The ancient temple contained the secret of a Jewish unity which the great Pompey could not understand. And when he found himself alone with what he thought was nothingness in the sanctum of the temple, he marveled how nothing could hold a people. I, myself, have, I believe, experienced Pompey's feelings. In the Orient, just as in the ancient world of Pompey, wooden and stone gods, death tablets, images, and other visible representatives of the supernatural, were so commonplace that one expected, as one saw the inside of a Shinto shrine, actually to see what Pompey thought he would see. Alone, I had the chance to enter a shrine deep in the mountains, a shrine with its Torii gates, representative, undoubtedly, of the ancient Egyptian eagle, which is found so plainly engraved on Mayan monuments in Central America. While I was not surprised, as Pompey was, at finding nothing, because my life had sensed the power of a spiritual control, I did learn that spiritual bonds held the souls of men we call pagans as it did our own. And again I sensed the universality of that spirit that could enlighten the souls of all men and the lesson of "at-one-ment" was mine again.

Born and raised in the neighborhood of the Mormon temple, Buddhist temples always attracted me. Their symbols fascinated me. and when, for example, I noticed first the swastika sign as a Buddhist symbol, I remembered seeing that symbol on American Indian pottery. Again world unity came to my mind. Such thoughts and many others like them undoubtedly contributed to my *World Unity Through Study of History.*

I had another temple experience at Jerusalem. I had seen the Russian pilgrims come up to the Holy City. I had experienced in life there the conflict of beliefs. I visited the Church of the Holy Sepulcher, and had many thoughtful musings over Gordon's tomb. I had wandered over most of the land, but the evening that Palestine impressed me most was when Mrs. Thomas and I sat on the Mount of Olives and looked across the valley to the place of the temple and the Mosque of Omar. While our baby gathered pebbles, we read the dedicatorial prayer offered by Orson Hyde on October 21, 1841, when the land of Palestine was dedicated by a Mormon elder sent by the Prophet Joseph Smith to dedicate Palestine for the return of the Jews. Here again deep, meaningful, long range spiritual understanding entered my soul. At the time I read the prayer, just twenty years after the dedication of our own temple, a few Jews were returning to Palestine to be buried near Jerusalem. Tel-Aviv was a doubtful venture, for in all there were only sixty or seventy thousand Jews in the Holy Land. Belief in the restoration of Jerusalem is part of my religion. In one of the Mormon scriptures is the prophecy that the Jews will return to Palestine under the auspices of the gentiles. Throughout the past two or three decades, when renewed interest in Palestine has come to the consciousness of the whole world, I have always been more than a mere observer of what to me is the fulfilment of God's promises.

The forty years spent in building the Salt Lake Temple was a period of poverty and always a time of trouble. To my mind, this was proof of what the spirit can do. The wisdom and statesmanship of

Mormon leadership is shown in this undertaking. An unemployed man is the most uneconomic of creatures, and idleness is the greatest destroyer of community morale. Both unemployment and idleness were avoided by the temple building. The possibilities of temple work for older people and those who find too much leisure time on their hands from whatever cause, has only begun to dawn. Lonesome, idle, purposeless old age is by all odds the worst time of life. Even if Cicero did say that old age is the best period of life, because then one may sit in the Senate, it just is not so. Few people sat in the Senate in Cicero's time, and fewer now can sit in our own or other Senates. But the possibilities of developing happy, useful, and healthful old age have not yet been realized. Aside from the religious aspects, the Mormon temples have justified themselves in producing the most spiritual minded and happiest old people I have observed anywhere.

The evening of the day that the Brethren decided to build the Hawaiian Temple I walked home with President Lund. He told me about the decision to build the Hawaiian Temple. When once a man has been given the Priesthood and presided over the Church's major activities, the spirit of his work never leaves him. Without thinking of the reason the Brethren might have had in building the temple, I said: "Isn't it remarkable, President Lund, that the first temple built outside continental United States should be built for the Chinese, Japanese, and Pacific Islanders!" President Lund looked surprised and said: "No, the temple is a monument to President Smith's first mission in Hawaii." Monument or not, the first couple married in the Hawaiian Temple, I have been told, were Chinese. The "work" for the ancestors of Japanese and Chinese members of the church has been started. The future will show that the temple will attract the worthy among the Orientals as no other Mormon activity will.

When the Arizona Temple was being planned, I was shown the artist's drawing for the frieze. The frieze depicted the carrying of the Gospel to the world. The Japanese group was to me the most beautiful. But at that time, and it was long before the war, the Japanese were not much liked even by some of our leaders. History was forgotten and the Japanese group does not appear on the temple frieze. Disappointment through lack of appreciation for work done affects one's spiritual growth quite as much as appreciation does.

In 1893, I saw President Cleveland. I had already seen President Harrison. Great men have always influenced my life. From each I have gained lessons. From mention of my father and mother anyone can see that I have a sense of filial piety. Many of our own people have influenced me greatly. Among the world's great who have contributed toward my life have been President William Howard Taft and William Jennings Bryan, both of whom came to Japan. But it was at the Conference of Governors, held in Independence Hall, Philadelphia, in 1918, when I represented my own Governor and when President Taft led out for the League to Enforce Peace, that President Taft became an influence. President Taft and I were the only two non-Governors in that conference, and he, in presiding, always linked my name with his when the clerk called the roll. He was a great inspiration. President Charles W. Eliot of Harvard came to Japan. From him I learned my greatest lesson in education. From Zenophon I remembered that "a question, then, is education." Great, retired, thoughtful, and wonderful, President Eliot spent his time with me not in giving information, but asking questions. Do not people ever stop studying, I wondered? I was with Wilson two days before he was stricken. There was our own Franklin D. Roosevelt, whom I learned to know so well, and who I think learned to know me, for he called me often to the White House. Senator Barkley and I were the last two men in official life who saw the President just before he left for Warm Springs. He called us down to the White House to ask about a bill which we were unsuccessful in having the Senate accept. I told him frankly that I thought we could not pass the bill. He was tired, weary, and as we left he held out his hand and said: "Well, Elbert, even Lincoln didn't always have his way, did he?" And I said, "No, Mr. President, he didn't, and it is probably well for the people of the United States that he did not."

In my travels men have meant quite as much as places. As a university sophomore, I reorganized the students of the University of Utah and wrote the constitution of the associated students, building that constitution around functional activities. When we set up the consitution, each student activity was in debt. When I got back to the University and began teaching, the constitution had not only survived, but it had made the student body a strong, solvent institution. Of that, I am more proud than my degree.

In international relations I have full faith in my country's purposes and with the strength of America on which to build, there seems to be nothing in the remaking of this world that America cannot accomplish, if she will but plan and work with the vision and faith of our Founding Fathers. As a child of the American Revolution, for me events in the world revolve around it—I have written in other places that the spirit and theory of the American Revolution will yet encircle the globe. I have interpreted the suggestions for world organization and the development of Democracy, since the invention of the American Federal system, with its concept of liberty and freedom, as part of the great "latter-day" movement. My concept of Mormonism puts meaning in all that is done. In the reading of history, events like those which took place in Europe in 1848 seemed closely related to what was taking place in America at the same time and even in the Salt Lake Valley. I would not like to be thought of as a world revolutionary, but Thomas Jefferson seemed to me to be a world revolutionary, even before I proved it to my own satisfaction in my *Thomas Jefferson, World Citizen*. And surely the toast offered at the great celebration at Philadelphia after the Constitution was agreed to—"To the United States and to the freedom of mankind everywhere"—was a rather broad toast, if men meant what they said. Is my idea farfetched, when we remember that Louis Philippe, Napoleon III, and Garibaldi, all had lived in America?

In Tokyo in 1911, just before the opening of the Chinese Revolution, I met Sun Yat Sen and his associates, including an artillery student, Chiang Kai-shek. They were all students of the American Revolution. Gandhi was influenced by reading our Thoreau. While it did not seem to have influenced him much, Trotsky had at least lived in the United States. In interpreting world history, I can never start, as most Westerners do, with Abraham, Palestine, and Egypt. I do not, as the Brahmans do, give Ganesa, the God of Wisdom, a salute. In fact, I slight India. I begin with the Canon of Shun in the

East and the Law of Hammurabi in the West, and work down, always pointing out the unities between the two. In the building of the future political world, I start with the Declaration of Independence, and, with the future spiritual world, I start with Joseph Smith's first vision. America is the center of each thought. When someone says Washington is fast becoming the capital of the world, I dismiss the statement as if it were an accomplished fact. I have known that all my life, for I have been taught it since babyhood.

The strongest challenge which has come to my revelation-inspired religion was that offered by a Confucian scholar. Because this experience added to my spiritual development, I think that it is proper here to point out the conflict that does exist between a religion based on revelation and one based on man's wisdom. This scholar was a Chinese-trained Japanese. He was an honest believer in Confucianism, and maintained that a peaceful world was possible only under Confucian naturalism. He attacked especially the West's concept of revelation. "That concept is a guarantee of strife, and even war," he said, "because men must be loyal to what is revealed to them from God. To die for a belief is the most honored duty Western civilization has yet produced." Speaking to me directly, he said, "You are now sacrificing the best part of your life to come here to try to teach me your religion. I honor you for it, and I also honor the West for what it calls its unselfish interest in all men. But I do not believe it is unselfish. I believe it is a selfish interest which you believe is necessary to prove your loyalty to God."

I became thoughtful about what the Confucian scholar had said, and I visioned the Roman Pantheon when the Roman people accepted the gods from all lands, and set them up side by side for any and all to worship. And I remembered that when the time came for putting up the Jewish-Christian God, peace in the assembly of gods ceased, because before the Jewish-Christian God could enter the Pantheon all other gods had to be knocked down.

On my next visit, I explained how we in America lived in comparative religious peace by separating church and state, and allowing freedom to and for religions. It was in these conversations that I, in defending the American way of religious life, traced the history of

religious strife in Europe and America through the periods of persecution, forbearance, and toleration. I admitted that we still had a
long way to go, and I advanced the theory that I wanted to see the
day come when appreciation might take the place of toleration. He
smiled and said that would not bring peace or remove the clash. He
pointed out that I liked to study the thought of Confucius or I would
not come back to see him, and he said he believed I truly appreciated
and admired the thought of Confucius. He said he appreciated but
did not admire our concept of revelation. And he said, "I will show
you the difference and prove to you that your system always ends in
clash. You teach me your beliefs and you say if I accept them and
believe, then I must strive to defend my belief, because the principles
I have accepted are God's principles and must be defended by my
life. I must willingly become a martyr, as you express it. But if you
become a Confucian, you need never die for your belief, because
you know that what you believe is merely Confucius's opinion, and
you need never die for that. Your loyalty is only the loyalty to a
friend's heart."

In 1901, while I was studying for the Oxford Rhodes Scholarship,
one of Utah's Patriarchs came to our home and I received my
"Patriarchial" blessing—a commonplace experience for Mormons—
but never commonplace in effect on the lives of those who respect the
blessing. Mine became another guide to understanding of events,
because nations, as well as persons, are mentioned in my blessing.
1893 and 1901, as much as being put on the Thomas Jefferson Memorial Commission, influenced my *Thomas Jefferson, World Citizen*.
Thus the child was the father of the man.

My childhood memories in Utah include the beginnings of political
parties there, carpetbagism, the struggles for statehood, and land
rushes, as Indian reservations were opened. Religion figures in all
these activities.

Women voted in the Utah Territory. The struggle my mother had
to face was to keep that franchise for the women. When the state
constitution was being written, an attempt was made to deprive
women of their suffrage "and make our state like most of the other
American states when we joined the Union." Memories flood my

mind here: the fight for suffrage in England, for I was there; the first election when women voted in France, for I was there; and then, one of my Japanese students wrote his thesis on women's suffrage, returned to Japan, fought for it, and ultimately won.

I saw the confiscation of Mormon property and the Mormon leaders disfranchised by the Federal Government. The first herd of sheep I remember had a red "U. S." branded on the back of each sheep. I suppose it was a herd owned by some Mormon cooperative.

My father had much to do with the gaining of amnesty for the Saints from President Harrison. I remember three conversations at the dinner table between my mother and father on what later in life I learned to realize were very important; first, concerning the granting of partial amnesty to the Saints by President Harrison and later full amnesty by President Cleveland. When I became a grown man one of the First Presidency of the Church, President Penrose, told me that my father had done much to bring amnesty.

Another time after Father was appointed with Henry Dinwoody a committee of two to furnish the Salt Lake Temple, he told of getting permission from the Brethren for hundreds of non-Mormons to view the inside of the Salt Lake Temple before it was dedicated. This did much to bring good feelings and helped with statehood.

After his return from a New York trip, about 1896 or 1897, Father told of advising bankers who had been approached for a loan of one half million dollars by Heber J. Grant, who was in New York offering all the security the Church could muster in attempting to get a loan. A banker told Father that the bank was not disposed to grant the loan because the security was of doubtful value. My father explained that if the bank got the names of the First Presidency of the Church on a note, all the Mormons everywhere would give their all to see the note honored, and that that was the only security they should demand. History tells us the loan was obtained and, of course, paid.

Another incident which did much to influence my youthful thinking occurred during the great drought of 1894 or 1895. Brigham Young, before he died, had urged the Relief Society Sisters to store wheat in preparation of need in case of crop failure. By 1895, many bushels of wheat had been accumulated. An uncle, a Methodist Minister whose church was in Nebraska, where the drought was, came to visit us. It was to relieve this condition that Congress appropriated money to buy seed for those distressed farmers, only to have the bill vetoed by President Cleveland, because he said the United States Government was set up to be supported by the American people, and not for the purpose of having the Government support the people. There was no relief for the farmers. My uncle knew of the Mormon wheat and pled with my father to plead in turn with the Brethren to send a train of wheat to his stricken friends. I remember so well Uncle's pacing back and forth and repeating that "surely the Lord would be happy if the Brethren would send some wheat." Our people were not greatly loved through those parts of America, and I am sure those big enough to realize it were pretty doubtful about wheat going where our missionaries had had so many unhappy experiences, but I was for sending the wheat. Uncle convinced me. Father suggested bed to us, and remarked: "I think, Samuel, the Brethren will send the wheat." I knew if Pa said it the Brethren would surely send the wheat, and went off to bed greatly relieved. The Brethren did send the wheat.

This story is hardly complete without telling another in connection with the Relief Society wheat. It was in 1919 when President Wilson was on his swing around the country speaking for the League of Nations. It was before he spoke in our Tabernacle. His speech in Salt Lake was one of the last he gave before he was stricken. I was acting as our Governor's aide and we had taken President Wilson to his hotel. He mentioned our wheat, and said he would like to thank the head of the Relief Society for it. On being informed that President Emaline B. Wells lived in the same hotel, he was guided to her rooms, and he there thanked her for letting the Government have the wheat. I have been told that the Sisters sold their wheat to the Government, and with the proceeds established maternity homes in communities where there were no hospitals. I was proud then of Brigham Young's farsighted statesmanship, proud of the honor President Wilson bestowed, and proud as a Mormon to have been a witness of these two great occasions where Mormon foresight came to the aid of a nation and those in need. The Church welfare organization today is large. Its capital investment and stocks now run into millions.

When about fifteen, I was called with three other boys on a special "mission" to visit all the non-Mormons in our neighborhood and attempt to interest them in the Gospel—a heartbreaking assignment if I ever had one. We made no converts. When I became a grown man I was assigned the headship of such a home mission, and the earlier task did teach me much. When I was nineteen, the old Salt Lake Stake was divided into four or five stakes, leadership became scarce as a result, and I was appointed a Mutual Improvement Association President. My appointment came not from merit, but because there were no other young men left. The people I taught were two young boys and several old men who came out of a sense of loyalty, because Mormons never let any announced meeting fail. There I learned that a teacher could learn much, even if he could not teach much. Readers, I would have never undertaken this task today if I had not learned that lesson in my youth. These early tasks gave me courage for future responsibilities, especially when I started my first Oriental courses, where I had no textbooks and no guides to lead the way. They also gave me courage to stand alone when the time came in interpreting the Chinese classics and history in my future studies. To pioneer a new field of study in an American university, is no easy task. To get Chinese scholars to change their interpretations of the Chinese classics, is also no easy task.

A man who goes into public life does not win all the time. I have won and I have lost. In losing there is sometimes a victory, because time and passing events change many circumstances. In reorganizing the student body at the University of Utah I had to win not only the students but both the faculty and Regents who opposed the "radical" change. My first political venture resulted in a crushing defeat, when I ran for Secretary of State in 1920. But my support of President Wilson's theories made me stronger for the United Nations contest. During the First World War I was able to convince our legislature that outlawing the teaching of German in our schools would not contribute to winning the war. This made me very unpopular, as I was in the Second World War, when I urged the acceptance of

Nisei in the Army by enlistment and through the draft. When I insisted on attempting to get a constitutional surrender from Japan, to avoid the anarchy incident to the complete destruction of the Japanese State, I was called a pal of Tojo. It is the first struggles that are hard. The years it took me to get our Government to accept the strategic materials act and to start stockpiling, is a good example. Even when we got the first bill passed, it was crippled by amendments in the Senate. I would have let the bill die, if it were not for the fact that I wanted to get a principle established. We therefore accepted the best we could get, and the bill was improved in conference, but not without my taking a terrible tongue lashing in the Senate for not standing by the Senate bill. That victory, disappointing as it was, was greater than I thought. The last strategic materials bill passed the Senate without a dissenting vote, and a national policy now is accepted by all. Can anyone separate the moral, spiritual, economic, or political influence on one's life from such experiences? As a man who has sponsored the creation of many public policies, his boyhood experiences in winning a just cause against great odds overshadows in importance many of the later accomplishments.

The presentation of copies of the newly translated Book of Mormon to the Emperor and Empress and the Crown Prince and Crown Princess seemed to us an impossible task—the Emperor of Japan was so aloof and we were afraid to ask diplomatic assistance—but it was done.

The Mormon boy is taught that there are two influences which are constantly struggling for supremacy over every man's life. The best way to keep in harmony with the good is to keep the Gospel's commandments and follow the dictates of the spirit. But the easiest way to do this is to "follow council." It is in this way that prophecy becomes so much a part of one's life.

I asked my father one time for money for a trip. He said, "Do not bother about going on trips. In your lifetime you will go everywhere and see everything. Wait until you have some reason for going." I have circled the globe and crossed the oceans so many times I cannot remember the number of crossings, but never once have I taken a pleasure trip.

It is inevitable that everything said by one of the leaders takes on the aspect of prophecy. It is a guide not only for the immediate task but will have bearing on the future. For example, when Mrs. Thomas and I were "set apart" for the Japanese Mission, the blessings were given by Apostles Heber J. Grant and George Albert Smith, both later became President of the Church. That in itself is significant and an honor. But just before Brother Smith blessed me, Brother Grant, who was the senior, suggested that I be ordained a Seventy and at the same time remarked: "Brother Thomas may be away a long time and have great responsibilities." Thus a simple sentence became a word of prophecy to me, and as life moved on to greater responsibilities I became convinced that President Grant had a purpose in what he said. Such simple prophecies influence a Mormon boy throughout his life. But prophecy is no good unless you live up to your responsibility. You yourself must do the doing. That cannot be left to God. He helps only when you do your best. Therefore be prepared for anything.

The Mormon missionary throughout the world today is recognized as a young college boy interested in athletics. He plays baseball and football where those games are played. And the Church today feels that the boy is living a natural life and that he is doing nothing which interferes with his labors as a missionary, but that was not always the case. Any new thing jars. I not only played baseball and basketball in Japan, but I let my missionaries play, and we became well known as a result. When the people at home began reading about this, I received a letter from the First Presidency, written, I am sure, by President Lund. It said in essence, "Brother Thomas, our people make great sacrifices to keep their children on missions, and when they read about their playing baseball, they wonder if they should not be preaching instead of playing." Then he went on to say, "We are not criticizing, because you deserve the guidance of the spirit in your mission, but be thoughtful and if you decide it is wrong to play ball any more, stop it." That is the way guidance comes, as I have experienced it, guidance full of love, understanding, and recognizing a man in his office half way around the world.

Another incident—the Book of Mormon translation into Japanese was about completed. Those who had worked the hardest got into a discussion over the translation of a given expression. The men came to me, and I took a stand different from either of them. Finally, it was decided to write the First Presidency. When the answer came, the First Presidency took a stand closer to my ideas than to the older men's. Immediately the two men accepted the advice of the Brethren, although it meant another whole year's work for both of them.

A baseball incident—the Tokyo-American team was made up of ministers, teachers, missionaries, and soldiers. We had a remarkable fan following. One of the most interesting of all the American bleacher-seaters was Bishop McKim, head of the American Episcopalian Mission in Japan. I was not a good player, but after a game wherein I had made a lucky catch and throw, and thereby won a game, as we walked off the field, Bishop McKim came over and put his arm around my shoulders. No sweating player, even if he is supposed to love his neighbor, reacts very affectionately to any kind of embracing at the end of a game. But I was interested in what the old Bishop remarked, "Oh, we do love to watch you Mormon boys play baseball. Some day we may grow up and invite you to come and pray with us." What meaning was there! After that I knew we did not have to stop playing.

I was President of the Japanese mission when Korea was annexed. The dedication of a land and a people to missionary work is something which our people take seriously. I was caught with a great question facing me. Did Korea belong to our mission as a result of a political action? From the standpoint of pride I, of course, wanted to take in all I could, but the restraint which comes from following counsel kept me from annexing Korea to the Japan Mission.

In 1911, the Minister of the Interior of Japan invited the leaders of all the religious sects in Japan to a conference. I was one. In his opening remarks he said the time had come in the development of Japanese nationalism for Japan to have a national religion and suggested that we work one out. I, of course, realize that the Minister did not quite mean it that way, but that is the way those of us from revelation-believing religions interpreted it. My answer was the same as most of the Christian, Jewish, and Mohammedan answers would have been, dominated by the concept of revelation which concept, of course, the Japanese Minister did not understand. My reply was, "Our religion is not made by man but by God. We believe that our religion is the best religion for the Japanese people. Therefore, we can take no part in trying to work out another." That seems harsh, but in the logic of authoritarian religions it is inevitable.

In the First World War it became one of my duties to suggest certain Mormons when the Army became willing to commission as chaplains three or four Mormon elders. That incident marked in my life a really remarkable culmination in the recognition of our Church. I, of course, had no authority to appoint the men either in the Army or to represent my Church in their selection, but I was asked to recommend. I had been a National Guard officer for years. I knew the struggle in the attainment of a proper place for local officers in the national scheme and I knew also the feelings which the national government might have in regard to recognizing a Mormon elder as a properly trained minister. When the CCC camps came into existence, I again had a chance to suggest to the Army that well trained Mormon elders would make ideal chaplains, and they did. When the Second World War broke out and, as Chairman of the Military Affairs Committee, I sponsored the bill giving general officer's rank in the Army to the Chief of Chaplains, I did all I could to make the Chaplaincy a religious activity.

When the coal mining industry was first started in Utah, Brigham Young sent missionaries to Wales and the coal mining part of England to gain converts. By my time these men had grown old but a few remained, and they were earnest members of the Church. I was called with troops during the general strike of 1922 to represent our Governor, when all of Utah's coal mines were put under martial law. The Governor had proclaimed that there should be no meetings. That, of course, meant schools and Sunday schools. Old Brother Llewellyn, who thought "Thomas" was a fine Welsh name until I told him it was Greek, came to me and pled the cause of the Sunday school children. I told him that the Governor's proclamation had to be obeyed, but that I was sure if I held a Sunday school the Governor would not get after me. Many labor leaders came to watch me.

One of them went off saying, "It was interesting to see Major Thomas standing there talking about the Golden Rule, but never once taking his hand off his gat." I guess I did rest my hand on my revolver because there was no pulpit. The Sunday school incident caused me to be looked upon by the workers as a sort of a man of religion. These people away from a priest when death struck a loved one became almost hysterical. I had never had that experience before. I did not know what to do, but I felt that neither the Lord nor any righteous thinking man who directed any church would chastise me for assuming responsibility which was not mine. I sent all people who came to me home, telling them that, of course, we could not get a priest because all were miles away, but I promised to act for them just as I did for the Sunday school kiddies. I do not know yet whether I did wrong, but many a soul was grateful.

Early in 1934, before I went to Germany on the Oberleander award, President Roosevelt called me to the White House because he knew I had been a missionary. The minor churches were having trouble with Hitler in Germany. My own Church was not having trouble, because a wise mission president was guiding affairs there. Roosevelt said, "Elbert, won't you tell me what to do in these cases?" And I did the best I could. It turned out all right and Hitler ceased abusing the minor sects. Great good came to our own people in Germany as a result of advice I was able to give later in regard to Church monies during the Hitler regime. The advice, which was followed, brought great benefit to the Mormon communities during the whole of the Second World War. The Mormon does not take pride in having accomplished any of these things. He credits to the guidance of the spirit whatever wisdom he seems to have at a given time. No one will ever understand the heart, the soul, or the actions of a Mormon, until he understands the fact that when once a Mormon gets the spirit and the responsibility of his priesthood, it is something which he never sheds. A partnership with God is not some vague expression to the Mormon boy. He accepts it literally. Throughout our experiences in the Orient, incident after incident occurred which to me made reading of similar incidents in the Old and New Testaments seem natural and ordinary. This contributed constantly to religious reactions. The Bible stories became more vivid and more vital, and the need for my own religion in the world became more convincing.

Before I was eighteen, when my mother and half of our family were in Europe collecting genealogical information, my father joined them, leaving me at home alone in charge of his businesses, as he told one of his friends, to teach me a sense of responsibility. That word again!

It was taken for granted in my youth that anyone in a government office was a carpetbagger. Some great men came, as I judge them now, but most of them were men who were transferred from the South out to our Territory. Carpetbaggism was taken for granted. The flagpole on the corner where the Liberal Party members held their rallies, instead of having an eagle at its top, had a carpetbag for a symbol.

In all my young days, strife was continuous, but no personal unfriendliness occurred. But out in the world it was quite different. I have never been hurt physically through what is called religious persecution or racial bias. I can assure you that experience does not make the skin tougher. In political life, opportunity after opportunity presents itself to get even, but it is never a temptation. In business life, I know of only three persons or institutions who were outright unfriendly to my father when he was passing through depression days. I read of all three crashing to the wall with the most direful consequences, without producing in me a feeling of satisfaction, but rather with a feeling of sorrow. I have seen Passion plays a score of times, wept each time, but never has one aroused hate in me. By nature I have a hot temper, and I am easily hurt, but a life's training has taught me that Mencius is right, and man's better nature can be made to prevail.

When I began the interpretation of history, I found that the Orient and my experiences in the Orient were so strong that I never left it out of my lectures or writings. To this day when it comes to religious questions, I interpret things from the fundamental thesis of my own Church. I have experienced the fire and water ceremonies of Shinto priests. I have seen the trances of the Dalai Lama priests. I have talked with various kinds of Buddhists. I have gone through the

Nichiren ceremonies of the heart. I have heard stories of how foxes get into men and how they leave great holes. I have seen the crudities of primitive religions, and heard of many miraculous healings, visitations, and, when strangely visited by an unknown individual, I had all of those ideas go through my mind. I have never seen anything or anyone, or gone through any experience that has caused me to change my faith. The philosophy behind what I call my religion is bigger and more all-embracing than any religious philosophy I have ever read. I sometimes think I see my own religion bigger and better than anyone else. But that cannot be a criticism of it.

In looking over my early writings, I ran across this sentence under a Cairo, Egypt, 1913 date and place line. I have forgotten the stimulus for it but it seems to have a place right here. "Religions generally are broad but religionists often narrow. Their cocksureness is the egotism of the ignorant." Man seldom knows about himself, but that sentence seems to me to reflect me and what I have been through. But please do not ask me what I meant and what the sentence means, because I do not know. Some religions I have known are very narrow, and some religionists so broad they did not seem to care, know, or understand anything. But some were narrow even to meanness, without having any reason to be.

Mormon care for children and youths, Mormon ideals for young fathers and mothers, Mormon interest in all from cradle to grave, seem to imply that there are only so many seconds in eternity and if one is wasted, it is gone forever. I have never known leisure. I have always had three men's jobs.

When I met Mr. Justice Brandeis he had read one of my books. He told me he was happy I got to Washington, but he added that he wanted to give me some advice. He said, "You know, Doctor, all that you have accomplished so far in your life you have done because you were able to get alone. Do not let anyone deprive you of solitude." Brandeis's advice was good, but the book he had read was produced in crowded hours.

Life to me is merely a learning process. I have never held back from new experiences. All seemed to be part of my education. On arrival in Japan I decided not to read foreign books about Japan, but to learn from my own experiences. This may have been a mistake, but it has kept me objective. Had I not assumed that attitude, never would I have braved Chinese and Japanese scholarship in my interpretation of Confucius. Had I not done this, the political East would have remained in my mind what Western writers had said it was.

The day I returned home, after circling the globe, I was asked to become an instructor at the University of Utah. A professor died the day we returned and I was invited to take his classes. I stayed twenty years.

In my legislative work, I have never been bothered by something I read out of a book. I learned my money economics from seeing and experiencing monies. I knew, for instance, that there was a difference between the silver in a tooth, the silver in a knife and fork, the silver in a dime, and the silver in the ground. When I explained this to President Roosevelt I pointed out that if he would give more for silver in the ground than he would for old silver, he could put men to work. Thus we got the differential for newly mined silver, and it did put men to work. That little lesson in simple economics has helped hundreds of thousands of people and created millions in wealth.

I unconsciously discovered a world unity because I had to make my lectures on the Far East to graduate students fit into something they already knew. If I had been book-trained I would have been frightened of my thesis in *World Unity Through Study of History*. I am not frightened any more.

One might get from this that I am not a supporter of formal education. This is not true. I took my doctorate after having lived in most of the capitals of Europe and Asia. My experiences were as broad as my instructors', but my whole graduate experience is one of the most satisfying of my life.

Three experiences in the Senate which came early in my first term are responsible for adding to my worth as a Senator. These were the work on the Civil Liberties Committee and the "Huey Long Hearings"—the Overton contest case. It was in my first term that I became a chairman of a major committee. This exceptional experience added greatly to my responsibilities.

As an educator, I think my Oriental courses contributed to a field of instruction our American universities could not longer neglect. As a Senator I think I have contributed to educational history, for the three great important accomplishments that have happened in the world's educational history all happened in America. They are the selling of public lands to aid schools, the Land Grant College Act signed by President Lincoln, and my Soldier Education Bill as it passed the Senate. Millions of American boys and girls have now had training in practically every university in the world. Nothing like that ever happened before.

I saw the first refugees arrive in Paris from the slave labor camps. Senator George and I visited General Eisenhower in his "little red brick school" headquarters. "Little red brick school" indeed! The atrocity camps, buzz bomb factories, and scores of other places in England, Belgium, France, and Germany, brought reactions to my thinking, but my Americanism and my Mormonism were the most shocked. Here was a man representing a religion and a nation whose fundamental principles are based upon the concept of the worth of the individual. I was invited to observe situations where individual rights, personal dignity, and governmental protection of the individual, were shattered. Throughout the whole of the Orient, where the individual rights are not stressed, I had never seen such indifference. Those experiences hurt me spiritually.

I had another experience which brought to my mind the early prophecies concerning the origin of my Church. It had taken my father nearly six months to get from London to Salt Lake City. I circled the globe in seven months' time. The end of the European war came while I was in Europe. When I returned in a single flight, with only four landings, the lights came on for the first time in London, in Paris, and, as we flew down in Washington our own Capitol was lighted for the first time since the war started. A commonplace experience, but not commonplace to the man who as a child was trained to watch the development of a "glorious work and a wonder."

Later in 1945, President Truman asked me to go back to Europe. I was entitled to a secretary. I invited the young lady who later became

Mrs. Thomas to go with me. From this came romance. But, romance, to the temple respecting Mormon that I was, had its religious significance. The journey to Europe resulted in another great religious experience. It became my task to speak for the bringing of a newly created government, Iceland, into the sisterhood of nations and also to make a plea for, and to succeed in obtaining, Italy's first invitation to join again an international organization. The speech I made for Italy was carried over all of the Italian radio stations. I was invited by the Holy Father to go to the Vatican, and by the King Regent to visit Rome. We had our own plane, with military and official attendants, totaling a group of about twenty-nine. I asked for a Mormon chaplain, but ended with three Roman Catholics, the senior, Colonel Turner, was the chaplain of President Truman's regiment in the First World War. Our party was a serious group. My thoughts during the journey were religious. For example, in an hour's talk with the King Regent, he attempted to maintain the thesis that bread for the Italian people was the thing that could hold his government together. I gave him the sermon "man cannot live by bread alone," and I told him that his government would not last, unless it was built on spiritual and educational bases.

The journey to the Vatican and the visit with the Holy Father was an outstanding experience of my life. We were alone for nearly half an hour. His goodness, his concern, his worldwide understanding, his desire for peace and decent living for all people, impressed me so greatly that my heart radiated his thoughts and words. After our conference, the Holy Father invited our whole group into his office, my future wife being the only lady present. The Holy Father read a gracious speech, centering around Elbert Thomas's work for peace. I was moved. As we were leaving, the Holy Father said he would like to give me a gift as a souvenir of our visit. I very frankly told him that if he was going to give me a gift, he would have to give me three, because I had three daughters. He gave me for them three white pearl rosaries and he also gave Miss Evans three. This experience marked for me not the beginning of meetings with great religious personages, and, as I review the great ones that I have met and the systems which they represent, I end where I begin, in deep respect for the simple words of Joseph Smith and the meaning of his first vision. To me it represents the greatest vision ever given to man, and Joseph Smith's own words in describing that vision are the most convincing scriptures I have read.

I had known the great Nicolai, the Russian who went to Japan in 1858 and established the Eastern Church there. Later I met the Patriarch of Jerusalem. My Confucian studies gave me an understanding of the difference between a belief based upon revelation and one based upon the wisdom of man. I had known the chief abbot of the Hon Kwanji Temple. His utter disdain of the body contrasted greatly with my Mormon and American respect for the sacredness of the human body. The abbot and I stood in front of an expensive coffin, bought in anticipation of the death of a rich man. His only remark was, "What a price to pay for something to put a smelling body in."

The story of Daruma and the contemplative priests, who live as Daruma taught, never satisfied me. I had accepted too fully the theory of revelation, ever to assume that I could sit down and think out the riddle of the universe. Shinto leaves me with a hollow feeling.

While I learned to admire the spirituality of both Hinduism and Mohammedanism, one left me feeling that a caste destroyed respect for the individual, and the other's history, not its beliefs, presented elements of religious zeal that ended in militancy. Not a day in the Orient passed without some religious reaction. Wherever I have gone, whatever I have done, even in my own land and in Europe, I have faced prejudices. I have tried always to appreciate and to learn.

In so rapid a review I have been unfair to all, including my own belief. I, in no case, belittle. The faith displayed by adherents of all religions is inspiring, and invokes appreciative respect in me. But I am left unsatisfied. My own religion, if I view it as something finished, does not satisfy either. But it is only a commencement of a great promised fulfilment, for is there not a need for a rebirth of the teachings of Jesus? Where in the world today do you find a complete fulfilment of the ideals of the Lord's prayer and the Sermon on the Mount? When I say that, I do not depreciate the worth of fine religions and splendid religious teachings, but the need of rebirth is everywhere. To me the world still lacks what a Jew would call justice; what a Christian would call love; what a Confucianist would call trust; what a Buddhist would call aspiration and a ridding of life's chains; what a Taoist would call a beginning of the understanding of the way; what a Zoroastrian would call that which makes you do for your neighbor what you would do for yourself. There is nothing in all of these systems of religion that could make me feel that mine was bad. Was there ever a people any poorer than my own people were in the beginning? It seems natural for me to say that all that they are today their religion made them. As an historian, an economist, and a political scientist, I know that there were other factors, especially the factor of America itself which contributed to what my people have made of themselves. But that does not make me unmindful of the fact that my father's life and my mother's life and my own life have each been made what they were and are by our religion. I have full faith that my children and my children's children will see as I do "this nation under God" as the source of mankind's political and spiritual redemption.

JUDITH BERLIN LIEBERMAN

To be born into a family which has produced men of great learning and of outstanding gifts of leadership can have a stunting effect upon the growing and maturing mind—especially as such assets are not passed on in the manner of some material goods. Fortunate are the children of such families if they are not made to feel the pressure of their heritage and if no unusual demands are made on them. Such was the spiritual milieu into which I was born. (My account will, therefore, include the influences exerted upon me by the three ancestors who were closest to me.)

The first time my curiosity was aroused in the history of our family was when in our travels we stopped off in Warsaw and visited the burial ground where my father's father had been laid to his eternal rest. The monument was a turretlike mausoleum surrounded by a low iron fence. Within the enclosure, the ground was strewn with pamphlets and papers yellowed with age. In the stillness of the air and the fervent attitude of father, there was the tremor of bygone years. The Hebrew characters on the slips expressed the urgent supplications and innermost yearnings of people who sought relief in their personal distress through the merit of the Good Deeds the deceased had performed in his lifetime. It was then that I learned that my grandfather had been a *Tzaddik*—a man who devoted all his life to study, to prayer and to the service of his fellow-men. He was the man who had trained a generation of the most outstanding Rabbinic scholars and leaders dispersed over Eastern Europe and other parts of the world.

My grandfather, Rabbi Naphtali-Zvi Yehuda Berlin—called for short the *Naziv* (from the contraction of the initials), a word meaning "governor" in Hebrew, came of a family that combined wealth with learning. At the age of twelve, he was admitted to the Yeshiva of Volozhin, which was the center of Jewish learning in the nineteenth century. He was a student of great ability and extraordinary application, and in a few years he became the son-in-law of the son of Rabbi Chayyim, the founder of the Academy and a member of the Dynasty, the term used to refer to the family. At the age of thirty-seven, the Naziv succeeded his deceased father-in-law as the head of the institution.

About grandfather's diligence, many stories bordering on the legendary, have been told. He would devote eighteen hours a day to study. To get some snatches of sleep, he would close his eyes holding a lighted candle of such a length that it could burn only fifteen minutes, then the burning sensation at the tip of his fingers would awaken him and he would resume his work. Such tales, however, do not illustrate the mode of life the Naziv would prescribe for the Yeshiva men. Of course, a student must not waste his time on worthless matters, but the Head would recommend habitual hours for sleep and regular times for meals. In his book, *From Volozhin to Jerusalem,* my father relates that grandfather was overheard saying to a very studious boy, "You devote so many hours to your books that you have no time to digest and master the material. If you allow more time for rest and meals, you will be able to fathom the meaning of what you have learned." Nevertheless, the voice of the Torah was never silenced in the hall of learning. There were always students who were bent over their books late at night, and others would come in after midnight and stay there undisturbed till early dawn. The only break in the monotony was the radiant appearance of the head of the school. When the town was soundly sleeping and enveloped in darkness, and the "old man" in his study was deeply engrossed in the big folios before him, he would suddenly rise from his place startled by some poignant recollection. He would close the tome, leave his house, and with resolute steps proceed in the direction of the "Holy Place of Study." He knew that many of his "children" would be pondering over the Talmud. He would walk the length and breadth of the large hall, take a good look at each figure, and pause over a youth who, overcome by drowsiness and heat, had dozed off in front of a burning charcoal fire. Grandfather would waken him with a gentle touch and warn him of the danger of a hot fire. He was anxious lest the overheated boy should take a cold drink and get chilled. There was hardly time to sound all these warnings when some hesitant steps were heard and a young student, who had been struggling with a difficult text, approached him. Grandfather, with kindness in his eyes and the friendly smile that always hovered on his lips, would gently stroke the young cheeks and patiently elucidate the difficult passage.

It is very likely that grandfather's reputation as a pedagogue has obscured his significance as a scholar. The spoken word can be heard and the magic of personality felt, but many years must elapse before the written word can be understood. Grandfather placed truth above all, and no trouble was too much for him to seek it. In those days, when modern research was unknown amongst Rabbinic scholars, and extensive travel unusual, he went by train to the capital of Russia to look for a manuscript of the work of Rab Ahai Gaon—a medieval scholar—and purchased it for a large sum of money. Unlike other Rabbinic scholars of his age, grandfather in his great commentary on Rab Ahai first tried to reconstruct the historical background and to correlate the work of Rab Ahai to those of the later codifiers of the Law, primarily to that of Maimonides.

One of the most impressive facts of the truly great Rabbinic minds was that their preoccupation with the study of the Torah never obstructed their view from the national needs of their people. Toward the end of the nineteenth century, when the idea of "Return to Zion" was still new, grandfather gave theoretical and practical expression to his support of the movement that later became known as the "Lovers of Zion." He found occasion to express his convictions on this head, in connection with the explication of certain passages of the Bible in his monumental Commentary. According to the Naziv, there is no place where the relation between the Creator and His people is as close as in the Land of Israel. The Jew can live a complete religious life *only* in the land of his Fathers, because a great part of the Law is applicable only to the Land of Israel. When the question of the Sabbatical year in Palestine arose, grandfather, moderate by disposition, insisted upon strict observance of the laws because he said, "We are ready for sacrifices not merely for the sake of furnishing the Land of the Philistines with inhabitants, but in order to settle the Holy Land with men devoted to the worship of the Almighty and the observance of His Commandments." No practical measures were too humble for the realization of this dream. A coin box was placed at the entrance of the hall on the eve of the Atonement services (an innovation in those days) and with grandmother's blessing, the son of his old age (the subsequent leader, Rabbi Meir Berlin) was put in charge of the collection.

Grandfather's second wife, my grandmother, was his close blood relation and twenty-five years his junior. The unusual match came about in the most extraordinary manner. Grandmother's fine bearing, personal charm, and intelligence attracted many suitors. She, however, had set up as her ideal her own scholarly father, Rabbi Michael Eppstein, author of many books that had become part of the standard equipment of those who practiced Jewish Law. She consented to marry a man of fine appearance and of considerable means, with the implicit understanding that he would devote time to gaining proficiency in the Torah. The young woman soon realized, however, that her husband had no penchant for the arduous task though he made an attempt. She felt she could not go on living a life of frustration. No pleading on the part of the young man (and of both families) could dissuade her from leaving him and hiding for months to escape the Russian law according to which the spouse had the legal right to force his wife's return. Finally the divorce was granted to her, and she returned to her parents' home strengthened in her determination to live a life that had inner meaning. Shortly after, an honored guest arrived from Volozhin with personal greetings from grandfather. When the conversation turned to family affairs, the visitor, realizing the wilfulness of the young woman, boldly suggested a match between uncle and niece. The parents were shocked nor could grandfather see his niece binding herself to a man many years her senior. The only one who welcomed the strange proposal was the beautiful and spirited woman. Months passed before the niece met her uncle, whom she had never seen before, and everybody felt that it was the hand of God when the union was shortly solemnized.

Grandmother, who was mother and pal to me the four years I was stranded at her house and later when she lived with us in New York, would keep me spellbound with the stories of her glorious past. Indiscreet as youngsters sometimes are, I asked her (as I blush even now to recall) whether she had ever regretted the decision about her marriage. There was something in her brown eyes and proud bearing which spoke of her happiness more eloquently than words could. Grandmother lived a full life, happy in the role of a helpmeet to the great man who was her life companion, content with the man who took great care of his appearance and was lovable in every way. Grandmother took complete charge of the finances of the institution, which in itself was a great challenge to her ability. Almost all the fellows—and they numbered 400–500—studied on a scholarship basis, and in order to free them of all mundane cares, their board and lodging were paid for. As a matter of fact, the Academy was the town's principal source of income. Harassed as grandmother was by these financial responsibilities, she had the satisfaction of being the mistress of a large household and the queen of the town.

About twenty years later, when I lived under grandmother's roof, the changed conditions did not affect grandmother's way of life. As the wife of a prosperous merchant and patron of learning (she had married again), she still assumed responsibility for the well-being of the townspeople and her house was always open to those in need of advice and financial aid. In keeping with Jewish tradition, the poor girl of marriageable age, the sick in need of medication, and the small businessman in times of economic depression, all claimed her special attention. With fires frequent and devastating in those districts of dense forests and straw-thatched roofs, many a Jew who had been rendered destitute, would be aided by her systematic plan of action. At a still later period, in Jerusalem, when grandmother reached the ripe age of eighty years, I was startled more than once by a hand (that was all I could see of the person in question) reaching from the outside for its share of the Sabbath loaves which had been lined up in a neat row on the window sill.

Amidst all this activity the grand old lady kept up her lively interest in men of learning and in the study of the Bible. She appeared to prefer the company of learned men to the prattle of women. She considered her day's work done only after she had covered a day's portion from the Torah and the Prophets. In winter her self-imposed assignment was the Book of Proverbs and in summer the Sayings of the Fathers. She was guided by these wise teachings in her personal conduct. She would overlook the failings of others and disparaging remarks about other people's doings would elicit from her the mild warning, "Do not judge your neighbor until you have been in his position."

She accepted the values of the new times and found fault with the past. "We girls were not taught like the boys, we were treated like a flock of sheep," she would complain of her early education. Though she valiantly tried to overcome her ignorance of the English tongue by taking private lessons and working hard on the *th's,* she felt unhappy because she could not master it. She followed my scholastic career with great satisfaction. If she ever had any feeling of envy it was, she remarked, for the opportunity the American woman had and the equality she enjoyed with the other sex. Her greatest fulfilment she found in her only son (the elder having passed away) and the relationship between mother and son was that of mutual understanding, deep love, and—on the part of the son—a certain element of awe.

In an attempt to sketch the main features of father's personality, elusive as they are (because the inner light he radiated diverts attention from the details), it becomes more and more obvious that the feeling of regard and consideration was the basic note in father's attitude to all fellow beings. Just as his belief in God was untroubled by any doubts, his trust in people was unshaken by any experience he might have had. Because of his fundamental fortitude, everybody around him seemed to gather courage and strength, and the impossible became possible, and the unreal real. Being the prime force behind Religious Zionism, and in any undertaking he associated himself with, his advice was always sought in times of crisis and his presence was essential in hours of weighty decisions.

If father ever transgressed any commandment of the Torah, it was the prohibition against favoring the poor. Of course, I do not mean that he showed bias in their favor in judging lawsuits, to which the passage in question (Leviticus 19:15) refers. But when there were people waiting for him in his office, it seemed as if his eye first recognized the one who sought his counsel, for among the host who sought him (besides those who conferred with him on matters pertaining to his party, the upkeep of many institutions of learning, promotion of journalistic and cultural enterprises) there were those who needed his personal help, whether in the nature of material or spiritual assistance. Nobody was turned away either at the office or his residence. "A man is a man," was his attitude, and no personal inconvenience to him or to his family, or threat to his declining health could restrict his activity. Regardless of his heavy schedule, he would personally contact endless lists for others when he was on his frequent (organizational) trips to distant parts of the world. To the public at large he appeared in the light of a great leader with a knack of stirring hundreds and thousands of people with the thundering quality of his voice, originality of thought, and fine delivery. In contrast to the soft-spoken man that he usually was, he would display a leonine pugnacity. Both his followers and anti-Zionists harkened as to one who spoke with the voice of tradition of the spirit of Israel. Though all his life he fought for a united Judaism and stood above party interests, he was the leader of the Religious front that wrested concessions from the Center Parties and the Laborites within the Zionist Organization. His stand was rooted in the vision of a Jewish State built on the principle of Torah-true Judaism and the spiritual values that have come down to us from the Prophets and the Rabbis. His firm conviction was that unless a majority of our people lives on the land promised by God and speaks the language in which the Bible was given, they are doomed to an existence barren of Jewish content and to ultimate loss of identity. Being both the man of action and the student, he could turn out a prodigious amount of work, no intrusions ever disturbing his serene flow of thought. He was the editor of the Talmudic Encyclopedia and the promoter of a new edition of the Talmud. Disregarding his physical weakness, he would stealthily disappear into his study at night and write long articles and essays for various publications with hardly any correction to mar the long white sheets of paper. Being one of the architects of the new State, he strove to promote legislation in the light of the Torah and on the basis of democracy. His political creed was permeated with a new hope for the future of the whole of mankind, and he envisaged American democracy and freedom of thought and speech established all over the world.

Father's attitude toward his children was "live and let live." No books were recommended that a parent felt children ought to read; no restrictions were made as to the choice of friends or places visited. At times the impression was created that father had little time to worry over his children's problems. As I look back, I can see that father jealously watched over his children's doings—though in the most unobtrusive way, as if allowing the young wings to unfold spontaneously. Want of over-protection early developed in me a sense of self-reliance and helped me to stand up to the trials of unusual circumstances in which I early found myself.

Throughout childhood there was the keen awareness of God, the Protector watching over our personal fortunes. The feeling was inculcated in us when my sister, having fallen through the broken bannister of a wooden shed escaped with slight injuries, or when she was restored to us after having been lost amid a hustling crowd on our arrival in a metropolis. When we joined father in Berlin, shortly before the outbreak of the First World War, the struggle for economic existence could not escape the attention of the youngsters. Though mother came from an affluent family, the dowry she had received was soon lost to a partner in a business venture in which father showed no interest. Our small apartment served as office for the promoter, editor, and journalist—all three combined in father—of the first Hebrew weekly in the German capital. Mother was the clerk, more hindered than assisted by me in the work of stamping envelopes and mailing the papers at the nearest post office. On Fridays our home would invariably assume a new glory, and all worry would disappear as if by magic. Dressed in our best, we would impatiently await father's return from the synagogue accompanied by the angels who were to usher in the Sabbath, the day of complete rest. Soon the sweet melody of "Peace Upon You" filled the air followed by "Virtuous Wife" in tribute to the mistress of the house. For it was she who on a snow white tablecloth had lit the Sabbath candles and prepared the fish and the coffee cake, the taste of which made us hanker for it the rest of the week.

It was left to mother, a graduate of a secondary school with a deep appreciation for good education, to supervise our formal training. Mother, far from resting on the laurels of the past, had great ambitions for her children. We were put into schools of reputable standing. The method of teaching the three R's may have had its merits, but little attempt was made to stir the pupil's imagination or allow for individual differences. Nor could the private teacher, to whom our Hebrew education was entrusted often at the price of a third of father's salary, awaken a lively interest in the matter taught. A Hebrew poet of note or a student of Semitics, who was thought most likely to succeed, could not be expected to give thought to the presentation of a passage in the Bible. As a result a stare of blank boredom was often concealed behind lowered eyelids.

I leave it to recognized authorities to determine the effects of the world wars and the resulting political upheavals on the forming of the personalities of our generation. The monstrosity of Hitler and the annihilation of all "inferior" peoples cut into the very being of a Jew. The rebirth of the Jewish State brought an upsurge of feeling and hope for mankind. By mere chance my personal fortunes were early bound up with the momentous happenings in the world. Having urged father to take me, a third-grader, on what was intended to be a two weeks' visit to my grandmother in Lithuania, a series of Odyssean adventures began. On the day we were to cross the border back to Berlin, war was declared. After months of waiting, our attempts to return together and rejoin the rest of the family in

Stockholm by the northern route were foiled by the good advice of a chance acquaintance not to expose a child to a voyage on icy waters. As I was left in the care of grandmother, my life took on something of an epic quality. I recall a covered wagon with the load of grandmother, her husband, myself, and some earthly possessions slowly moving through a blizzard in the wake of retreating Russian regiments into the capital of White Russia. Vivid are the recollections of the rejoicing of old and young after the fall of tyranny and the exalted spirits with which the new era was awaited. Important to mental growth was access to a private library that contained the best of the world classics. Tolstoy, London, Byron, were read avidly and the morbid characters of Dostoievski were gleeful topics for lengthy discussion by adolescent girls. I sought answers to the questions "how" and "why," in pictorial abridged editions of Darwin and Haeckel. But whereas the young minds gloried in the rationalistic approach to the creation of the world, whereas all tradition was discarded with ease, I found reassurance in the memory of grandfather standing on the eve of Yom Kippur on the threshold of the House of Learning and asking for forgiveness of those whom he had harmed unwittingly. There was also the feeling of spiritual nearness to father and mother beckoning to me from across the seas of the New World where they had settled, and strengthening me in my beliefs.

My reunion with my father after the armistice in 1918 was an overpowering experience. Coming home to the blessed shores of the United States was a most welcome relief from the complex system of passports and other restrictions on personal liberty in Russia. New life began and new interests were awakened. At Columbia University the study of the principles of democracy underlying the political order of the New World and the constitutional history of the United States and of nationalistic movements with Muzzey and Hayes, respectively, inspired me to make a study of the doctrines of liberation in the light of English literature. Inspiring were the seminars of Professor Bernard Fehr, head of the English department at Zurich University and formerly of Cambridge, England. Professor Fehr, who was the rare combination of a brilliant scholar and an artistic temperament, could draw with masterly strokes the Englishmen of letters and men of thought, and in his lectures poets such as Milton and Blake came to life again. It was at that time that I began to question the reliability of some footnotes made to Robert Browning's poems which had been inspired by Jewish sources. Whereas the commentators relegated some of the verses to pure "fancy," they were in truth images taken from the Midrashic and Talmudic treasures. In particular one poem entitled, "Ben Karshook," which is omitted from many selections of the poet's works, led me to look for parallelisms between the writings of the English poet and Hebraic lore. The remarkable similarity in the story of Rabbi Perida between the wording of the poet and a passage in the Talmud inspired me to delve into the poet's past, to scan through the complete list of books found in his private library as catalogued by Sotheby & Company, to inspect the Hebrew writing in the original manuscripts in the Bodleian Library and to come across an unrecorded manuscript of his father's commentary on the Bible.

My interest in Hebrew learning was further stimulated by life and work in Jerusalem, marriage to a scholar, and educational work in the United States. Life and work in Jerusalem required the harnessing of all human power in the country. In the twenties immigration laws permitted thousands of young men and women to enter the Land where they hoped to see the fulfilment of the Promise given to the Fathers of the Jewish people. The vision of a People with all its attributes never looked brighter. Neither limitation of funds nor restriction of space could deter the new generation from breaking up their homes and setting forth to Zion, where the name, David, was to mean again inner strength and implicit trust in God and the memory of Sarah, the protecting arms of a mother. The hold of a ship could be miraculously stretched. Money was procured with the willing assistance of more fortunate passengers. The blue skies were a marvelous setting for merry song and gay laughter. On one such voyage, we exchanged our berths for deck chairs so that the difference in the cost could be applied to purchasing additional tickets for new immigrants. The arrival at Tel-Aviv or Haifa was heralded by more song and carefree laughter. The stucco buildings exhaled warmth of temperature and warmth of feeling and the sidewalks resounded with the noisy, hurried clatter of footsteps and the hubbub of voices. There was no time for sleep. Structures rose like mushrooms, and new enterprises blossomed overnight.

People with some systematic training in the fields of pedagogy were absorbed by the expanding communities. Teaching of European history and literature at a teacher's training school for girls, whose cultural backgrounds and training were as varied as the countries they came from, presented a great challenge to an inexperienced teacher like myself. There was excellent material from Western Europe, but haunted by the memory of broken families, and the shadows of the dead. There were girls of darker shades from North African countries, whose families abandoned their cavelike dwellings and set out on their long trek to Zion on a donkey. One such girl lost her father when he fell off the donkey while stumbling through the sands of the desert and reached Jerusalem with a sick mother and three smaller children to care for. The equipment of their one-room dwelling consisted of makeshift mattresses and sacks of burlap for protection against the cold winds.

At the completion of a four-year course all differences were ironed out and after rigorous finals in Bible, Prophets, Hebrew Literature, and pedagogy, the graduates were competent enough to staff schools in both large and small settlements set up by the Education Department of the Jewish Agency.

The recollections of my visit to the communal settlements are most vivid. These settlements are a form of life that can hardly be found anywhere else. Private interests were entirely subordinated to the good of the community. The house became the property of the collective, and the tractor was acquired with the pooled resources of all members. In the Mizrachi communities, one of which was named after my grandfather, "The Well of Naziv," prayers were said at dawn and after a heavy day's work, young faces and eager eyes were bent over the large folios in the pallid light of the barn. Sabbath was a day of complete rest, and the milking of the cows was permitted in order to bring relief to the animal, though the milk could not be drunk or put to any use. The greatest favor asked of a visitor was the negative of a snapshot taken by the American camera. The objects to be snapped were in the following order of importance: first the cow and plough, then the newborn baby, and finally the adult. Most of the children were, as in other communes in Israel, blue-eyed and fair-haired.

The radically changed conditions in the thirties presented new challenges and called for new educational projects. In an air charged with tension, when shots were heard intermittently, and many victims were felled by Arab snipers, it became imperative to found all-day nurseries to enable mothers to take the places of their husbands on duty elsewhere. I felt that the obligation to establish such institutions in Jerusalem especially for religious groups, fell on me. We organized all-day summer play schools to care for undernourished children who in peaceful time might have vacationed on Mt. Carmel or on the shores of the Mediterranean. Though additional activity was accompanied by physical hardships, there was the satisfaction that an earnest effort was being made to prevent the lifelong ill-effects that are known to have resulted to the mind and body of some of the youthful population from the disturbed conditions of those years. A most rewarding project was the founding of a dormitory for the young women at the Mizrachi Teachers' Training School for Girls, who with limited means of their own could find congenial living conditions and be assured of a bright future as career women in their own country and in many distant lands such as India, where the need for trained Hebrew teachers was very great.

In 1940, I returned to the United States with my husband after days of flying over the sandy wastes of the Middle East, a stop-over at the British oil wells of Bahrein and days spent at Bombay. My return made me painfully conscious of the sad fact that the world at large had still to learn much from America. Though "the idea and example" of America had invaded the world, the virtues of political freedom and belief in personal liberty still had to be accepted by many countries in order to make democracy work. We received a hearty welcome from the customs officer in New York who had heard of the great institution of learning to which my husband had been called. Subsequent association with men and women of high

moral qualities and great scholastic attainments, and lifelong friendships which have been formed, have mitigated any hardship which
might be felt by the wife of a scholar wholly devoted to study and
research. Precious have been the moments to me when my husband
has been able to tear himself away from his work in order to illumi-
nate the gleanings of Jewish treasures not only with his erudition but
with the moral strength drawn from the wealth of Torah that has
motivated every action of his life.

My husband, though by nature disinclined to express his personal
beliefs, has brought to bear upon me, by his mode of living and
conduct, the great force that Torah has been in the destiny of our
people and in the lives of Jews as individuals. He helped me to gain
an insight into the role that the Jews play as individuals and as a
people in the community of nations.

Jews have survived anguish and physical torment because they
were imbued with the teachings of the Torah. They knew that the
cause for which they were suffering was worthy of their sacrifice.
Thus suffering, instead of breaking them, gave them spiritual depth
and strength and even satisfaction, as it frequently does to people of
noble character. A striking example of this phenomenon was the
reaction of the German Jews to the events of the nineteen thirties. In
most cases it was those who were ignorant of or estranged from their
spiritual heritage that committed suicide. Those who had preserved
Jewish learning and observance found the strength to go elsewhere
and take roots in a new environment.

In Jewry, the Torah has been an affair of the masses. The Torah
specifically commands every Jew to study it, and the passage in
question is included in the *Shema,* which every Jew repeats twice
daily: "And ye shall teach them (the words of the Torah) to your
children, talking of them, when thou sittest in thy house, and when
thou walkest by the way, and when thou liest down, and when thou
risest up" (Deuteronomy 11:19). For since the Jewish people was
chosen by God to keep His commandments, the Jewish people
must spend all the time it can studying His commandments.

How this peculiar feature struck the eye of an outsider is eloquently
attested by a German officer who was interested in biblical studies.

While serving in the German Intelligence Office in Warsaw during the First World War, this writer records, his office learned that something very mysterious was going on in the Jewish section. It was said that coachmen would come one after another without passengers and disappear mysteriously into a certain courtyard. The writer continues that he went to investigate for himself and arriving at the place in question with two detectives, stood and watched. It was true. Coachman after coachman was driving in with no passengers in his cab. All of them disappeared into a courtyard into which the scholarly writer followed. He finally came into one of the upper stories of the building. There he opened the door and saw two long tables, surrounded by coachmen who were sitting in their high hats, bent over books, and listening attentively to a man who was expounding something. The officer realized at once that there could be no question about a plot being fomented against the government. Nevertheless, he stood, dazed. He reports that he remained motionless, observing the occupants of the room without being able to comprehend what was going on. Finally he motioned to one of the listeners, for until then no one had even taken notice of the intruders. Utilizing his imperfect knowledge of Yiddish, the officer asked the Jew, "What is this?" "Why, this is a synagogue," the Jew replied. The officer repeated his question, "What is this?" "Why, they are sitting and studying the Law." The officer asked, "Is today Yom Kippur, a holy day?" "No," the Jew said, "This is what we do every day." "You mean to say that every day you come here and listen to a lecture on the law?" "Why, certainly," the Jew said. "After a hard day's work?" "Yes, that is what we do." The officer was convinced, and he concludes his account saying: "It is amazing. It is unthinkable. It is inconceivable that German drivers should come every day to the University and listen to lectures on law!" The officer, of course, could only have realized dimly, if at all, what the Torah had meant to the Jews through the ages, how, like a lone beacon, it alone had relieved some very gloomy pages of Jewish history, and how the Jew clung to it and found comfort in it.

It was this evaluation of the Torah that strengthened me in my resolution to do my small share in the restoration of Zion, the center whence Torah shall come forth. Early in my college career, I joined the Mizrachi Organization, the Orthodox branch of the Zionist movement, of which my father was the leader. The essence of Mizrachi ideology is: Israel restored on the principles of the Torah. Such doctrines as universal brotherhood of man in God's image, the Messianic dream of permanent peace, the doctrine of the sovereignty of every soul as expressed in the complete physical rest on the Sabbath, are to the Mizrachi the *conditio sine qua non* for the structure of the Jewish State. An Israeli whose only cultural mark is the ability to speak Hebrew would be an Israeli bereft of all the other spiritual values which have come down to us. In order to build for the future, we must return to the past.

In the capacity of national political chairman of the Mizrachi Women's Organization, I have been called upon to clarify our stand in the political setup of the Zionist Organization. The central idea of building a Jewish State on the land of our Fathers is common to all Zionists. Just as the essence of sugar is sweetness to all human beings, so Zionism is to all Zionist parties the restoration of the Jewish State. The lump of sugar, however, can also convey a variety of meanings. Whereas to the peasant it is sweetness only, to the physician it is primarily a means of nutrition. Moreover, to the industrialist it is a substance to be exploited for industrial purposes, and to the chemist it conveys a distinct chemical formula. Yet the sweetness of sugar remains the basic feature to all. In the same way, the restoration of Israel has to the Mizrachi, besides the meaning common to all, an additional significance. This is an Israel based on its spiritual heritage. Roots steeped in the past give the State not only a firm hold on the present, but lend to it that spiritual content which makes its existence worthwhile.

The practical work carried on by the Mizrachi Women's membership has been in the direction of establishing projects in Israel where cultural possessions could be transmitted in the most up-to-date fashion and in an adequate physical environment. The institutions in Israel established by the Mizrachi Women's Organization of America, whether they are schools, where all kinds of vocations are taught, or whether they are children's villages and social welfare centers, take great pride in their lovely exteriors, progressive approach to education, and Jewish spiritual content. As a member of the National Administrative Board of the organization, it has been incumbent upon me to share the task with other members to guide those thousands of co-workers who have dedicated themselves to the practical aspect of our work.

As I look back upon the latter years of my New York period, I become keenly aware that my preoccupation with the Bible, Prophets, and Commentaries has given me a great deal of inner satisfaction. It was also in a sense a fulfilment of my nostalgia for these subjects which in the past did not form the central theme in the education of girls. I consider it a great privilege to have been instrumental in elevating the teaching of Bible and the traditional commentaries to their rightful place in the curriculum of the Shulamith School for Girls. This institution, founded by a group of parents and friends, wholeheartedly devoted both to the ideas of American democracy and to the Jewish heritage, has been inspiringly successful in carrying out an integrated program of bilingual cultural experience. The name, Shulamith, which is that of the heroine of the Song of Songs, and the motto of the school, "Return, oh, Return," are evocative of the spirit which has formed the curriculum of the school. The revival of the study of sources on the elementary level meets the desperate need for filling the void felt by the Jewish child—the desire for roots, the yearning to "belong." In the Bible, the child learns of the beginnings of his own history, of the pride and greatness of a people, acquires a knowledge of and love for the Hebrew tongue, and encounters situations which help him resolve his own difficulties.

The wholesome tendency to integrate the past with the present is illustrated by the following incident at one of the Bible classes on the adolescent level. The teacher explained the meaning of "Do not gossip," and how base it is to engage in gossip, a vice which tends to befall the idle. The following day, in the course of the lesson, one of the girls suddenly raised her hand and made the following observation, "Teacher, yesterday while taking a stroll we made up our minds to abide by the law and not to gossip. To our great consternation, we had nothing to talk about." Whereupon another girl, from the opposite corner of the room reiterated the same thought. "It is true," she said, "we could not make any conversation, we did not open our mouths." The children preferred for once not to talk, as a result of reading the wise words of our sages who regard the "evil tongue" as only less serious than bloodshed.

Precepts like these and stories centering round such ideas as Abraham's hospitality and Moses's simplicity, give the child a positive image of human nature and enable him to find faith in himself. A positive version of the world was recently unfolded by a third-grader in the words which closely resemble ancient prophecy: "I dreamed that God created the world anew. He created one people and one language. The word, 'death,' was not known and the dead came to life again."

The Haggadic literature which I have been trying to integrate into Bible teaching, opens a gateway to a storehouse of untold pleasures to our pupils. At the same time, I do not lose sight of the prime importance of teaching the great moral foundation upon which American life has been founded. A perfect example of such an integrated lesson—the teaching of a democratic philosophy—is afforded by the Rabbinic speculation about Jeremiah's ancestry. The theory that Jeremiah was descended from Rahab may strike most readers as merely a simple Rabbinic whimsy. But as a teacher, I try to emulate the Rabbis who insist upon making it a lesson in democracy. "Let the son (Jeremiah) of the reformed wanton, the Rabbis teach, come and reprove the wanton son (*i.e.*, the prophet's contemporaries) of the paragon (meaning Israel's forebears)."

In the mere existence of such variety of educational institutions, there lies the strength and glory of American life. The freedom to express oneself freely and to preserve one's cultural heritage will bring out the best that is in all peoples in America, and will mold a form of life whose unity will grow out of its diversity.

CHANNING H. TOBIAS

I was born on February 1, 1882, in Augusta, Georgia, a city whose founding dates back to pre-Revolutionary days. It is such an interesting city, and had such a decided influence on my early life, that I must take the time at the outset to say a few things about it.

It is thoroughly steeped in Colonial and Revolutionary traditions. There is a monument on one of the principal thoroughfares of the city to George Walton, a resident of Augusta, who was a signer of the Declaration of Independence. Like Charleston, South Carolina, Savannah, Georgia, and Macon, Georgia, Augusta was a cultural center during the period immediately before and after the Civil War. Two or three poets were residents there, the most noted of whom was James Rider Randall, the author of "Maryland, My Maryland." The nationally known poet, Sidney Lanier, who wrote such popular poems as "A Ballad of Trees and the Master" and "The Marshes of Glynn," lived nearby in Bibb County.

It was inevitable that in such an atmosphere as this there would be a cultural spillover into the Negro community. Two Negro writers, Silas X. Floyd and Wilson Jefferson, wrote poetry that was considered of a fairly high order. I recall a couplet written by Wilson Jefferson, who was the son of a cobbler, and was often taunted by the men who worked in his father's shop for being a dreamer. He countered by writing these lines:

> Pity him not who in the world sense fails,
> Whose task truth-seeking, trails

A light afar;
But rather pity him who still assails
Pregnable heights,
And never sees a star.[1]

I am sure you will agree that this is real poetry.

Augusta was one of those cities in the deep South that established a public school system for Negroes as well as whites immediately after the Civil War. Of course the double standard existed then as it does today, under which there is a disproportionate expenditure of public money for the education of white children as over against the amount spent for colored children, but, in spite of the disadvantage of such disparities, the public school officials were conscientious in bringing in as teachers the best trained Negroes who could be secured at that time. The chief training center for Negroes for the entire state was Atlanta University, an institution that was founded by Northern philanthropists immediately after the Civil War. In the nature of the case the training for Negroes in the early days did not go beyond the elementary grades. After sufficient students had passed through these grades, a high school was set up that was presided over by Richard R. Wright, a graduate of Atlanta University, who afterward became president of Georgia State College for Negroes, and in later years moved to Philadelphia where he entered the business field as a banker, and served in that capacity until his death at ninety-two years of age. He had the distinction of operating his bank through the trying depression years without loss of funds or prestige. When he passed away in 1948, the President of the United States took notice of the contribution that he had made in education and business.

Distinguished contemporaries of Dr. Wright in these early years in Augusta included Judson W. Lyons, who first was a teacher and afterward a highly controversial political figure. He was appointed postmaster of Augusta by President William McKinley, but the reaction of the Augusta public was so hostile that the appointment was revoked, and he was made register of the Treasury of the United States. Charles T. Walker, a famous Baptist minister of worldwide

[1] Wilson Jefferson, *Poems,* Richard G. Badger, Boston, 1910.

reputation who was popularly known as the Black Spurgeon, was as acceptable in the pulpits of London and New York as in his native Augusta. John Hope, afterward president of Morehouse College and Atlanta University, was born and received his early training in Augusta. While Augusta was in the pathway of Sherman's march to the sea, and has never forgotten that devastating destruction of property and life, it has risen above most communities in the State of Georgia in the pattern of race relationships that has been developed there through the years. There prevails what is commonly known as good relationship between the races, but of course all within the framework of segregation, to which Negroes rightly object. Perhaps the absence of the kind of prejudice that is found in many other parts of the State is due to the cultural background I have described, and to the fact that, for over one hundred years, there has been a daily newspaper published in the city, the oldest newspaper in the South, the *Augusta Chronicle,* which has kept the public informed of what has been happening beyond the borders of the community, thereby making it a less provincial community, which always means a less prejudiced community. The fact that I was born and grew up in such a city, accounts in part for the lack of bitterness with which I have been able to approach consideration of racial relationships in the South.

In spite of the fact that colored children were given in the public schools the kind of elementary training that I have described, there was a set pattern of employment for the Negro part of the population. The men were permitted to become artisans, working as bricklayers, carpenters, shoemakers, etc., etc. The women were, for the most part, employed as domestic servants in white families. My mother, although fairly well trained, was a domestic servant. My father, who was even better trained, having spent a short while at Atlanta University, could find no higher occupation than that of coachman— forerunner of the modern chauffeur. Both were loyal members of the Colored Methodist Church, but neither was what might be called devoutly religious, in the sense of regular attendance upon all the services of the Church. My sister, three years older than myself, was the only other child. Neither of us lived with our parents, because they both worked out and were not able to give us their personal care. My sister lived with her paternal grandmother, a woman of unusual intelligence, beauty, and personal charm, who was fairly well provided for economically through inheritance. I lived with a widowed friend of my mother, who was illiterate but highly intelligent. This foster mother, though never a member of any church, nevertheless saw to it that I attended Sunday school and church services regularly.

It was at one of these church services, when I was about ten years of age, that I heard a man preach who was destined to exert a great influence on my life. He was a white man from South Carolina who had come to Augusta to establish a private church school for the training of Negro youth. No single word of his sermon remains with me, but the image of the man is as clear as if I were looking at him now—his alert, soldierly bearing, his sparkling blue eyes, his well trimmed Van Dyke beard, and the kindly tone of his voice as he placed his hand on my head after the service when he was greeting the departing congregation at the door and said: "My little man, you were very attentive today. One of these days, when you have finished public school, I want you to come to my school." I never forgot that invitation. When I finished grade school I had the choice of three high schools, including the school of this white friend, Dr. George Williams Walker, and I insisted on going to his school, Paine Institute, as it was known then, although it was the poorest equipped of the three. It was literally true that the buildings consisted of converted stables, and a president's home that was partly used as a girls' dormitory. In my student days the story was told of a visit to the school by the noted evangelist, Sam Jones. In taking Mr. Jones through the buildings, President Walker entered a room containing a few shelves of well worn volumes, and said: "Mr. Jones, this is the beginning of our library." "Pardon me, Professor," said Mr. Jones, "but it looks like the end of it." Of necessity in those early years the Institute was one run by white people for colored people. The main teaching responsibilities were carried by President Walker, Professor Robert L. Campbell, both of whom were Confederate veterans, and Mrs. M. Z. Hankinson, a woman of fine cultural background who, like Dr. Walker, had felt the call to give her life to this type of educational service.

The time soon arrived, however, when the cooperative principle found expression. One of the first students of the school was a country boy named John Wesley Gilbert. His mental alertness at once convinced President Walker that he should be encouraged to go to college. Accordingly, his regular school work was supplemented by special college preparatory study under the direction of President Walker, himself. In due time young Gilbert entered Brown University, from which he was graduated with honor, and pursued postgraduate studies in the classics at the American University at Athens, Greece, which led to the granting of the Master's degree by Brown University. On his return to America he had many attractive offers to teach, but chose to return to Paine, and became the first Negro to be associated with Southern white people in the education of Negroes. From that day until this, Paine College, as it is now known, has been a place where highly trained white and colored people join hands and work side by side in the training of Negro youth. I, myself, joined that faculty after receiving my A.B. degree at Paine College and my Bachelor of Divinity degree at Drew Theological Seminary, Madison, New Jersey. The first six years of my working career were spent at Paine College. The old teaching staff of four has grown into a first class faculty, and the instruction given is officially recognized as Grade A by the Association of Southern Colleges. Thus you can readily realize the effect upon me of my close contact with the type of Southern white people whom I have described, a contact which is unbroken at the present time, because I am now serving as Vice President of the Board of Trustees of Paine College alongside of the President of the Board, Bishop Arthur J. Moore, a Southern white man who presides over the Methodists of Georgia.

I can never utter wholesale condemnations of Southern white people, in spite of the fact that everything within me revolts against the Southern pattern of double standards as affecting white and Negro citizens. And the reason I take this position is inherent in such experiences as I have described. Even though it meant defiance of the customs and traditions of his own people, George Williams

Walker believed in a single standard of citizenship and in the sacredness of all personality, white and black. The fact that I knew him and worked by his side, and have known hundreds of others like him since, imposes an obligation upon me to consider questions involving race relationships on their merits, rather than in terms of the geographical backgrounds of the persons concerned.

Perhaps this is as good a point as any to state my position on race relationships in America. But before I do so I want to make it clear that the extent to which I insist upon no deviation from a single standard of citizenship, is due as much to the example and teaching of this Southern white man, who was my college president, as to any influence which has been exerted upon me in later years. I think it is important to repeat this, because so often today the enemies of civil rights in the South attribute any opposition to the traditional Southern point of view on the part of a Negro to the fact that he has been influenced by exposure to the North.

My position on race relationships can be briefly stated, for it involves mainly one practice, namely, segregation. *I am unalterably opposed to segregation based on race, creed, or color, and for the following reasons:*

First, it cheapens human personality and leads to crime against the group affected by it. To illustrate: when a lynching occurs, most people hasten to condemn the lawless element responsible for the actual perpetration of the crime, when, as a matter of fact, the real responsibility rests with the respectable citizens of the community who, through custom or law, impose a double standard of citizenship upon the community. I maintain that every law on the statute books and every well established custom of a local community or state that assigns a group, because of racial, religious, or color considerations, to live in a segregated part of the community, contributes to the cheapening of the personality of that group. Therefore, when an inhabitant of such a community is made a victim of mob violence, those who are responsible for the making of the laws and customs that have cheapened the personality of the victim must share the guilt.

Second, segregation is unAmerican in spirit and practice. American citizens are supposed to enjoy freely all public privileges without discrimination as to race, creed, or color. When certain groups of citizens, because of economic power or superiority in numbers, arrogate to themselves the right to circumscribe life, liberty, and happiness for minorities, they have violated the most sacred of American principles.

Third, and most important of all, I object to racial segregation, because it is an insult to the Creator. The individual or group who segregates is put in the ridiculous light of questioning the wisdom of Almighty God in creating people physically different from themselves. Racial segregation is indefensible on religious grounds, because it is based on something that the individual is powerless to remove. If a man is discriminated against because he is unclean, he can bathe and overcome the handicap. If the discrimination is because of ignorance, he can study and learn and meet the conditions. But if he is discriminated against because he is black, or brown, or white, the discrimination is based on something that he cannot remove, and would not if he could, and is therefore a sin, not just against the man himself, but against the God Who made him as he is.

One would think, from all the noise and furor coming up out of the South following the Report of the President's Committee on Civil Rights and the issuance of the President's Message on the same subject, that life itself depended upon the segregation of the races. Mr. Truman has been accused of blasting at the white supremacy rock of ages, simply because he has insisted that it is not necessary to do violence to the personality of one racial group in order to uphold the dignity of the other. There are thousands of white people in the South who agree with the President but who are not disposed to argue the case once politicians have raised the cry of Negro domination. But there is an ever increasing number of Southern people who are growing weary of the wolf calls of the politicians and are becoming articulate in the interest of a single standard of citizenship. I quote directly from a deliverance by a group of white church women assembled in 1948 at Orlando, Florida:

We recommend that women of the Methodist Church seek to remove every barrier that separates members of the family of God in the Church, and to build a Christian fellowship where ideas, experiences, facilities and action programs may be shared with freedom on a basis of full participation.[2]

That part of my life that has been devoted to better understanding and cooperation between the races has been based upon the principles that I have just enunciated. With reference to these principles, there are four principal classes of Negroes. I wish to name them and in so doing point out the group with which I claim to be identified.

First, there is the Negro who considers every problem from the viewpoint of his own personal advantage. He is willing to lie about conditions and what is in his own heart. He is willing to bend and bow obsequiously before white people who demand subservience, if by so doing he can get what he, personally, wants from these white people. Such a character is viciously selfish and dangerous.

Second, there is the Negro who is not vicious and not particularly selfish, but who is weary of the struggle, and is willing to agree upon any course that will permit him to pass his days without coming into open conflict with other people. He is popularly known as the Uncle Tom type. As I have said, he is not vicious. He is simply tired— and I might add, is becoming more and more out of date.

Third, there is the ultra-radical type of Negro who believes in agitation for the sake of agitation, and is not eager to find a solution of the problems of which he complains, because then he would be deprived of the one occupation for which he exists, namely, disagreement for the sake of disagreement. Fortunately, his number is too small to merit serious consideration.

Fourth, there is the Negro with whom I count it a privilege to be identified, namely, the Negro who will not bow or bend obsequiously before other people in order to gain something for himself, who will not lie about conditions, or about what is in his own heart, who is willing to cooperate, but only on terms of mutual respect. This is the group with which all who are interested in true democracy for America will have to deal.

It is because of my strong conviction that it is possible within

[2] 1948 Report of the Southeastern Jurisdiction of Women's Society of Christian Service, Methodist Church.

the lifetime of the present generation to see true democracy in the ascendency in America, that I have identified myself with many movements that are working to that end. I think of such movements as the National Association for the Advancement of Colored People, the National Urban League, the American Council on Race Relations, the National Committee on Segregation in the Nation's Capital, the philanthropic boards, such as the Phelps-Stokes Fund (of which I have the honor to be Director), the Marshall Field Foundation, the Jesse Smith Noyes Foundation, the Southern Regional Council, the National Council of the Churches of Christ in America, the Young Men's and Young Women's Christian Associations, and many other organizations that in one way or another seek to bring about the realization of a single standard of citizenship in American life.

I think I should take the time also to mention the names of some persons who have been an inspiration and a help to me, as I have tried to work cooperatively and constructively at this task of human relationships. Among them are Robert R. Moton, who exhibited patience and fortitude under trying circumstances but never sacrificed the vital principles for which he stood; John R. Mott, world citizen and advocate of Christian democracy for all peoples; William A. Hunton and Jesse E. Moorland, pioneers in the extension of Y.M.C.A. work to colored men and boys, who enlisted me in the service of that organization; William Jay Schieffelin, quiet but nevertheless forceful advocate of human brotherhood; Anson Phelps Stokes, pioneer in many ventures across racial lines that have brought mutual understanding and goodwill between white and Negro people; Edwin R. Embree, interpreter of the art contributions and possibilities of Negroes through his work and writings; Will W. Alexander, Southern pioneer in movements for equal opportunities for white and black people in the South; Mary McLeod Bethune, one of the great women of the world, whether judged by the depths from which she came, or the most modern standards of educational and social leadership; Wendell L. Willkie, whose strength of personality and political honesty made a great impression upon me as we worked intimately together on certain social and political problems; Charles E. Wilson, outstanding executive of the General Electric Company,

who presided sympathetically and impartially over the sessions of
the President's Committee on Civil Rights; Rabbi Stephen S. Wise,
preacher of righteousness and brotherhood; and James Weldon
Johnson, whose poetry in this field of human relationships will live
forever. Who can ever forget his challenge to the South epitomized
in the following verse:

> How would you have us? As we are?
> Or sinking 'neath the load we bear?
> Our eyes fixed forward on a star?
> Or gazing empty at despair?
> Rising or falling?
> Men or things?
> With dragging pace or footsteps fleet?
> Strong, willing sinews in your wings?
> Or dragging chains about your feet?[3]

There are three other persons with whom I have been associated
in connection with questions of civil rights and race relationships
about whom I desire to write at greater length:

First, Franklin D. Roosevelt, Sr. One incident will suffice to
indicate the working of his mind on the problem of Negro-white
relationships. It has reference to an order from the War Department
for the establishment of redistribution centers for returning soldiers
in the late months of World War II. One day a group of about ten
Negro leaders was called to Governors Island for a conference with
General Terry, then in command of the Second Army, for the purpose of sharing with this group the plans of the War Department. I
was a member of the group. Soon after we sat down in the general
conference room, the General imparted to us the information that
the Pershing Hotel for colored people on the South Side of Chicago
had been taken over by the War Department as a redistribution
center for Negroes, and that the Theresa Hotel in New York City
would soon be taken over for a similar use. One after another of the
Negro leaders gathered around the General's table told him that

[3] James Weldon Johnson, *Fifty Years and Other Poems,* Cornhill Company, Boston,
1917, 1921.

they were not interested in cooperating with him in carrying out the order to take over the Theresa Hotel, because they did not agree with the plan and would do everything possible to have the order of the War Department revoked. The General thanked us for our frankness, and the conference ended rather abruptly. Later in the day the group instructed Walter White, the Executive Secretary of the National Association for the Advancement of Colored People, to write to President Roosevelt, protesting against the discriminatory order of the War Department. About a week later President Roosevelt summoned Walter White, Mary McLeod Bethune, and myself to the White House to discuss the protest of our group. At the time of the conference the President had with him his Special Assistant, Jonathan Daniels. (Following a brief discussion of our complaint, the President said that he regarded the order as a stupid one to start with and had conveyed his personal reaction to the Department through Mr. Daniels.) Then the President asked Mr. Daniels to state that a new order had been issued and to read that order for the benefit of the group. The substance of the new order was that the Pershing Hotel on the South Side of Chicago would be returned to its owners, the Theresa Hotel would not be taken over, and colored soldiers would go, with the exception of the deep South, into the regular redistribution centers for United States soldiers.

Second, Franklin D. Roosevelt, Jr. I mention him especially because of the contribution that he made as a member of the President's Committee on Civil Rights in connection with a discussion of discrimination in the armed forces. Before referring directly to young Roosevelt's statement on the subject, I want to say concerning him that for the ten months that he and I worked side by side on the President's Committee I never heard him sound a false note or avoid a ticklish issue. He was always the forthright and unequivocal advocate of a single standard of citizenship for all Americans regardless of race, creed, or color. On the occasion to which I have referred, a member of the Committee had said that he thought the question of segregation in wartime should be left entirely to the Commander-in-Chief. To this Mr. Roosevelt replied in the following words, as quoted from the record:

I think if we rely on the Commander-in-Chief's judgment, we are liable to fall into a pitfall, because ultimately, as Commander-in-Chief, he is going to rely on the opinion of his top military and naval commanders. I saw this first-hand during the war. The argument always was: "Well, let us do it slowly, let us work into it." We tried to do it slowly. In war you are teaching men how to operate too many gadgets to teach them how to overcome their prejudices. The result was that we did not get top Negroes in the right spots and I felt that the whole thing would have been an awful lot better if we had just completely eliminated segregation and separate units. Negroes have not gotten the rights for which they really thought they were fighting. If we had done away with the whole idea of segregation in the units, in the separate ships in the navy, we would have overcome this thing over night.

Third, Harry S. Truman. All sorts of motives have been attributed to President Truman for appointing the Committee on Civil Rights. Many people have believed that it was an act that was politically inspired. I can state the facts because I was present at a meeting in his office when he decided to appoint the Committee. I had just returned from a trip to West Africa in late August of 1946, and had been asked by Walter White, in his capacity as Executive Secretary of the N.A.A.C.P., to join a small group that would call upon the President to bring to his attention a wave of mob violence that had swept over the country, culminating in the lynching of four persons, two men and two women, in Walton County, Georgia. At the time appointed, September the 19th, the group went to see Mr. Truman. There were six of us: Walter White; Leslie Perry, Secretary of the N.A.A.C.P. Branch in the District of Columbia; Dr. Frederick E. Reissig, representative of the Federal Council of Churches of Christ in America; Boris Shishkin, economist of the American Federation of Labor; James B. Carey, Secretary-Treasurer of the C.I.O.; and myself. Mr. White recited what had happened in Georgia, to which the President replied, "It's a terrible thing, but I doubt if the people realize how helpless the Federal Government is in protecting its citizens in their rights." In reply to this Mr. White said, "If that is true, Mr. President, it would seem to me that we should try to find some way of determining how the Federal Government can protect the rights of its citizens." I said to the President, "Mr. President, it is less now a question of what can be done to relieve the situation in which Negroes of this country find themselves, than it is of what must be done to safeguard American prestige among the nations of the world. I was in London at the time of the Walton County lynching and read the account in the London papers, and it did not make good reading for an American abroad." The President replied, "I know it." Then he turned to David K. Niles, his Special Assistant, who was seated behind him, and said, "Dave, there must be some way in which a great country like ours can protect its citizens, and I want you to get in touch with Attorney General Tom Clark immediately and ask him to arrange to make a study of the whole question of civil rights." That was, as I have stated, in September, and in December following the President's Committee on Civil Rights was appointed. As is well known, the Committee consisted of fifteen persons, forming a cross-section of American life as to race, sections of the country, religious groups, and labor and management. It was my privilege to serve on that Committee. I recall the day when, after ten months of work, the finished Report was presented to the President. Mr. Charles E. Wilson, Chairman of the Committee, in a few choice words presented to the President the special volume that had been signed by the members of the Committee. The President took the volume, fingered the leaves for a moment, and then said, "I have stolen a march on you. I have already read the Report, and I want you to know that you have done not only what I consider to be a corking good job, but you have done just what I wanted you to do." I think it is to the everlasting credit of President Truman that in spite of storms of protest that have broken about his head since the Report was released, he has held his ground.

Most of what I have recorded up to this point has dealt with my interest in human relationships. I come now to my interest in religion. The early religious influences that affected my life have already been described. What I say here will bear upon the religious thought and experiences of my maturer years. I have stated that I was reared in the Colored Methodist Church. Two Bishops of that

Church, Lucius H. Holsey and Robert S. Williams, were my spiritual advisers at the time that I decided to study theology. They were self-made men of strong personality and deep religious experience. Their theology was conservative and would be considered today as out of harmony with progressive trends in religious thought. But I feel a deep sense of obligation to them in spite of this fact, for they were sincere, and according to their light rendered highly significant service to the Kingdom of God as they conceived it. These men have long since passed on, but their mantles have fallen upon other Bishops with whom I have maintained contacts and from whom I have received inspiration, namely, Charles H. Phillips of Ohio, Randall A. Carter of Illinois, J. Arthur Hamlett of Missouri, and William Y. Bell of Georgia.

The Drew Theological Seminary of Madison, New Jersey, where I received my theological training, had as its President when I entered in 1902 Dr. Henry Anson Buttz, a distinguished Greek scholar. He made a deep impression upon me, not so much on account of his scholarship, as because of the kindly spirit that he manifested in personal interviews with entering students. He realized that my residence up to the time of my entering Drew had been in the South exclusively, and he knew from long experience the difficulties facing students who had to adjust themselves to a new environment. The kindly manner in which he talked with me about my personal problems gave him a place in my heart which he will always occupy. Other members of the faculty who exerted a great influence upon me included Robert W. Rogers, Assyrian and Babylonian scholar under whom I studied Hebrew for the three years of my stay at the Seminary, and Alfred Faulkner, distinguished church historian.

It might seem that one whose early religious training was received in a Methodist Church and a Methodist school would embrace a theology narrowly sectarian. Such has not been the case with me. I believe firmly in the character and teachings of the Founder of Christianity. But I have always reserved the right to make my own interpretations of the Christian Scriptures, and my own appraisal of the teachers of religion with whom I have come into contact. I think it is important to be loyal to the great principles of religion, regardless of whether they are enunciated by leaders of one's own faith or of some other faith. It happened that two great characters outside of the Christian faith greatly influenced my religious beliefs. They were Julius Rosenwald and Mahatma Gandhi.

I first came into contact with Julius Rosenwald soon after he had visited Tuskegee Institute for the first time, and had made a remarkable philanthropic offer after walking with his friend, Booker T. Washington, along the country roads of Macon County, Alabama. The substance of his offer as expressed to Mr. Washington was this: "Seeing how terribly inadequate these country school houses for Negro children are, I will give a third of the money, if you will get a third from the Board of Education, and a third from the people of the community, white and colored, to erect a decent school building for colored children in each community throughout this County." Mr. Washington accepted the challenge, and succeeded in meeting the conditions of the offer for the County. Mr. Rosenwald then extended the offer to include any county in the South that would meet the same conditions. Before the building campaign closed a few years later, five thousand modern school houses had been erected for Negro school children in the South.

Simultaneously with this campaign, Mr. Rosenwald did another magnanimous thing. Impressed by the efforts of colored people in Chicago to raise money for a Young Men's Christian Association building, he made a personal contribution of $25,000 for the erection of a Branch of the YMCA in the Negro community of Chicago's South Side, and followed this with an offer to contribute $25,000 to any city in the United States that would raise a total of not less than $100,000 for the erection of a Young Men's Christian Association building to serve primarily the needs of colored men and boys. Twenty-seven cities of the country qualified for this offer and in each instance he contributed $25,000. It was in connection with working out the terms of this offer that I met Mr. Rosenwald. The meeting took place in his private office at the Sears Roebuck plant in Chicago. As I sat at his desk and talked with him, I noticed that on the wall directly in front of his desk was a splendid painting of Booker T. Washington. The fact that this man of great wealth, a member of another race, and a communicant of another faith, could find his daily inspiration through looking into the face of a distinguished Negro educator, made such an impression upon me that it led me to reexamine my Christian faith. I said to myself: "Why should I assume that I have more in common with the white Baptist or Methodist preacher in Macon County, Alabama, simply because we both call ourselves Christians, than with this man, a Jew, who has in his spirit, and in his acts, more thoroughly demonstrated the teachings of the Founder of Christianity than those who call themselves Christian leaders?" For decades these Christian ministers had passed by the shacks in which these Negro children of Alabama attended school, and never once had it occurred to them that the inequalities that existed in the facilities for the training of white and Negro children should have been removed; while one look at the situation by Julius Rosenwald, the Jew, was sufficient to move him to action. From that day until now I have determined to be loyal to the expression of the heart of the Founder of Christianity, whether such expression emanates from a Christian, a Jew, a Mohammedan, a Hindu, or one of any other faith. For thirty-five years I was an employed officer of the Young Men's Christian Association, and throughout that period of service worked to carry out the splendid program of that organization. But I can never forget that it was a Jew who dramatized the needs of colored youth for a Christian movement that up to that time had shown no marked enthusiasm for bringing this youth into fellowship with the youth of other races, or making adequate provision for service to them in Branches set apart for them. Therefore, I am not disposed to question the validity of the faith of any man who lives and acts in accordance with the spirit and content of the Golden Rule, simply because he is identified with a faith other than my own.

Now as to the effect of Mahatma Gandhi upon my religious thinking. Thirteen years ago I attended a conference of the World's Committee of Young Men's Christian Associations at Mysore, India. On the way to India I visited Palestine. While I was deeply moved by many of the sights that had association with early church history,

I was disappointed in some things that I heard and saw. For instance, when I visited the Church of the Nativity at Bethlehem, I learned of the bitter rivalries between the various Christian communions for places of priority in the Christmas Pilgrimage to the birthplace of Christ. When I went to the Church of the Holy Sepulcher, my guide noticed that one of the lamps above the Tomb needed adjustment to its frame. He called to a passing attendant to ask that the adjustment be made. With a look of anger the attendant turned abruptly and went away. I asked what the trouble was. My guide replied that the lamp was an Armenian lamp and that the attendant whom he had asked to make the adjustment was a Greek, and that a Greek did not dare touch an Armenian lamp, even above the Holy Sepulcher. When I proceeded on to India and finally had the opportunity of meeting Mahatma Gandhi, I could not help but contrast my experiences in Palestine with the experiences that I had in connection with my meeting with Gandhi.

An Indian friend who was attending the conference at Mysore, and who was also a close friend of Gandhi had wired to Gandhi's home in Central India to see if I could have an interview with him. A wire came back saying that Gandhi had left home, was making a brief stop at Poona for the purpose of arbitrating a labor dispute, and would proceed after a day or two from Poona to Travancore, the southernmost state of India, going by way of Madras. My friend in Mysore then wired to Poona that I would meet Gandhi's train at Renigunta, a small town two and a half hours away from Madras, which was quite convenient for me since I was on my way to that city. On the day appointed I reached Renigunta two or three hours before the time for Gandhi's train to arrive. It was a Monday, and I knew that this was Gandhi's day of silence. I had no hope that I would have the opportunity of conversing with him, so I wrote out the questions that I wanted to ask him, a question to a sheet, with space beneath the question for him to write his answer if the opportunity presented itself. I was uncertain at Renigunta what class ticket I should buy, for there were three classes of accommodations on most trains. I took a chance at buying a second class ticket. I should have known better, for when the train finally arrived I noticed the crowd rush to the third class coach. Then I knew that Gandhi was in that coach.

Fortunately for me I had an a topi, or sun helmet, which proved to be the means of my identification, since the Indians either wear turbans or no head covering at all. As I elbowed my way through the crowd, I noticed a tall man open the side door of the car, look down upon the crowd, and then, recognizing me, beckon to me to get into the coach. As soon as I was safely through the door, he took the papers on which my questions were written and then said to me, "You will be glad to learn that Gandhigi is going to break silence at 4:30 so that he may talk with you personally about America and the problems of your people." This man was Mr. Desai, Gandhi's secretary. The first thing that impressed me as I was ushered through the door of a partition running through the middle of the coach to the other side where Gandhi was sitting, was the rugged simplicity of this third class car on which the greatest man of India, and one of the greatest men of all the world was riding. Although he remained in silence, he recognized my presence and bade me sit down in front of him while he continued to operate his little spinning wheel, and, as the train stopped at station after station, passed out fruit to those who were able to get close enough to reach through the window. The people, in turn, threw in bunches of yarn for his spinning wheel, garlands of flowers, and small contributions for his work among the Untouchables. All the while he spoke not a word, but with the Hindu greeting from time to time acknowledged the plaudits of the people.

Finally, at the hour of 4:30, he arose, shook hands with me warmly, and asked me to sit down beside him. His first words were these: "You will be interested to learn that I have read everything that I could lay my hands on that was ever written by General Armstrong and Booker Washington." Then he proceeded to tell me how closely he watched the development of race relations in America. Finally, we began to talk of world conditions. There were two wars at that time: the Italian conquest of Ethiopia had just been concluded, and the Spanish war was still in progress. As we discussed war in general, he said substantially this: "You people of the West have a war, and then you have a so-called peace conference following the war, which you might just as well have had before the war and possibly have prevented it. Then in the so-called peace conference you sow the seed for the next war, which means an unending cycle of conflict."

One of my written questions was answered in a way and spirit that I have never forgotten. I quote:

Question: Negroes in the United States (12,000,000) are struggling to obtain such fundamental rights as freedom from mob violence, unrestricted use of the ballot, freedom from segregation in all forms and an opportunity to find employment in skilled, as well as unskilled forms of labor. Have you out of your struggles in India a word of advice or encouragement? I ask this fully appreciating how differently situated the two peoples are.

Gandhi's reply: I had to contend against some such thing, though on a smaller scale, in South Africa. The difficulties are by no means yet over. All I can say is that there is no other way than the way of nonviolence—not of the weak and the ignorant but of the strong and the wise.

For an hour and a half we had communion together before the train arrived at Madras where Gandhi was greeted by approximately 20,000 people in the public square. After acknowledging the demonstration, he was driven quietly away to the Temple to be in prayer for the three hours before the departure of his train for Travancore. Both through his word and his actions he had convinced me that he was the greatest spiritual leader of our time. While we were still in conversation I had said to him, "I have often wondered what it is that gives you your power. I know that you have no army, no navy, no wealth, but people all over the world, great and small, lend attentive ears to whatever you have to say." No teacher of my Christian faith ever made the impression upon me that this man made, because he was the living embodiment of what he taught.

I have given this fairly lengthy account of my meeting with Gandhi for the purpose of suggesting how important it is that people of different faiths find common ground on which to stand as they seek the realization of truth.

In this atomic era the only alternative to destruction is cooperation, and cooperation is not something that can be worked out in science laboratories. It is definitely spiritual. Hence the importance of the interfaith religious approach to present day problems of human relationships at home and abroad. I stress interfaith because no one religion or denomination is adequate to express all the longings and desires in the hearts of men of many nations, races, and cultural backgrounds. I do not believe that it is necessary to bring about creedal, doctrinal, or organizational uniformity, in order that people of different faiths may cooperate in the interest of the realization of certain common spiritual objectives. Men always have and doubtless always will approach truth from different angles. Therefore, Lutherans will continue to be Lutherans; Baptists will continue to be Baptists; Catholics will continue to be Catholics; Jews will continue to be loyal to the Jewish faith; but at the same time it is possible for all to be striving to discover some means by which they may speak with one voice and move with united action for satisfying those deep yearnings of the human heart that are common to all nations, races, and tongues.

It is in the interest of bringing about this kind of religious unity that I am devoting much of my time today. Therefore, I hope you will bear with me as I elaborate more fully upon what I believe to be involved in bringing to bear upon the present world situation the impact of the true essence of religious faith. I think I should say first of all that I believe that it is impossible for society to be redeemed from the selfishness, greed, and exploitation so prevalent in the world today, until those who constitute society are made free to participate in the redemptive processes. In no nation in the world does such freedom exist today. The totalitarian states, with all their boasting about social democracy, make voting by the masses a sham and a mockery, because the decisions that count are made by the rulers and handed down to the people, with conformity demanded sometimes at the peril of imprisonment or death. Even in a democracy like the United States of America, freedom of expression at the ballot box and freedom of participation on terms of equality in government are denied to a large segment of the population on account of race. Important decisions involving the social welfare of the people are often influenced by the use of money, or the threat of loss of employment. Colonial powers are still dragging their feet on extension of self-determination to the people of their colonies. The debate before the United Nations General Assembly on whether or not Southwest Africa should continue to be held in trust by the Union of South Africa, clearly indicated a determination on the part of the Union Government to insist upon the trusteeship on its own terms, regardless of the desires of the Africans, themselves, who constitute four-fifths of the population. The present demands of the Italian Government that its African colonies be returned to Italy for the economic advantages that it would derive from these colonies, with little thought being given to the welfare of the people, or to their desires with regard to Italian sovereignty over them, bear out my contention that there is need for emphasizing the right of all people to participate directly or indirectly in the making and execution of the laws by which they are governed. This is something so basically moral that people of all faiths and divisions of faith should unite to bring it to realization.

The task of translating these principles into action is, as I intimated at the beginning, too great to be accomplished by the efforts of man alone. Science in and of itself is powerless to work out solutions for such intricate problems of human relationship. Some time ago I read a news story which stated that a distinguished Columbia University professor had discovered a shift on the part of present day students from science to the humanities. This is not strange in view of the inadequate answers of science to the perplexing problems confronting students today. After all, it is impossible for anyone to contrive a scientific bath in which one may dip and be washed of hatred and suspicion of his fellowmen. It is my belief that we cannot do other than seek the help and guidance of the supernatural as we deal with these problems that are too difficult for the mind of man to solve. This falling back upon the resources of the Infinite is a universal instinct. I am sure that you who have visited most of the countries of the world will bear witness to the truthfulness of this observation. I saw it at the Wailing Wall in Jerusalem. I experienced it in the hour with Gandhi that I have described. I saw it in a Congo mission service. I saw it in Roman and Greek Catholic cathedrals in Europe. I have seen it in Methodist camp meetings. I have seen its spontaneous expression, without the aid of church or cathedral atmosphere. It is as universal as the presence of man. And it is this fact that suggests the possibility of a worldwide interfaith movement for focusing attention upon the welfare of human beings, above considerations of politics and economics. It would be a great thing for a bewildered and pessimistic world if the leaders of the great religions and denominations could sit around a common table—Jews, Mohammedans, Hindus, Buddhists, all divisions of Christians—for the sole purpose of calling attention to the broad principles upon which it is possible to unite in the interest of bringing understanding and peace to mankind. The very fact of the meeting of such a group would be significant and impressive, to say nothing of the impact upon world thinking that could be brought to pass through such united suggestions as such a group would make. With a group of such wide differences of background and custom, any suggested program of action, as I have said before, would of necessity have to be very broad. Perhaps the suggestion that the hungry people of the earth be fed, and that this be done, not in a spirit of charity but of sharing, and not according to selective processes by which friends would be favored and enemies denied, might be the only program upon which there could be immediate united agreement. Perhaps our first reaction to such a proposal would be that it is too naive, too simple to be taken seriously. This may be true, but I would remind you that the same criticism was made of the Gospel of the Kingdom of God as preached by Jesus of Nazareth. And then there may be those who would shudder at the thought of cooperation with those outside the household of their own faith. I would remind such that on more than one occasion Jesus did exactly that and found great satisfaction in the experience. Then there may be those who feel that the difficulties in carrying out such a proposal are insurmountable. To this I would reply that all things are possible with God, and as the alternative to a peaceful world may be the destruction of civilization, it is worth trying. One thing is certain—whether our united actions take this form or some other, we must do something and we must do it without delay. This is no time to beat our denominational war drums in a crusade for church expansion that expresses itself merely in saving souls from heathenism. This is no time to proceed in the spirit of the crusaders of old who waged wars for the recovery of a holy vessel. This is no time to work for the revitalization of our denominational patriotism, simply to be able to compare notes favorably with other denominations. This is no time to put great emphasis on benevolence as such, remembering that the test of faith today is not so much in what the church and synagogue are willing to give, as in what they are willing to give up for the sake of righteousness. As I have said repeatedly, purely humanistic efforts to bring peace to the world have failed, and are destined to further failure. There is only one hope left, namely, an appeal to the hearts of men. This is the responsibility of the united religious forces of the world, and now is the time for these forces to spark the conscience of the human race into a chain of action that may lead men away from suspicion, distrust, and enmity to righteousness and peace.

And now for a final word that I have reserved for this concluding paragraph. I mentioned at the beginning the persons who, in the plastic period of my life, helped to set the patterns of my thought, my ambitions, my aspirations. In this closing word I must acknowledge the debt that I owe to those who have been closest to me in the mature years of my life—my wife and my two daughters. My wife, who passed on not many months ago, was in the truest sense of the word a sharer of my struggles and a contributor to any worthwhile services I may have rendered. My elder daughter, who was educated at Barnard and Wellesley Colleges, passed on at an early age, but not before she had given four years of her life to building up the biology department of a Southern college. My younger daughter, product of New York University and Columbia University Graduate School, now the mother of two precocious youngsters, and pursuing a business career in a field open to few of her race, is a constant source of encouragement and inspiration to me. Without these three there would have been no life story worth recording.

DAVID de SOLA POOL

I am not a self-made man. The self-made man often worships his maker. I realize only too well how little I owe to myself. Yet, in the retrospect of nearly two-thirds of a century, I see, and those who know me must see even more clearly, how far I am from attaining the standards and the ideals of which I speak and which fifty years ago seemed so close to me. The little that I may have achieved is heavily indebted to forces around me—home, family, friends, and a serene background now almost unknown.

I was born into an English Jewish family that lived its life in a largely Jewish milieu. This basic fact made it easy for me to grow up as a Jew. Ancestral influences helped set the compass of my pilgrimage along paths held in honor in the family tradition. Pictures of rabbinic ancestors hung on the walls of the London home where I was born and where I lived through my childhood and youth. One of these was a picture of a great-great-grandfather, Raphael Meldola, a scion of many generations of Italian rabbis, who was chief rabbi of the Sephardim in England. A great-grandfather on the de Sola side, a family which traces its family tree back to the ninth century in Spain, was D. A. de Sola, known in his time as "the learned *hazan*" of the London Sephardic community. Many of the Hebrew prayerbooks and other books of Hebrew learning which he published were in current use in my home. In the generation of my grandfathers, two other members of the family, Abraham de Sola of Montreal and Samuel de Sola of London, served in the Jewish ministry. In the generation of my father, three members of the family, H. Pereira Mendes and Frederick de Sola Mendes of New York, and Meldola de Sola of Montreal, were notable religious leaders. The rabbinic tradition was a part of the home atmosphere.

There was also in the family a tradition of physicians that went back some centuries, and we had among us a number of moderately successful business men. Therefore, had precedent from earlier generations or environment been the determining factor in my choice of a life's work, I might equally well have yielded to the prospect of greater financial rewards by following my paternal grandfather who was a flourishing importer of cattle, or my maternal grandfather who had been a pioneer in the manufacture of sewing machines. But from an early age I had looked forward to becoming a rabbi or a physician, with a preference for the rabbinate.

The environment in which I lived was quiet and simple. Though I grew up in London, the world's greatest metropolis and the heart of the world's greatest empire, life as I recall it was not speeded up to the intensity that we know today, be it in New York, London, or Tel-Aviv. I recall the birth of the automobile, the bicycle with pneumatic tires, and the moving picture. My evenings were illumined by gas lights. We had yet to see the first radio or airplane. I moved through early childhood at the leisurely pace of the horse drawn omnibus, or at what was looked on by my parental generation as the daring, breathtaking speed of the safety bicycle. Even politics was mild and urbane. The most radical kind of decision that I was called upon to make was to be "either a little liberal or else a little conservative." No anti-semitism, no migration, no undue struggle, no harsh change of fortune, no world war, marred the even tenor of the home in which I grew up. Unlike the children of the world of today, heirs of two world wars, I knew of death only as something that naturally befell old people.

School was of the typical late Victorian style, both good and bad for scholastic education. It meant much in companionship and sport, including the ancient sport of scrambling for prizes; but it was almost as remote as medieval Scholasticism from the psychologically child-centered school that we know today. Almost exclusively it stressed factual knowledge. The memorizing of remote names and dates of the English kings and queens including all the wives of Henry VIII, and the correct use of the subjunctive in French and in Latin, stood out among the most important knowledge that had to be acquired. My teachers were often uninspired educational hacks. But I gratefully recall J. L. Paton, then the headmaster of University College School in London, who had vision and personality. He helped me gain a broader outlook.

My synagogue meant much to me from my earliest days. Because our group lived some three miles from the historic Sephardic synagogue in Bevis Marks, we developed a neighborhood *"esnoga"* of our own. This was a small brick building in a back yard in Mildmay Park in North London. It had hard wooden benches and a seating capacity of about 120. The congregation of that little synagogue was bound together by a warm feeling of family intimacy and personal participation in its services. Every one of us counted, even the little boys, for they formed the remarkably effective choir. We boys were actively and happily at home in it. There I learned to know the traditional ritual of Jewish worship, and Hebrew Psalms and the hymns of the millennial prayerbook became familiar on my tongue long before I knew their meaning, for our Hebrew prayerbooks usually had no English translation. The teachings of Moses and other biblical passages became known to me through their repeated readings at the Sabbath services. Not a few of us boys if called upon could readily have conducted some of the Hebrew services. Indeed, some of us were often called on to lead in reading parts of the Sabbath morning service. Though we had a regular reader for the services, we had no rabbi or preacher. I recall but two sermons being delivered in that building in the first two decades of my life. I owe much of the foundations and the pattern of my religious life to that little synagogue where the congregation generated its own religious feeling and expression in happy intimacy and unquestioning loyalty.

My deeply rooted attachment to Judaism owed something also to negative forces from the outside. Thus, one of my neighbors, a middle-aged woman as I remember her, was annoyed at something done by a group of us boys. While upbraiding us, at one moment she turned from the Christian boys, and with an ugly gesture said to me harsh and insulting words about Jews as moneychangers whom Jesus drove out of the Temple. Her contemptuous remark was a turning point in my Jewish development. I was about eight years old at the time. I did not then know, as this woman did not know, the necessary function of those who by changing money in the temple area served the needs of worshipers bringing their offerings. But my whole being rose up spiritually in defense of my people and their religious tradition which I knew she had slandered. In our synagogue our religious leader served through the whole year and conducted all the services virtually without pay. My father in his devotion to the synagogue never received or looked for a penny for carrying out the multifarious duties of honorary secretary of the congregation. The leader of our choir freely gave his constant service as a labor of love. We boys of the congregation attended choir rehearsals and sang regularly in the choir entirely for the love of it. There were no "moneychangers" in our synagogue, no trafficking, no selling of honors, no seeking of business advantage. Inarticulate as I was, deep in my soul I knew that I had nothing for which to apologize. I winced at that woman's words, for that was my first experience of "religious" illwill. But I left her presence a stronger, more consciously Jewish child.

At the other extreme was another neighbor who spoke not in harsh tones of intemperate prejudice but with a gentle and affectionate voice. One day, when I was a very young child, she appealingly asked me if I would not like to be saved as one of the little lambs of Christ. Her desire to share with me the spiritual gifts which her religion brought to her might have stirred a response had I been a homeless, hungry-hearted orphan. But my religious life was rich because of the happy and vivid Jewish character of my home. The word of God attached to its doorposts and the biblical fringes which I wore beneath my outer clothing so infused the word of God into my life, that I felt no call for the symbols of another religious tradition. The permeating Jewish discipline of the Levitical and rabbinical dietary laws, the color, the poetry, and the glamor of the religious ceremonial in my home, and, most pervasive of all, the Sabbath's spiritual uplift and religious joy, left no room in my soul for the message of another faith. To me the Sabbath had nothing of austere Puritanical solemnity; it was a warm and vivid experience of family love in the home, as well as an active happy participation in the chanted prayers, colorful ceremonial, and religious teachings of the synagogue. My religion was felt and lived in the eagerly looked for observances of my daily life; it was not designed to lead me in flight from a sinful word to an apocalyptic new Jerusalem.

The month of December brought me an eagerly anticipated vacation from school; but I had no need of a Christmas tree and its candles, for my heart was aglow with the light from the Hanukkah candles which at that season every evening for eight days I kindled in my home with blessing and song. The family ritual around the table on the Passover eve—with its deliberate appeal to the interest and heart of the children, its striking exotic ceremonial, its playful words of profound instruction, its hymns, psalms, and happy songs, and its bitter herbs, wine, and unleavened bread—left me with no longing for the hot cross buns which were featured in the windows of the bakers, or for the Easter eggs which were the joy of my friends among the Christian lads of my age. My own religious experience was happy, integrated, natural, and fulfilling, and the invitation from the sweet lady on the other side of the garden wall to join the happy Christian flock struck no responsive chord in me.

Moreover, her missionizing invitation fell on uncomprehending ears, for religion as I knew it had an appeal that was different in character from that which I had heard addressed to my Christian neighbors. It is true that I scarcely knew the inside of a church; but what I had gathered from the Salvation Army meetings held outside the drink purveying London public houses was a reiterated emphasis on sin that had little meaning for me. Except on the New Year and the Day of Atonement, my religion did not stress that I was the victim of sin. In my life, "hell" and "damnation" were words used by coarse persons who swore. The Jewish men and women whom I knew were not notably sinners, and I saw no reason for them to be "saved." They did not know what the inside of a "pub" looked like. They were sober, decent folk who loved us children, and who gave us a sweet and happy home life. They were kind folk who when we came to visit them welcomed us in their homes and gardens, and treated us to chocolates, or oranges, or what was then the English child's delight, ginger beer.

Yet, in various ways my consciousness was markedly influenced by the dominantly Protestant Christian civilization in which my childhood was spent. I was deeply stirred by such books as Ingraham's *Prince of the House of David,* or Dean Farrar's *St. Winifreds* and *Eric.* These books brought to me an uplift of soul that was lacking in the sea stories of Captain Marryat and the fighting stories of G. A. Henty which nourished my boyish spirit of adventure. At a boarding school which I attended for one year my principal teacher was a pious young Christian who used to tell me of his desire to become a missionary in Africa, and who later became a minister in the Church of England. Such literary and personal religious influences made a deep though undenominational imprint on my spirit.

When the *Sturm und Drang* days of adolescence came, I moved on from the gallant stories of Henty and Marryat to Byron whose vigorous thrusts were applauded by my questioning soul. The rugged, fighting optimism of Robert Browning struck so responsive a chord that in my twenties I not infrequently lectured on his poetry at Browning societies. Ruskin's righteous indignations and enthusiasms were a revelation to me, and I read whatever I could lay my hands on of his writings. It was a meaningful day for me when I first came to know Emerson's essays; their sententious wisdom sank deep into my spirit. There was also at the time a young writer named H. G. Wells whose *Anticipations, Mankind in the Making, A Modern Utopia,* and other works envisioning new possibilities for human society, stirred my imagination with an optimism for mankind that two world wars have cataclysmically assaulted, but have not been able to overcome.

Alongside of these more spiritual influences my high school adolescence came to recognize such immutable facts as that $(x+y)^2$ always equals $x^2+2xy+y^2$, that in dynamics action and reaction are always equal and opposite, or that the action of sulphuric acid on chalk always produces calcium sulphate, water, and carbon dioxide. The unfailing constancy of such natural phenomena and the ability to reduce them to absolute mathematical formulas, brought me face to face with universal law. As my studies progressed and broadened, ever newly revealed marvels of nature held me in thrall. Underlying them all I felt the presence of an all-pervading unity. The more I delved into the physical phenomena of life, the more these spoke to me of a unifying, universal God. This upward look through nature to nature's God has never failed me. It kept me from yielding to the lure of rationalism, humanism, materialism, and Haeckel's monism, all of which for a time appealed to my adolescent pride in a newly revealed intellectualism.

The influence of individuals, which necessarily plays a large part in the lives of all of us, seems in retrospect to have been relatively limited in my spiritual development. But one name I gratefully single out in blessing, that of Michael Friedlaender, the head of Jews' College in London. He was the exemplar of spiritual learning and learned spirituality. His modesty, gentleness, spiritual humility and saintlike piety, exercised a sweet and chastening influence on all who were privileged to know him. Israel Abrahams, too, meant much to me with his easy mastery of *le mot juste,* his amazing command of facts, his familiarity with so many diverse fields of knowledge, and his unfailing human touch. His stimulating and scintillating mind, and later his personal friendship, remained as an influence throughout the years.

The part played by the visual arts in my spiritual growth has been, I regret to say, a small one, though in my adolescent years of travel I came to know many of the great galleries of Europe and I felt the beauty of the great cathedrals. Perhaps the overriding denominationalism of so much of this art prevented its becoming fully and freely an abiding part of me. On the other hand, from my earliest years I responded to the appeal of music. It spoke to me in universal accents which transcended sectarian theologies. I have always been moved by such melodies as Schubert's *Ave Maria* or the Bach-Gounod *Ave Maria,* or the *Pilgrims' Chorus* in *Tannhaeuser,* or the hymn, *Adeste Fideles,* as unreservedly as if these melodies had no theological associations. To me they have sung in the wordless language of the human soul as thrillingly as do such undenominational melodies as

Schubert's *Staendchen* or Bach's *Melody on the G String*. I owe much, very much, to music for giving me sustained uplift of soul.

This I drew also from the beauty of nature itself. When I was a youngster in my early teens, a climb to the top of Mount Rigi engraved on my soul an unforgettable impression of the glories of the physical setting of human life. There I saw unfolded the magnificent panorama matchlessly portrayed in the One Hundred and Fourth Psalm. I cried out with the Psalmist then, as I have done so often since that day, "How manifold are Thy works, O Lord! Thou hast made them all in wisdom; the earth is filled with Thy handiwork." Ruskin had taught me to look with esthetic wonder on the skies, clouds, and sunsets; but such experiences in the mountains of Switzerland taught me to look also for man's place in God's nature.

Yet, despite the euphoria of my sweetly blessed early years, man did not always make it easy for me to see the divine in life. I began to read the newspapers, and their record of man's inhumanity to man gave me many a rude shock that influenced my thinking and feeling. From endless newspaper headlines there beat in on my youthful consciousness the story of the Dreyfus case in which one Jew became a world symbol of the struggle of justice and truth against injustice, falsehood, and reactionary prejudice. My Jewish soul began to be stirred with an active reaction against the anti-semitism which I had hardly known from personal experience. The Kishinev pogrom of 1903 completed this formative phase of my Jewish development and made me articulately one with my Jewish people everywhere, although the language and the inner life of Eastern European Jewry were still closed books to me. I, who had grown up as a Jew in free and happy England, began to realize my obligations to all Jewry. The words and the work of Theodor Herzl and the other far visioned Zionists of those days commenced then to have a meaning in my life which has deepened with the years. My active Zionist interests began through a paradox. At a meeting of the London Jewish Students' Association my brother and I led a debate on Zionism, he arguing for it, I against it. At the end of the debate I found myself a convinced Zionist!

At that time the studies which I was pursuing at Jews' College began to make the Jewish past an exciting personal reality. They were no longer literary exercises or academic preliminaries to a university or a rabbinic degree. The luminous words of the Hebrew Bible, the penetrating sayings of the rabbis in the Midrash, the constant talmudic search for justice, the spiritually yearning songs of the medieval Hebrew poets, the persuasive living convictions of Judah Ha-Levi's *Al Khazari,* ceased to be printed words. They leaped from the pages and took on meaning in my life. The services and readings in the synagogue became for me more than recurrent obligations conventionally required, as they challenged me with their demand for articulate expression in life outside the synagogue walls.

With the passing of childhood and the waning of the impatient eagerness of adolescence, I was rapidly realizing that this was neither the best of all possible worlds, nor one that the optimism of late nineteenth century Victorian England would soon bring to a glorious climax of Messianic fulfilment. Fifty years ago, both the first Zionist Congress and the first meeting of the Socialist International were held. Then in editorial comment the *London Times* told both the Jews and the poor not to be concerned with the unrealistic visions of these congresses, as both anti-semitism and poverty would soon disappear from the world. But it increasingly seemed to me that Jews and the poor were suffering too organically and too grievously for such bland optimism to be acceptable. I was finding in our manmade world all too many generally accepted limitations on the application of justice and love, though the centuried traditions of the Judaism that I was learning to know demanded them for both Jew and Gentile, for poor and rich alike. I felt that all over the world the Kishinevs where unhappy men lived must be saved from the vileness of further outrages. This could come about not through protest meetings, nor even through Socialism, though the applied social justice of Fabian Socialism appealed very strongly to me, but only through men everywhere learning and living the religious teachings of their Jewish victims. A Jewish mob howling for blood was unthinkable. It seemed to me that the world's primary need was the religion I was studying. More and more the conviction strengthened itself within me that my chosen life work must be to teach that religion. By making it better known to my own Jewish people, I would thereby also help make it known to a world that so sorely needed its healing balm.

One day an uncle, very much a man of the world, speaking to me about my studying for the rabbinate, said, "You don't want to go into all that nonsense; you should study for the Indian Civil Service." But his counsel came too late; I was then set and determined on the religious path I wished to follow. Kipling's call to assume the white man's burden no longer appealed to me.

One of the religious leaders of the London Jewish community also might have swerved me from the call I felt. In conversation with my parents he said in my presence, "What do you want for him? Do you want him to have all the heartbreaks I have known? Let him follow the suggestion that has come to you from Dr. Mendes in New York that he go to the United States." What sank deeply into my consciousness from his words was not his implication of ampler perspectives in the rabbinate in America, but his depreciation of the rabbinate in England. At the time I had little concept of the wider vistas before the rabbi in the United States. Not uncontentedly I saw before me the prospect of becoming the preacher-reader-teacher-pastor of the Anglo-Jewish ministry of the time, and this rabbi's words were deeply discouraging to me. But the sense of call persisted and triumphed over these and other discouragements. For the challenges which life presented to my adolescent questionings, and the special problems and sufferings of my Jewish people, had convinced me that no service which I could give would be more fruitful than that of a religious ministry.

I then learned to know the London ghetto. It had heretofore been to me largely a *terra incognita* because of its insulating distance of a few miles from my home and its difference of language. In my childhood I had known of the existence of the Jewish underprivileged masses in London, for my father had been continuously active in the work of the Jewish Soup Kitchen in the East End, and in the Board of Guardians of the Spanish and Portuguese Synagogue, and my mother was for years secretary of a grocery fund. But the time had now come when I had to outgrow this attitude of comfortable benevolence. The London East End was no longer to me only slums, calling out for settlement workers and philanthropy. It was a place to which I could turn for stimulation of Jewish living and Jewish learning, and for a time I went there regularly for additional instruction in Talmud. It was also a place where I could the more fully realize my newly discovered oneness with all my Jewish people.

My moving out beyond the happy though limiting home walls of the little synagogue which had delighted and satisfied my soul, was completed when after graduating from London University I passed on from my rabbinical training school of Jews' College in London, and went to Berlin for postgraduate work. On my first day in that city I saw a printed announcement of a students' anti-semitic meeting to be held that evening. I said that I would be interested to attend, but I was warned that it might be much safer for one with my non-Nordic looks to keep away.

In the university of Berlin I learned in some classes what it meant to be segregated on special benches to which some pre-Nazi Teutonic students limited their Jewish fellow students. But it was in Berlin that I gained compensating Jewish strength, as I learned in the Hildesheimer Rabbinerseminar more of the rabbinic micrology which gave a consistent rationale to historic Jewish religious tradition. I learned from Professor Ismar Elbogen of the Lehranstalt fuer die Wissenschaft des Judentums how Jewish religious learning could be linked with and expressed in service to the community. Browsing in Berlin's Juedische Lesehalle, I learned how in the teachings of Judaism one could find the foundations for virtually every social and spiritual cause for the blessing of mankind. In Berlin I also learned how the language of the ancient Bible had again come to life, and was once more expressing values which could be uniquely characterized only by the Hebrew tongue. And there in the vibrant Berlin of the first decade of the twentieth century, within my chosen milieu I felt the heartbeat of a Jewishly informed and religiously loyal great Jewish community possessed of Western culture, while the chilling blasts of German anti-semitism without helped me feel the more warmly at home within the haven of that

Jewish community. There my adolescent doubts were resolved, as traditional Judaism become merged within me in an organic harmony with the finer aspects of modern life.

At the close of two years of postgraduate study in Germany I felt myself at length ready to enter the active rabbinate. I then responded to the call which I had not accepted when it had come to me officially two years earlier, to serve as assistant to Dr. H. Pereira Mendes, the spiritual leader of the historic Spanish and Portuguese Congregation Shearith Israel in New York City. In the esthetic devoutness of the services in its synagogue I have found the beauty of holiness. The complete freedom of its pulpit has given me an ever growing opportunity for religious self-expression. In the broad concept of communal service which had been developed by Dr. Mendes, I have sought opportunities for larger fields of usefulness than were ordinarily open to the Jewish ministry in England at the beginning of this century.

From that day in 1907, forty-five years ago, when I first began my rabbinical ministry in Congregation Shearith Israel, the continuation of my religious story would be a recounting of many things attempted and perhaps of some effective service; but it was all along a pattern which was set at the start. For when I entered the religious ministry at the end of my student days, I had found the spiritual bearings from which subsequently I have not markedly swerved.

I have cause to be grateful to the Zionist youth organization, Young Judaea, of which I was president for a number of years, for it was through it that I met Tamar Hirshenson who was to become my wife. She, the understanding daughter of a rabbi distinguished by his profound learning and brave originality of thinking, has given me a perfect fulfilment of my prayers and of the fondest hopes I cherished on our wedding day, and has sensitized and deepened all my spiritual reactions.

Within the expanding field of my ministry I have tried broadly to express the message of religion through work for Jewish and general causes. However, one hurdle has always stood between me and a common run of organizational activity. I have never been able to work effectively through the instrumentality of rigid sectarianism or party politics. A regimented partisan alignment, exclusively under group A or under group B or either for this party leader or for that one, has always alienated me by its strabismic falsifying of perspective values, and its frequent setting of secondary interests above the supreme cause. Sometimes when a great issue has had to be fought through, such as the question of partition of Palestine that was debated at the Zionist Congress at Zurich in 1937, a convention has been for me a soul-stirring experience; but I can find little place on the credit side for religious or social work done through disputatious sectarianism or organization politics.

In the day by day opportunity to give service which has come to me in the pulpit, or at personal religious functions such as weddings or funerals, as well as on the lecture platform and before the radio microphone, I have tried to apply the eternal truths of religion to the problems of the day, in the spirit of the social idealism of the prophets. I am afraid that I have borrowed little from their matchless gift of moral denunciation. There has, therefore, been nothing sensational in my message. Indeed, reporters asking me for advance publicity must often have found me apparently uncooperative. For there is no recognized publicity value in such emphases as that religion is the supreme essential for mankind's enduring happiness, nations should act toward one another and cooperate in a spirit of justice and brotherhood, war must cease, social justice alone can end class war and give assurance of man's abiding well-being, under-privileged peoples must be accorded their rightful place in the unity of mankind, etc., etc. However, my views on religion have found frequent publication, such as in the article on "The Place of God in Modern Life" published in the *Columbia University Quarterly,* or in the annual pastoral messages dealing with the place of religion in life that I have issued to my congregation for the past quarter of a century.

My religious views have perhaps come to their fullest expression in the English translation of the Sephardic Hebrew prayerbooks on which I have worked for twenty years. From the centuried Hebrew page in those prayerbooks rise all the overtones of the passionate soul of the Jewish people in its transcendent joys and its unequalled sorrows, in its sobbing humility and its loftiest aspiration. On the corresponding English page, which usually bears a literal translation, that soul speaks in narrower terms. This is in part due to the semantic limitations imposed by the dominantly non-Jewish associations of the English phraseology. Still greater inadequacy is imposed on the English translation by limitations in the spiritual perceptions and sensitivity of the translator. Yet, the thousands of revisions progressively made in the English translation of the later volumes in the series give some indication that there may have been a continuing spiritual development in the translator.

Both World War I and World War II diverted me in a measure from the usual rounds of congregational and communal activities into pastoral work for uniformed men. In the First World War I helped organize Jewish Welfare Board service for men in camps in New England and in the Southwestern and Western States. In the Second World War as Chairman of the Jewish Welfare Board's Committee on Army and Navy Religious Activities it was my lot to give a great deal of my time to developing Jewish religious service for men in the army, navy, and air force. This was carried out principally through the work of the 311 Jewish chaplains who came forward, not at the call of a draft but each in response to the call of his own conscience.

The First World War left me an articulate and ardent pacifist. I remained a pacifist so long as the world remained relatively sane. But when faced by the maniacal obscenities and horrors of Nazi Germany, I felt myself compelled to sacrifice the sanity of non-violence and pacifist absolutism. If six million Jews and countless myriads of other peaceful men, women, and little children had to give their lives before the sadistic blood lust of the Nazis, it were better that they had not gone as sheep to the slaughter, but that they had gone down fighting to destroy evil incarnate.

The First World War, waged, as we then hoped, to destroy German militarism, brought on the Second World War. Must this in its turn prove to be but the prelude to still another war, a world destroying war of atomic bombs or hydrogen bombs? The Kellogg-Briand Peace Pacts, the League of Nations, and the other instruments so far forged by man to create peace, have failed. These failures and the vileness and the infinite sufferings created by the World Wars have come perilously near to shaking my faith in man; but my faith in God has not been shaken. Religion and only religion still offers the ultimate hope of saving mankind from a self-destruction brought about through unmastered human bestiality.

After the First World War, there came to me an invitation to go to Palestine as a member of the Zionist Commission. This Commission was charged with helping implement the Balfour Declaration that in Palestine would once more be established a national home for the Jewish people. My congregation had generously given me leave of absence during the war to travel continuously far and wide throughout the United States to help bring Judaism to the men in service. But now the war was over, and I could not persuade my congregation to give me another extended leave of absence to work in what seemed then to be far away Palestine. Yet the moment was historic. I felt that I had to make my own decision to follow a compelling call. That decision gave me a precious and an unforgettable experience. I am deeply grateful today that for three years I was associated with the setting of stakes in a Palestine that was pioneering for the rebirth of Israel.

It was the beginning of the year 1919 when Mrs. Pool, our baby, and I set out from New York. After nearly three months of travel in a war ravaged world we came to Palestine. There it was my good fortune to be assigned work that was almost a continuation of one aspect of my ministry, for it fell to my lot to take over the work of the Joint Distribution Committee in Syria and Palestine. From 1919 to the end of 1921, I found myself engaged primarily in the life giving task of directing postwar relief and reconstruction. This meant not only concern with the externals of budgets and accounts, allotments, expenditures, and deficits. It also demanded the reality of care and aid for widows and orphans and helpless old men and women. It called for creating opportunities for work for old and for young. It involved giving a hand to refugee immigrant pioneers (*halutzim*). It meant establishing a loan bank. It expressed itself in helping sustain rabbis and students in the talmudic academies (*yeshivot*). It involved providing for the blind and other physically handicapped. It brought me close indeed to the heart of my Jewish people struggling to reestablish themselves after the sufferings of the war, and it enabled me to express the ministry of neighbor love.

Moreover, the Jewish roots of my spiritual life were deepened immeasurably by contact in Palestine with both ancient Biblical Zionism in action and also with modern collective settlements, with the pious rabbis of the talmudic *yeshivot* as well as with the road-building and marsh-draining *halutzim,* with the Wailing Wall of the past as well as with the old-new throbbing Hebraic culture of the nascent Jewish state. As I worked for Zion of today and of tomorrow, for three years I walked the streets of Jerusalem with the Psalmist, with Isaiah, with Jeremiah, with Ezra, with Rabbi Johanan ben Zakkai. I was one with my spiritual ancestors, one with my Jewish people of today striving to make itself free, and one with my Jewish people of the generations to come. In Zion, the spiritual center of the Jewries of the world, I found within my spiritual being an achieved harmony of both time and space. In the Holy Land I completely found myself as a Jew.

At the end of 1921, this opportunity for postwar service in Palestine came to an end. I then returned to the United States and helped develop the work of the newly organized Jewish Education Association of New York City. But when in 1922 a renewed call came to me from the congregation that I had served for eleven years before going to Palestine, my inner being had no choice but to respond. There had been in me no spiritual break, for the three or four intervening years had given me a deeper understanding of the problems and the aspirations of Jewish life, and of the rabbinate as its workshop of service. With, I hope, a broader vision of human needs and values and with wider worldly experience, I returned to my chosen rabbinic field of work the more assured that in the ministry I could express the deepest yearnings of my soul.

In a public life now covering more than four decades I have tried to serve not alone the one congregation to which I have ministered but also many public causes. In that service I have attained a unity of faith in my Jewish people and its religious tradition, and in mankind's future under God. I have discovered for myself Judaism's deep truth that Israel, the Land of Israel, the divinely revealed Torah, and God are one, and that under God man is one. May such days as may still be given me in life never shake this inner spiritual unity and peace.

BASIL O'CONNOR

The very phrases, "Spiritual Autobiography," and "Spiritual Self-Portrait," are upsetting to me—yes in fact, terrifying. They were all of that when they were first directed to me by our good friend, Dr. Louis Finkelstein, and I do not think I would be honest if I did not say frankly that for the past several months I have been walking around them if not away from them. To compile a "Spiritual Autobiography" covering a period of almost three score years would, I suppose, involve an ability to psychoanalyze oneself which this one, at least, does not possess, and probably result in entanglement in a controversy between the Freudian school and the religions. On that altar, I am certain, no layman should knowingly lay himself!

Well, to allay my fears, I have exercised the right of construing what is meant by the phrase, "Spiritual Autobiography," to mean a statement of those thoughts one has and of those things one believes which presumably made him the individual he is at the moment, without involving the necessity of reaching a conclusion as to whether or not the result is good or bad. I suppose it means, too, a consideration of what has motivated one to do or not to do those things which one has or has not done.

In my own case, those things which make for being extend back to the very beginning and cover a multitude of fields of activities. I suppose it is impossible in any scientific sense to measure the degree to which any particular phase of life has affected one more than another, and yet I suppose in the over-all canvas we are bound to highlight some things that are vivid in our recollections, as indicating in some way the kind of person one is or thinks one is.

Almost fundamental in the creation of the present being, there was inculcated from the beginning and existed during the process, the idea of a sense of fairness as a prerequisite to the proper and happy existence, not only as related to oneself but in reference to one's co-existors. One of a people that had experienced what it considered unfair treatment for many centuries, I came into the world at a time when that group—in this country, at least—was throwing off its shackles and being accepted by others as proper material for assimilation. As is not always the case, that arrival led one's parents and, in due course, oneself to realize fully the delights of the absence of persecution (in the large, at least) and a concomitant desire that those delights be shared by others, regardless of their previous condition of servitude, their race, color, or religion.

Nothing stands out clearer in my mind, as a youth, than the teachings, both at home and at school and all the way through college, of the righteousness of doing the fair thing toward others, and, incidentally, toward oneself. The fair thing meant the *right* thing; it meant not doing to oneself those things that disturb one's conscience and it meant not doing to others those things that disturb the tranquillity of their existence. Over all this, doing the fair thing meant making life pleasant for all—meant, of course, recognizing that all were alike. It meant recognizing the Brotherhood of Man.

Today, I think we think more of the necessity of the Brotherhood of Man. In the days of my youth we thought more of the *goodness* of the Brotherhood of Man. It goes without saying that we, of course, were taught, participated in, and recognized the conception of the Fatherhood of God, but I have a distinct feeling that we felt that, to the extent that that concept called for implementation, it found its best expression in the actual practice of what is meant by the true vision of the Brotherhood of Man.

In a smaller locality, even in a smaller country than we have now, the feeling that one had neighbors, the sense that they were brothers, was unquestionably more intimate than it is at the moment. Size in any activity presents problems—some that can be solved happily for the advancement of civilization, and some that, at least until they are solved, seem to be retarding the spiritual progress of mankind. Size was not at all as important a factor a half-century ago as it is today—socially, economically, or governmentally. The recognition of the spirit of the Brotherhood of Man could frequently be—and usually was—accomplished on the intimate personal basis, whereas today, more and more, that end has to be secured through mechanisms of large units and large organizations—yes, even in the churches.

But some of us, at least, of those who had that early inculcation of the real spirit of the Brotherhood of Man, like to think that we have been able to retain much of it through our whole life. There is not any question that it has affected us fundamentally in whatever activities we have engaged. We have always felt, I think, that the fair thing is the right thing, and that the fair thing to others is the right thing, regardless of its cost to oneself.

When one is deeply imbued with the real spirit of the Brotherhood of Man, I think it carries one much farther than simply doing to others in one's daily contact, those things that are right. I think it makes one seek to be of affirmative assistance to one's fellowmen whenever and wherever help is needed. I think one is apt to find one's self as I have found myself, engaging willingly and happily as a volunteer in great humanitarian organizations, such as The American National Red Cross, The National Foundation for Infantile Paralysis, Tuskegee Institute for colored students, and The National Conference of Christians and Jews—because through such organizations one finds that one can share with others that part of one's self of which one is glad to give as it is needed. In fact, that desire exists in all of us, if we are but given an opportunity to express it.

One of our great problems today, confronted as we are with size, is to see to it that the individual is not deprived of that opportunity to express himself in terms of others, which is a necessary part of his mental, and, in fact, spiritual existence. If there ever comes a time when no one can do anything for others, we will have a world that none of us these days would recognize.

I think the whole concept of fairness involved many other things that impressed some of us during all our lives. I think it carried with it the implication of merit—that merit should be recognized, that merit should be rewarded, and that the opportunity should be given to enable one to establish and to demonstrate one's merit. I have said time and again, and I repeat it now—in my opinion the essence of the democratic way of life is the merit system. Eliminate that and democracy falls. Choose men for office, lift men to high position regardless of merit—and you have a political society that is in no sense described by the word, "Democracy." It may be difficult to define "merit." It is difficult to define many other things that we readily recognize in our existence. But I think we all know well what we mean by "merit." Unless people are given an opportunity to demonstrate that they have merit—yes, in fact, unless they are given an opportunity to use that which they have acquired through merit, you have what we frequently see—not fairness, but unfairness. So long as we have a society in which it is established that those who through the normal processes acquire worth in their various activities shall in general reap rewards, we shall have a happy and contented people. If that condition of affairs does not exist we shall have, as I think we have had in this country in the past half-century, times when people are extremely disgruntled and discouraged, and we shall have—as we now have—a very unhappy world. The possession of power through happenstance or through force, whether it be in the hands of an individual or a nation, can never make for happiness or peace. It is only when those in the place of authority are respected, as being there meritoriously, that localities or the world pursue the even tenor of their way in the spirit of the Brotherhood of Man.

An integral part of the merit system was work.

The unwillingness to labor or work, the desire to enjoy the fruits thereof without the toil therefor—have caused the downfall of nations and empires and the ruination of countless individuals otherwise endowed with ability and intelligence. "Observe," said Sophocles, "without labor nothing prospers."

Some time ago I said that a nation is only as strong as its people are well. Probably it would be much more accurate to say that a nation is only as strong as its people are well *and willing to work!*

To the truth contained in this simple statement, we are too frequently blind.

It may seem strange to us in this day and age to come face to face with the thought that work or labor has not always been an honorable institution. While Lowell was exclaiming, "Blessed are the horny hands of toil," Hawthorne was writing the sour lines, "Labor is the curse of the world, and nobody can meddle with it without becoming proportionately brutified." Sometimes I think that Hawthorne's idea seems to be recurring!

The truth of the matter is, however, that during only a relatively short time in the history of the world has toil and labor been considered a noble pursuit to be followed by man. It has not always been true that, to quote Mrs. Osgood, "Labor, all labor, is noble and holy."

Prior to the time of the advent of Christianity, work was always the province of the slaves—the lot of the conquered—degrading, and humiliating, and a pastime in which the so-called free man or noble man did not indulge.

The concept of labor in medieval times can be no better described than it was by Langenstein when he said:

Heavy laborer's work is the inevitable yoke of punishment which, according to God's righteous verdict, has been laid upon all the sons of Adam. But many of Adam's descendants seek in all sorts of cunning ways to escape from the yoke and to live in idleness without labor, and at the same time to have a superfluity of useful and necessary things; some by robbery and plunder, some by usurious dealings, others by lying, deceit, and all the countless forms of dishonest and fraudulent gain, by which men are forever seeking to get riches and abundance without toil —not so, however, do the reasonable sons of Adam proceed.

I think one would not be exaggerating unduly if one made the observation that some of the descendants of Adam are *still* seeking "in all sorts of cunning way to escape from the yoke" of labor.

With the advent of Christianity and the teachings of its leader, new thoughts and ideas were presented. And among the boons which Christianity has given to mankind, none has had a greater impact on the thinking of men than the idea and conception that work and labor *are* noble. With the upheaval accompanying the teachings of Christ, as J. G. Holland tells us, came for the first time the thought, "We work and that is Godlike."

Industrial work (says Levasseur) in the times of antiquity had always had, in spite of the institutions of certain emperors, a degrading character, because it had its roots in slavery; after the invasion, the grossness of the barbarians and the leveling of the towns did not help to rehabilitate it. It was the church which, in proclaiming that Christ was the son of a carpenter, and the apostles were simple workmen, made known to the world that work is honorable as well as necessary.

There are indications here and there, at various times, that work and labor are unnecessary and ignoble; but I think civilization has progressed sufficiently far since the advent of Christianity to make us all realize full well that work and labor are not only noble, but necessary for our very welfare.

It is to labor (says McCullough) and to labor only, that man owes everything possessed of exchangeable value. Labor is the talisman that has raised him from the condition of the savage; that has changed the desert and the forest into cultivated fields; that has covered the earth with cities, and the ocean with ships; that has given us plenty, comfort, and elegance, instead of want, misery, and barbarism.

Let no one tell you otherwise—labor is the law of happiness. "To labor rightly and earnestly—is to adopt the regimen of manhood and womanhood." Holland goes on to say, "It is to come into sympathy with the great struggle of humanity toward perfection. It is to adopt the fellowship of all the great and good the world has ever known."

Well, we felt that way about work. In what might be referred to as "my day and age" we felt that work was the common and happy condition of man. We felt that it was through work, through occupation, through healthy occupation, that man not only achieved accomplishment but participated in what Holland called "The fellowship of all the great and good the world has ever known." And our parents knew—at least, some of them knew—that no matter what the level of the occupation was, the greater the knowledge one possessed, the better work was done and the happier its performance.

And that, in turn, led to a desire for more knowledge, more knowledge through education—through education at all levels, with the result that real efforts and sacrifices were made to attain that education which gave one a better understanding of the life in which one lived, and in which one had to live, including a greater respect for those who had to live that life with one. And the urge for education which seems to me to have existed in my day was founded on the belief that it was worthwhile intrinsically and that it had value as related to life and the problems of life. Education was not sought because others were seeking it, or because it was "the thing to do." It was sought because it was believed to be good.

Out of all this, as hazy and indefinite as it may seem to you, I think there came upon some of us a definite feeling that we lived not alone in this world; that we were not to lead our lives as *we* saw fit; that we were not to be wolves seeking only to pounce upon the defenseless. I think we realized that life could have meaning only if we knew that we were but one of many and that there could be no success or happiness—no *real* success or happiness for anyone of us, unless in a very general sense it was shared by all. And I think from that point we charted a course and set out on a journey to attempt to bring to others a participation in those good things in life which we might acquire on the way. We may not have succeeded in that to any great extent, but without that purpose—a purpose shared of course by millions of others—what relatively little has been done would never have been accomplished.

While we have been on that journey, and as aware as we have been of man's fundamental *spiritual* requirements, we have made an inventory of the human being's mundane necessities, and have, of course, listed food, shelter, clothing, freedom, and recreation as essential to the enjoyment of a happy life. Yet all of these, even though they were possessed in abundance, would be of little, if any, value unless there were added to the asset side of the balance sheet that all-important item, good health.

During that journey to which I have referred it has been impossible, of course, for each of us to gather and bring to others all of those assets which make for man's happy life. We have from sheer necessity had to limit ourselves to some items that appealed to us, for some reason or other, more particularly. And so it has been that in my own case, of those necessities that mean so much to the normal worldly life of man, health has interested me particularly. Without sound bodies, without minds functioning normally, there can be no enthusiasm for living, for "Life is not to live but to be well" (Martial).

But more important than all that, without health there can be no clear, sound thinking or reasoning—lacking which there can be no worthwhile social, political, or economic progress. Without health, sorrows are deeper and joys lose their zest. As Sir William Temple put it, "Health is the soul that animates all enjoyments of life, which fade and are tasteless, if not dead, without it."

Those interested in the cause of health—as I am in the fight against infantile paralysis—know all this, and they are anxious, therefore, that every possible effort be made to prevent any lowering of the standard of the health of our people.

Frequently we hear interesting stories, and, in fact, much has been written, about the great accomplishments in history of those unfortunately not possessors of good health. All that those tales contain is undoubtedly true, but no one ever tells us (because no one ever can) what greater accomplishments might have been achieved by those same individuals had illness not retarded them.

And here again we must recognize the simple fact that health is the *normal* condition and *ill* health or lack of health the *abnormal* or *unnatural* condition. Some of man's ailments are unquestionably due to factors over which science has not yet been able to gain control. Others, in turn, are due to neglect where neglect is not necessary.

All that can be done in the first of these two classifications is to continue every effort of scientific research and the medical profession to conquer the unknown. The accomplishments of the past in the great wars against disease which have been waged so persistently and so sincerely by men of science, are our justification for believing that each year will reduce that field where now there is no knowledge. That is the kind of fight we are carrying on against infantile paralysis.

Where unnecessary neglect impairs the well-being of the individual, we can only hope that through a continued educational process, he will be brought to the full realization that he and he alone is his own worst enemy. An Arabian proverb says: "He who has health has hope and he who has hope has everything." We must strive to teach the individual—particularly the youth of our country—that improving the physical condition of a people is not merely for the purpose of extending the span of life. Far better is it that while we live, we live well. And let us hope that we may convince them, too, that the acquiring and possessing and enjoying of good health is not a pastime to be postponed and indulged in in old age. Health or ill health is here now—it will be here tomorrow—and the next day. If eternal vigilance is the price of liberty, constant attention is the price of good health.

But there is another and much larger field than the two to which I have referred, where illness and sickness are not due to the unknown or to unnecessary neglect, but to the lack of opportunity for maintaining normal health. And here, just as in the case of the man willing to work, the man who wants to be well, wants to have all his faculties sound and intact, must be given the chance to have and possess good health.

No one is more fully cognizant than am I of the great contributions that have been made to the health of mankind by our great foundations and the medical profession itself. Nor is anyone more keen in his awareness of the work the practicing physician has done and is doing throughout the world for humanity, without thought of fee or compensation. But the task is enormous and is never done.

The discovery of the cause of a disease or the method of preventing its spread does not conclude the subject. Generations succeed generations; people must be kept informed and advised of the knowledge that exists while discoveries go on in attempts to solve the unknown.

More and more we are all coming to the clear realization of the fact, particularly as society becomes more complex, that there are certain activities in our life of such importance and of such magnitude that, if they cannot be properly and fully performed by individuals and private organizations, they present fields in which government may properly participate more than it has heretofore. If in harboring such views we acquire unsavory titles, we are not deterred.

Some of us, at least, who see the real necessity of health for the individual, if he is to have happiness and contentment, and who visualize the enormity of the task of giving him the opportunity to possess it, are not overwhelmed by the fact that the field of health seems to be particularly one in which government, not only may, but should, continually take a part and actively engage. And such participation need not in any sense eliminate, or reduce, or impair the work being done at the present, or to be done in the future by already existing health agencies or the medical profession.

If we must think of kings, we all like to think of a benevolent king; but whether a king be benevolent or not, whether he sincerely have at heart the health of his people, because he is interested in their happiness and success, or whether he be one of those bad kings of history, interested only in using his subjects for the purpose of conquest of others—in either case he must have great concern if a large percentage of his people are ill.

A nation is only as strong as its people are well—and that will always be true, whether the times be warlike, and those people are used for what seem to us to be futile purposes, or whether the times be peaceful, and people are interested in spiritual, political, economic, and social advancement.

As we journeyed still farther along that road to which I referred, we realized all too well that if there is to be fairness and happiness and brotherhood in this life, some of us, at least, must devote ourselves to the elimination of those prejudices that make the survival of the Brotherhood of Man seem somewhat doubtful. The dreadful events of the past few years have taught us that in this one world no nation can be wholly free unless *all* are free and that prejudice and hatred *any*where are a threat to peace *every*where. The infection of animosities that set men in hostile camps in any country seeps across national boundaries, is airborne across oceans, and contaminates the world. As it was once said that the United States could not exist half free and half slave, so the free world of today cannot long survive, if brotherhood is anywhere flouted and denied.

The Jewish, Catholic, and Protestant faiths, whatever their differences, alike teach the Brotherhood of Man under the Fatherhood of God. They stress the religious character of the obligation to practice the Brotherhood of Man. That practice is the logical sequence of their religious profession. The simple fact is that no *man*made sanction will support brotherhood in any and all circumstances or among any and all people. Any sanction that man makes he can unmake. Any obligation that man *im*poses he can *de*pose. If there is an obligation forever binding on all men to treat all other men justly and fraternally, it can only be an obligation that comes from outside man himself. That is the simple fact. The Founding Fathers of the American Republic, whose world was nowhere nearly so upsidedown as ours, saw that very clearly. They said that all men are equal and are endowed with inalienable rights, including life, liberty, and the pursuit of happiness—precisely because they were so created and so endowed by their Creator.

Whether one has had a definite philosophy of life which one has followed unswervingly and continuously, or whether one has subconsciously pursued a line of activity that has imprinted its mark on one's existence, I cannot say. For myself I can say only that, because they *were* created and endowed by their Creator, I have always believed that all men *are* equal and *are* endowed with inalienable rights, including life, liberty, and the pursuit of happiness, and that those activities which have interested me most have been of a nature through which I believe men will be more likely to reach those ends.

WILLARD L. SPERRY

I was born into a Congregational parsonage in Peabody, Massachusetts, in 1882. After a second pastorate in Manchester, New
Hampshire, my father became president of Olivet College, Michigan.
I graduated from Olivet in 1903, and therefore lived at home, not
merely as a child, but during the years of school and college.

Father, as a student at Andover Seminary, in the 1870s, belonged
to the generation which was throwing off the last remnants of the
hereditary Calvinism of New England Congregationalism. He was
an excellent preacher, a beloved pastor, and a wise teacher. His
interests were warmly human, and he took little interest in systematic
theology. He never preached at me or tried to indoctrinate me. His
influence on me was largely that of his unconscious example. When
I finally left home he said, "I suppose, now you are going away, I
ought to say something to you. I think that all I have to say to you
is what the Lord said to the prophet Ezekiel, 'Son of man, stand upon
thy feet!'" I have been grateful over all the years for those few,
reassuring words.

Mother was the family theologian. To the end of her days she took
a keen interest in matters of Biblical criticism. She had something of
Newman's dread of liberalism. She looked with apprehension at the
pronouncements of the higher critics and often spoke with distaste of
the works of a German gentleman whom she insisted on calling
"Karnak." She spoke the word with the same contempt which
Churchill used to put into his references to the "Nazzys."

Such matters were much to the front in table talk in our home. I remember the distress with which mother told father that our new minister in the village church at Olivet, a fledgling graduate of Union Seminary, was rumored not to believe in the Virgin Birth. Father seemed not to share to the full her fears and scruples. Overheard conversations of this sort familiarized me as a boy with the fact that the letter of the faith once delivered to the saints was in process of change. Awareness of this fact saved me, during my own theological studies, from the shock often experienced in seminary years by more innocent students. I knew that damnable errors and heresies were abroad in the land, and never was thrown into any panic by that awareness. Indeed, I am inclined to think that the memory of those earlier years persuaded me that if there is a theological skeleton in the closet, it is no use to lock the door and throw the key down the well; it is much better to open the door and have a look at the brute.

Meanwhile much of my formal religious training was had from my mother. She made me learn by heart many of the Psalms. I can still remember sitting on the floor on the far side of her sewing machine, pumping up and down the shaft which connected the foot pedal with the apparatus overhead, thus easing her work for her, and reciting to her the majestic text of the 104th Psalm. To this day it is hard to dissociate those words from the physical sensations which went with the first pronouncement of them. I still feel that working one's arms up and down, as the Psalm is said, is the orthodox liturgical and ceremonial procedure.

But, if the theology of the ancients did not persist unchallenged in our home, the traditions of Puritan culture were still in force. The tabus against all the supposed vices of the world were strictly observed. In particular, Sunday was scrupulously kept. It had its prohibitions against all games. The only exception allowed was a game of biblical cards, in which, as I now look back on it, we substituted the names of Bible heroes and heroines for the kings and queens and jacks of the devil's playthings. In retrospect those stirring games seem to me to have had little real religious content, and to have been by any modern standard pedagogically most irregular. As for books, those of travel were allowed and long hours were spent over Dr. Kane's Arctic explorations. Hence a much later enthusiasm for books about the Poles and the Everest expeditions. I sometimes wish that I could recover the mood of those boyhood Sundays. Our modern secularized Sunday, which has succeeded its Puritan predecessor, has cost me something of my childhood feeling for the Wholly Other, which ought to be a part of any religious experience. Church bells on a Sunday morning sounded differently in those days than they do today. So, again, I remember the awe almost to the point of holy fear, with which I sat beside my parents in church, while they received the bread and wine of the Lord's Supper. That experience gave me some childish clue as to what Otto means by the Numinous. I still feel that there ought to be in any religion an element of mystery, and am constitutionally averse to what Whitehead has called the vice of over-simplification.

Matters of conscience were all important to both father and mother, although I should say, if there be any distinction between religion and ethics, that the latter field was my mother's special bailiwick. We children—and there were two sisters as well as myself—were brought up with a dread of lies. The lie was the all but unforgivable sin. The tests for truthfulness were rigorous, and we were sometimes sorely vexed to know what the truth about some past fact had been. However, that discipline persuaded me that sincerity is a cardinal religious virtue, whatever the price for its observance or penalty for its abuse. I have at times wished that in my boyhood and youth there might have been a hint of the world of the Cavalier, some concession to life's "cakes and ale," but in spite of its rigors it was a happy, wholesome life, and its accepted usages were a good preparation for exactions met in later years. I was familiar from the first with the fact there are in life such processes as self-examination and self-discipline, and such valid requirements as reverence, truthfulness, and duty. On the whole, I am grateful for this Puritan heritage, although I realize that I am by no means in these later years a conspicuous exemplar of some of its one time *mores*. I mention these facts because in such matters "the boy is father to the man," far more so than we commonly suppose.

As a matter of course and custom I joined the church in my mid-teens. I do not recall any particular insights or emotions connected with that act. It was merely one of the things one did at about that time of life. Indeed the whole conventional apparatus of religion existed as something more or less apart from my own inner self. I have never been able to believe that we are all born not merely innocent, but fully endowed with some innate religion which subsequently becomes soiled by the stain and slow contagion of the world; in short, that a first hand religion of childhood turns into a second hand and conventional religion in maturity. The fact is that we all inherit what is to us at first a second hand religious heritage which the happenings of later life may turn into a first hand experience. There is something to be said for the principles of Anabaptism. Such would seem to be the meaning of those otherwise meaningless words of Jesus, "If ye have not been faithful in that which is another man's, who shall give you that which is your own?"

As an undergraduate at Olivet, because the college was at that time unequivocally denominational, I had to take a course in Christian Evidences. The course was given by a hard, doctrinaire old gentleman whose rigid mind and dull lectures were guaranteed to discourage any possible interest in religion. His nature and character were anything but an evidence of that which he professed. He never touched the mind, let alone the heart, of the healthy young pagans who sat before him.

On the other hand, we had on the faculty a young professor of English, a devout man with real imagination who taught us our English literature; in particular Carlyle, Tennyson, and Browning. In so far as I have ever had in my life anything corresponding to sudden conversion, that experience came when I was reading, as part of the assignment for the day, an early chapter of *Sartor Resartus* in which Teufelsdroeckh looks down at night time from his watch tower upon the seething caldron of the city beneath. Books, which until that time had been something outside me, passed miraculously inside to take up their permanent lodgment there. So, a little later in the course, Browning's *Epistle of Karshish* and his *Death in the Desert* became, not merely a living introduction to the Bible, but more than that, an intimation of Christianity itself.

During my undergraduate days, in so far as I had thought about my own future, I planned to go into medicine and perhaps into surgery in particular. Hence most of my electives in college were in the fields of chemistry and biology. In the latter field I had the friendly guidance of a first rate biologist, and with him did some work on unknown material, dredged in the Japan Sea and sent to our laboratory for study. There were no books to tell us what to look for, only the pickled specimens to look at. Thus necessitated, first hand venture into the unknown gave me some hint of what the scientific method really is and how it works. If I am today merely a lapsed scientist, the mood and method of that laboratory gave me at least some slight understanding of the ways in which modern science sets about its task. That brief insight yielded me a fellow feeling for the scientist and has been of much incidental help to me as a preacher and teacher.

In my senior year in college a boyhood friend with whom I had grown up and gone through college died a sudden and tragic death. He had developed a serious brain trouble and had been told the diagnosis. I have always supposed that he committed suicide, in order to throw off the burden of what promised to be an insupportable life, and to save his family from the burden of such a problem. The shock of that experience shook my whole world off center and out of line. I felt I had to find for myself some answer to the tragedy which had befallen him. It shifted my thinking from natural science to reflective religion of a much more intimate sort than any I had previously known.

I had been active in the college Y.M.C.A., and one of the national officers of that organization suggested that I become a travelling student secretary. Not knowing where to turn or what to do next after graduation, I accepted his proposal, and became circuit rider for the Y.M.C.A. in Kansas, Oklahoma, and parts west. It was not an experience which I enjoyed or on which I look back with any satisfaction. It was, for one thing, too desultory. But beyond that the theological dogmatism of the movement at the time, and more particularly its rather superheated emotionalism were not my affair. Robert E. Speer, who had an almost magical influence on the students of those days, advised me not to try to make "student work" a life work. He said that a man was too apt to find himself in midlife at a dead end in that setting, and told me, if I wished a religious vocation, to enter the regular ministry of the church.

Meanwhile, in the course of my wanderings in the wide open spaces of Kansas a letter came from my father, saying that he had been appointed one of a committee of three college presidents in Michigan to choose the first Rhodes Scholar from that state. He enclosed all the preliminary publicity from Oxford, saying that he thought I might like to glance at it. I not only glanced at it, I decided on the spot to try for the scholarship myself. When father heard this he resigned from the Committee, and I found myself in due time the elected Rhodes Scholar of the inaugural year, 1904.

I only knew, in a vague way, that I wished to study theology at Oxford. I wrote the Rhodes Secretary, saying that I was planning to enter the "Nonconformist" ministry, and asked him to choose some College in my behalf, which was on the whole liberal and low church rather than ultra conservative and high church. He chose Queen's College and no choice could have been happier or more fortunate.

This is, perhaps, the moment to enter on the record one of my inferences as to life from my own experience. None of the really important happenings in life have been of my own planning. The opportunity to go to Oxford came unexpectedly out of the blue. So with other and later events. So far from having planned them for myself they have had the quality of seeming to be done on me rather than planned and executed by me. I can understand the writer of the apocryphal gospel who said that his mother, the Holy Spirit, seized him by the hair of the head and carried him to Jerusalem. Call it grace or foreordination or election or determinism, or what you will, my own experience has been strangely wanting in fulfilled forethought, and has been instead a matter of yielding to sudden and wholly unexpected imperatives served on me by the outside world. My religious experience has never been a matter of mere subjectivity. Objective realities have come and laid their claim on me, and I have had no option but to consent. Hence a certain skepticism as to one's ability to plot one's life in advance on the basis of some five year or ten year plan.

The three years at Oxford, 1904–1907, were indubitably "formative." I was fortunate in entering Queen's College just at the time that Canon Streeter came to it as Dean and Theological Tutor. The tutorial system at its best is by far the most effective medium for education. I knew it at its best. Streeter was not overworked with tutees and gave me unlimited and generous time. At our first meeting he set me the task of writing for our next meeting a paper on Paul's idea of salvation by faith. I knew nothing about it, but got some most useful information from the Sanday and Headlam *Commentary on Romans*. I duly relayed this information to Streeter. He said, "I think this is rather dry bones, don't you? I know that is what Sanday and Headlam say. But what do you think about it? Go back and write a paper of your own." These colloquies went on in that vein for three years. My debt to Canon Streeter remains to this day a major obligation which can never be repaid. The academic relationship matured into a lasting friendship. His scholarly standards were high, and he was one of the best New Testament critics of his day. But he was also a warm hearted and shyly affectionate human being, with a sympathetic interest in all sorts and conditions of religion, and I was never made aware of any national or ecclesiastical gulf between us. We were in close and constant touch with each other, until the day of his tragic death on an airplane flight over the Alps.

The Oxford curriculum, in so far as there was any such fabric, looking to the Final Examination in the Honour School of Theology, coming as a single test at the end of the three years, was concerned wholly with subject matter, and not with professional ways and means. Not only so, but, beginning with the Song of Deborah, it concluded with the Council of Chalcedon. The work was mainly Biblical and historical. My window in Queen's College looked out over a lane to the old church of St. Peter's in the East, Saxon in its crypt, and Norman in its entire superstructure. The sight of that church, as I lifted my eyes from my books, gave me a sense of the continuity and stability of the Christian religion, as it has survived the vicissitudes of many centuries. To this day being a Christian means to me the consciousness of standing in a living succession of unbroken, organic experience, rather than belonging to some hastily and mechanically assembled set of ideas or group of persons. Thus, in a time of radical change in our political, economic, ethical, and theological systems, being a Christian seems to me to be a matter of trying to maintain the continuity of the Christian spirit, whatever its immediate formulation. I want to keep that interlocked life of our religion over the years unbroken and inviolate.

An American friend had advised me just before I went to Oxford to make my personal friends among the English, and not to live a clannish life with fellow Americans. I have always been glad of that shrewd word, which I took at its face value. I might add that his suggestion did much to foster what has become a fixed habit of seeking and finding many of my more intimate personal friends outside the boundaries of my own profession and the walls of my particular sectarian sheepfold. My closest friend over those years was a young Irishman from Dublin, Charles Bennett, who lived on the same stair in Queen's College, and who spent the latter years of his life as a Professor of Philosophy at Yale. I used to visit him in his home during vacation time, with the result that I became engaged to his sister. She was one of the first two or three women to receive a degree from Trinity College, Dublin, and had spent much time studying in France and Germany. Her church affiliations were with Anglo-Catholicism and have remained such. I have never been allowed to proceed on the assumption that Congregationalism is the only divinely ordained polity, and the good humored give and take on these matters has saved me from too facile provincialism. We were married in Ireland a year after I had left Oxford and was launched in my first parish. Canon Streeter came over to officiate at the wedding. Meanwhile I had succeeded in satisfying myself and the examiners that an education in a small midwestern American college did not disqualify me for work in a great and ancient European university. I had entered Oxford with many misgivings at this point.

There followed a year at Yale Divinity School given largely to work in philosophy under Professor Bakewell. I occasionally turn

the yellow leaves of a thesis on Aristotle's criticism of Plato's doctrine of ideas, which earned me a modest M.A. I brought my church
history on down after Chalcedon in the class room of Williston
Walker. He was by all odds the best lecturer whom I have ever heard
in any college or university. I got also a hint of authentic saintliness
from the lectures of Frank Porter. Academically the year was useful,
but I had come back to Yale mainly in order to have some point of
departure into the American ministry.

The manners of my hereditary American Congregationalism
seemed to me, as they still seem, rather sloppy and untidy beside
the ordered dignity of Anglicanism as I had known it in Oxford. My
father had been a Congregational minister. But on my mother's side
of the family there were Episcopal rectors. It seemed to me that I
might be more at home in the Episcopal ministry. I therefore stated
my case and my dilemma to the Reverend James DeWolfe Perry,
who was then rector of a New Haven parish. He entirely agreed that
I belonged in the Episcopal ministry, and advised me to explore ways
and means of entering it with Dean Hodges of the Episcopal Theological School in Cambridge, who was preaching at Yale the next
Sunday. I did so. The Dean put me on the mat as to my position on
the Virgin Birth, the bodily resurrection of Jesus, and the like. I relayed to him my general opinions—rather than convictions—on such
matters as I had formed them under Streeter's tutelage. The Dean
shook his head and advised me not to apply for Episcopal ordination.
I think he felt, not without warrant, that he did not know what he
might be letting the Episcopal Church in for, in the case of an unknown Congregational maverick tainted with modernist heresies
from England. That settled the matter. Over all the intervening years
I have met Episcopalians who have said to me, "You ought to be in
the Church." Culturally I agree, but I have always replied, "That
matter was settled by yourselves, adversely, some thirty or forty years
ago."

During the year at Yale, having been rebuffed by the Episcopalians,
I applied to the New Haven Association of Congregational Ministers
for a license to preach. I had to appear before this group and make a
brief statement of faith. Matters of faith were then, as they still are,

matters also of conscience. I presented a brief statement of my convictions and belief, which cost me much travail of soul to formulate, and I then ended with the historic words, "Here I stand, God help me, I can do no other." That quotation was greeted with a howl of laughter from the assembled company of ecclesiastical thugs. If they had taken a snake whip and struck me across the face, they could not have hurt me more. The pain of that cruel laughter still lingers in my mind and heart as a wound which has never healed. In my own experience it was my taste of the brutality of organized ecclesiasticism. True, at this distance I can see the discrepancy between the Diet of Worms and my appearance before the New Haven Association. But the heartless reaction of that gang of theological ruffians gives a clue as to why some sensitive and conscientious young men do not enter the ministry today.

In distress as to whether I was fit for ordination into any Christian ministry I went to Dr. Newman Smythe who was at the time minister of Centre Church on the New Haven Green. I laid my problem before him. My initial concern for religion had grown out of my brooding over the death of my friend, and then later the untimely death of my father. The mystery of human life and the meaning of eternal life were much to the front in my mind. Such questions as that of the Virgin Birth were incidental, peripheral. Dr. Smythe gave me some of the wisest advice I have ever had. He said, in substance, "Most men enter the ministry with no strong conviction at any point. All articles of the faith are equally real to them and none very real. You have the immediate disadvantage, but the ultimate advantage, of feeling with force the truth of two or three articles of our faith. Your task is to stand fast on the rock of the convictions you already have, and then to extend the area of that conviction, as men building a platform for a lighthouse on a single lonely rock extend the base of that platform for their finished work." Reassured by those words I went on to enter the ministry of the Congregational Church into which I had been born.

In the autumn of 1908, I went to Fall River, Massachusetts, to become associate minister of the First Congregational Church. The minister was William Wisner Adams, then in his late seventies. He was a man of great physical and mental vigor. He rose every morning about five o'clock, took a cold shower bath, ended his dressing by pulling on by their straps a pair of knee length leather boots, and settled down to work at his desk by six. He was an avid and omnivorous reader. He kept abreast of most of the more important theological literature of the day, which at that time was mainly concerned with biblical criticism. Much of it went beyond his own position, and the margins of his books were cluttered with his single devastating comment, "Bah!" However, he knew what was going on. From his watchtower on the walls of his church he looked out over the confused theological scene, and reported back to his parish that, although there were many foes in the field, the faith was still intact.

I learned much from him. He had a precise mind, and on Monday mornings, after I had preached on the previous day, he would seat me in a chair, surrounded at his study desk by a battery of books he had assembled for the occasion, and commenting directly on some misstatement of fact which I had made, would say, "Never let me hear you say that again!" He habitually preached over the heads of his congregation and told me that he would be ashamed not to do so. They, in turn, felt honored at the compliment he paid them, though often they had no idea what he was talking about.

I owe to Dr. Adams a moment of insight into the nature of religion, which was, again, little short of a kind of conversion in maturity. My generation of theological students had been much under the spell of Tolstoi. His uncompromising ethical interpretation of Christianity set before us an absolute ideal which was a challenge to the conventional and easygoing Christian morals of our Western world. We were not yet aware of the theoretical exception which Nietzsche was taking to the validity of the Christian ethic. Indeed, the subsequent discovery that there were serious persons in our world who questioned the validity of that ethic was the one bad theological shock that I have ever experienced. Our concern at the time was whether the Christian ethic was practicable, and if so, how? Preoccupation with this problem ran true to what had been with me a semi-mystical devotion to the person of Christ.

Dr. Adams preached to his people an annual sermon on the latest discoveries in astronomy. This sermon usually ran to undue length. On a given Monday morning after one of these sermons I ventured to ask him what use his sermon was to a congregation absorbed in making and selling cotton cloth. He replied with a certain fine indifference, "My dear boy, it's no use at all, but it greatly enlarges my idea of God." The words came almost as a revelation. In so far as I had ever thought of God, it was only as a hazy Veiled Being in the background of Christ. But from that day to this the idea of God, rather than the ethic of Jesus, has been the center of my religious thinking. Nothing seems more important than "greatly enlarged ideas of God." I have not given up my initial concern for the ethic of the Gospels, but that ethic is now set in the framework of my thought of God, and does not stand or fall as an independent system. Hence, I have never been able to share what was, some years ago, the attempt to isolate and salvage the ethic of Christianity, while letting its theology go.

My most interesting venture in that parish was a Bible class, attended every Sunday noon by a group of men who were the leading mill treasurers, and bankers of the community. Over a succession of years I inducted them into the methods and findings of modern biblical scholarship. We began with the Hebrew prophets, passed on to the historical books of the Old Testament, came on down to St. Paul's Epistles and thus finally to the Gospels—and not merely to the Gospels, but to the apocalyptic interpretation of the Gospels as found in Schweitzer's *Quest of the Historical Jesus*. They followed along with mounting interest, and were loyal to the end. This experience persuaded me that, given time and opportunity to do so, it is not impossible to interest the laity in such matters. But it cannot be done in any single thirty minute sermon.

We often came up against the sharp contrast between the ideal and perhaps unworldly ethic of Jesus and the concrete moral problems of everyday life. A prominent mill treasurer in the class agreed that his people were poor and underpaid. He said he would give me the help of a chartered accountant and turn me loose on the books of his mill. If the two of us would discover any way by which he could pay four per cent interest in the stock, which he regarded as fair return to the investor, at the same time meeting the mounting competition of the Southern mills which were undercutting the whole New England textile industry, and find an available balance still standing to his credit, he would gladly give that to his employees as increased wages. Needless to say, I did not have the wit or courage to accept his offer. But that experience prompted a seminar which I now conduct in our Divinity School on The Ethics of the Professions and of Business. The seminar aims to intimate to preachers-to-be how difficult are the concrete moral problems which men face in doing the work of the modern world, and thus to save them from platitudes and glittering generalities in the pulpit.

Dr. Adams died while I was in the parish, and I duly succeeded him as minister. Then, in 1914, I went to Boston as minister of the Central Congregational Church. This parish was one of the problem churches of the community. It was in the Back Bay, and I was often chided by critical friends for settling down too comfortably in the lap of a supposedly rich congregation. Nothing could have been farther from the fact. The financial problem of the parish was always a serious one. The congregation was made up mainly of professional people: doctors, teachers, librarians, secretaries, nurses, and the like. We took especial pride in a loyal member with a wooden leg who sat on the sidewalk selling pencils hard by the Back Bay Station. The student work in those Back Bay parishes was, and still is, a considerable part of their opportunity and mission. One way and another a good many men from the Massachusetts Institute of Technology turned up at our services or student clubs. I may have tried to make a virtue out of my necessity, but preferred working in a downtown church to life in a suburban parish, where a carpet slipper mentality is apt to assert itself. I had eight good years at Central Church.

Six months after my arrival there the First World War broke out in Europe. I was still living in the afterglow of my Tolstoian period, and once the war was on in Europe, though before we entered it, hazarded some account of Tolstoi's doctrine of non-resistance. The people in the pews did not understand it. However, the chairman of the parish committee said, "I don't agree with you, but we don't want a man in this pulpit who changes his convictions merely because the times have changed." That generous vote of confidence in the liberty of prophesying, meant much to me then, as it still does in retrospect. I do not know that I was ever fully committed to the doctrine of non-resistance; I was rather exploring it. When the time for decision came I found myself unable to part company with youth going off to battle and tried to do what I could for them. But I have never been at ease, through two world wars, at the moral dilemmas in which war involves us, and have always been aware of the tensions of a permanently uneasy conscience over the whole problem of militarism and pacifism. It is, theoretically, easy enough to live in one of these worlds at a time; it is not easy to try to live in both worlds at the same time without suspecting oneself of cowardice or compromise.

While I was in the Boston parish Dr. Albert Parker Fitch resigned the presidency of Andover Theological Seminary, which had moved to Cambridge in 1908. The Trustees of the Seminary came to me and asked me would I be willing to come out to Cambridge on two or three afternoons a week to give instruction in homiletics. The invitation was attractive and I accepted.

Shortly after my acceptance three gentlemen waited on me at my home, explaining that they were the Visitors of Andover Theological Seminary, and had come to take my subscription to the Andover Creed. This historic instrument was—and in history still is—an implacable transcript of the most pitiless Calvinism. I knew there was such a document, but had never studied it. As they read its paragraphs, I was dismayed to discover to what sentiments and purposes I had committed myself. They finally asked me did I believe all this. I said, "If, in reading me that creed, you mean do I think I stand in the historic succession of orthodox New England ministers the answer is, 'Yes.' If you mean, do I believe those particular propositions the answer is, 'No.' As far as I know my own mind I dissent from practically every one of them." They replied that this was precisely what they meant and was entirely satisfactory. On this basis I became a lecturer at Andover. That seminary was now living cheek by jowl with Harvard and in academic affiliation with the institution from which it had fled a century before. This move back from Andover to

Harvard had prompted the wry remark, "Jonah returns to the belly of the whale."

The two schools were in 1922 eventually brought into a "closer affiliation," with a united faculty and a single student body. At the time this closer affiliation was proposed President Lawrence Lowell sent for me and asked me to become Dean of the joint faculty. I told him I thought this was rather a bad joke. The faculty had as its members a number of older men, many of whom were scholars of national and international reputation. I should be not merely the youngest member of the group, but from a scholarly standpoint the most illiterate. I said that I had always thought that had I gone on with theological studies after my years at Oxford and Yale I might have done a little something with scholarship, but that I had been fifteen years in the parish ministry, occupied with unacademic matters, and that, whatever qualifications for scholarship I might once have had, my tools were now rusty and dull and it was too late to sharpen them up. Mr. Lowell asked me if I knew a scholar when I saw one. I replied, "Oh yes, I know a scholar when I see one." He said, "That's all a Dean has to know." On this basis I came to Harvard in 1922 as Dean of the affiliated schools, and there on this same basis I have been for thirty years. Our closer affiliation was dissolved by the Supreme Judicial Court of Massachusetts in 1926, as the result of action brought by the Andover Visitors, but Mr. Lowell simply told me to carry on as Dean of Harvard Divinity School. Ten years later I became, also, Chairman of the Board of Preachers to the University, *i.e.,* minister of the "college chapel."

I had been reluctant to leave the parish ministry, and over the past twenty years have welcomed such opportunities for preaching and pastoral work as the University Church has offered. The American college chapel, in our privately endowed universities having no single denominational tie, is a unique phenomenon, unmatched as far as I know elsewhere in the Western world. It is a House of the Interpreter where preachers and students from many denominations learn that there are in our world sheep of folds other than their own. It is, to this extent, an unofficial but nonetheless effective laboratory in which to work out experiments in church unity.

There is abroad a suggestion that a minister of religion is a cabin'd, cribb'd, confin'd person, shackled by creeds and dogmas, but that a college professor is as free as the winds of heaven. I have not found this so. The issue is not as simple as that; it is the generic problem of the relation of the single individual to an organized society, in short, the problem of all institutionalism. I can only say that thirty years in a university have not made me think worse of churches. A minister in the pulpit who speaks the truth *in love,* as he sees it, is about as free in our America as any man can be who has accepted life in an institution. It is loveless truth telling in American pulpits that gets ministers into trouble, or else the resentment of a people (who are theoretically the minister's first loyalty) at the fact that their minister leaves them sitting at home evening after evening while he is off with some siren at a political or economic night club. In short, I am still a believer in our churches, and have had no sense of relief in exchanging a parish for an academic post. I might add that when I came to Harvard I had a single line from Alexander Meiklejohn, who wrote, "Another damned fool who has left a perfectly good job and gone into an office!"

My decision to come to Harvard was adversely commented on by some of my more ecclesiastical friends. They said that a non-denominational divinity school was a contradiction in terms. Harvard Divinity School is, by its constitution of 1816, a non-denominational, non-sectarian school of theology. For the first fifty years of its history it had been, as far as its faculty was concerned, mainly a matter of Greater Boston Unitarianism. In the 1880s President Eliot courageously implemented the constitution by beginning to invite to the faculty members of other denominations. That policy has been progressively developed for the past seventy years, so that on the faculty in 1950, we have not merely the original Unitarian group, but also Congregational, Methodist, Anglican, Episcopalian, Presbyterian, Quaker, and Jewish members. The same is true of the student body, which regularly includes some twenty to twenty-five different denominations. These men live together in perfect amity. Over all these years we have had mutual respect as between any two antithetical positions—ranging all the way from extreme Fundamentalism at the right to unequivocal humanism at the left. The School is, I suppose, culturally liberal, whatever that word means, but its liberalism is undogmatic. We have not been agitated or divided by controversy, either on the faculty or in the student body. I know of no other similarly constituted school, or no academic faculty where the total "sense of the meeting"—to use the Quaker phrase—has maintained such unity. This is true in the fields of politics and economics, as in the field of systematic theology. My own life in the School has been happy, and there are no sores or scars left by the memory of ungenerous controversy. I like to think that to this extent our School may be contributing, and will continue to contribute, its modest achievements to what is, in the broadest sense of the word, the ecumenical movement. The moral desire for more and better understanding of the commonalties of our religious life, is one of the dominant tempers of our time. It is my belief that the non-denominational school of theology has, today, because of the changing concerns of the time, a new and unlimited opportunity to serve the total religion of our land. Such a school is far from having supplanted the strictly denominational school, but like the college chapel, it is doing a pioneering job.

I have never had any quarrels with the chores of a dean's office. The fact that I have always been able to make my peace with them, I attribute in part to a Puritan heritage from my home and my consent to the ideal of duty as the "stern daughter of the Voice of God." But this hereditary habit has been much fortified by the witness of two distinguished men as to their own work. Canon Sanday of Oxford used to say that "three-quarters of all the honest intellectual work of the world is pure, unrelieved drudgery"; and Charles Eliot has been quoted as adding that nine-tenths of his work as President of Harvard was honest drudgery. This does not mean that such drudgery is meaningless. Indeed, it is my own conviction that such inspiration and first hand insights as most of us get, lie on the far side of much work which at the moment may seem unrewarding drudgery.

Chapter V of Newman's *Apologia Pro Vita Sua,*[1] headed "Position

[1] Cardinal Newman, *Apologia Pro Vita Sua,* E. P. Dutton & Company, New York, 1921.

of my Mind since 1845," the date of his entry into the Church of
Rome, begins with the statement, "From the time that I became a
Catholic, of course I have no further history of my religious opinions
to narrate." We know what he meant and why he said it; nevertheless this has always seemed to me one of the most melancholy bits of
religious autobiography on record. However, when I consult the
history of my own religious opinions since I took my present post, I
find little that is novel.

I am somewhat reassured when I remember that William James
used to say that few men have any fresh ideas after they are twenty-
five years old. The direction of life is fairly well determined by that
time, and most of us spend our more mature years trying to make
good in achieved fact the ideas and ideals of youth.

My own inner history has been in more recent years a thing of
contradictions. I have tried, conscientiously, to extend the circle of
my religious acquaintances in ecumenical and interfaith groups,
serving for instance as chairman of one of the four commissions
which did the preparatory work for the Edinburgh Conference on
Faith and Order, and working with more than one of the pioneer
groups which are trying to create greater comity between Catholic,
Protestant, and Jew. The ecumenical movement, as one saw it in
Europe, taught all Americans how provincial their indigenous Protestantism is, and how small a body like my own Congregationalism
bulks in the totality of Christians. Interests of this sort are a wholesome discipline in a proper humility and charity of mind.

But I have never had any interest in what might be called theological eclecticism—picking out the best in all faiths and assembling
these fragments as a kind of a mosaic faith. Coleridge says somewhere that efforts of this sort are as if a painter trying to portray the
face of Helen of Troy should take the forehead of one woman, the
eyes of another, the nose of a third, and the lips of a fourth. Religions
are grown, not mechanically assembled. Not only so, but each of us
probably makes his best contribution to the total cause of religion by
maturing the insights and leads of his own tradition. As one cannot
in midlife learn to eat rice with chopsticks, so one cannot successfully affect a religious culture that is wholly alien to him. He may use

the intimations of such a culture as a valid criticism of certain over-emphases or defects in his own tradition, and apply such criticism to self-correction, but this should be done within what is still his heritage and his mental second nature.

So, also with one's conception of the church and its mission in the world. The idea of church unity based on some lowest common denominator of all the faiths involved is an uninspiring one, for religion is a maximizing rather than a minimizing affair. Hence, for most men, the futility of shopping around from one denomination to another for a church which precisely fits his measure. Father Tyrrell says that ecclesiastical vagrancy of this sort is much like trying to find the ideal house. The house that we now live in has poor plumbing, so we move out into another house, only to find that the roof leaks. All we do, on most such occasions, is to exchange one type of institutional problem for another. I have been at home in the church of my fathers, and despite my early attempt to go into another church, have been content to stay where I was born and where I have lived. This does not imply any denominational pride or com-placency. But I have always advised divinity students to stay in the churches to which, individually, they belong, unless as a matter of naked conscience the position is intolerable.

In matters of this sort sincerity is, of course, of the major impor-tance. But one must not identify minor irritation at this or that phase of the faith and practice of a church with the imperatives of conscience. The chronic ecclesiastical nay-sayer is not necessarily the historic and authentic conscientious objector. The great religious reformers have never left their churches at a first moment of their holy impatience. They have stayed as long as they could and exhausted the meaning of their tradition before parting from it. That time may come to any man, but it should come later rather than sooner in his history.

Hence it has been a fortunate thing for me, given this concern for the continuity of one's religious life, that the past thirty years of my life have been lived in the oldest of our American universities, where there is a strong feeling for the three uninterrupted centuries of our life on this soil. Not only so, but in a Divinity School which shares the tempers of its University and which, as a matter of theological disciplines, approaches religion mainly by the historical method, at the cost of what may be more contemporary approaches.

Any one who has been in the ministry for forty years has seen ecclesiastical attempts to reanimate moribund churches by means of one or another of the many stresses which have been proposed. The Layman's Movement, the Religious Education Movement, the religious drama, the enriching of worship, and more latterly the psychological reinterpretation of pastoral care. All these are important, some more so than others, but no one of them, if it is a matter of chafing the extremities of the institution, will effectively reanimate it, if its mind is going and its heart failing.

Merely keeping an institution alive, when the idea which originally occasioned it no longer inspires it, is mere ecclesiasticism, and mere ecclesiasticism is once removed from the vital concerns of religion itself. The case for churches will be won or lost on prior and more central grounds, man's faith in God, the continuing validity of the whole Jewish-Christian ethic, the value of the single individual as against the aggression of mass man. These concerns antedate, and will probably outdate, every temporary shot in the arm given to American churches by ingenious practitioners.

I have no fears for the future of the Christian religion. It is too true ever to be permanently outmoded. The forms of our faith and the patterns of our church life may change with changing times. No single doctrinal system or particular polity has any advance assurance of immortality in history. It is one of my pet beliefs that theology ought to be always in process of becoming heretical, while religion is and ought always to be orthodox. I am more concerned for the orthodoxy of religion, *i.e.,* the basic constancy of its experiences, than for theological orthodoxy. Most of my preaching and writing can probably be appraised in those terms, though I have not been on every occasion conscious of that motive.

I have enjoyed preaching and have worked hard at it. But the sermon which was once the end all and be all of my professional life no longer holds that prominent place. I thought at first that I should live to preach; today I live and preach. The sermon is a byproduct of other concerns. It takes much less time in preparation than once it did; it is in any given instance the formulation of convictions that have grown up without immediate reference to the pulpit, but rather to life itself and as a whole. The only technical homiletical discipline to which I have consciously and conscientiously stuck is the endeavor to learn how to handle words. They are so elusive and deceptive. They are such an imperfect medium for self-expression and are so often misinterpreted. But one of my secret and imperfectly realized ideals is that, somehow, I might be able to make words obey, to make them come to heel, as Milton and Wordsworth have done in their sonnets. The problem there is, of course, not that of the words themselves, but of the ideas behind the words. But I still maintain that a preacher in a pulpit ought to be able to handle the English language with decent competence.

As to our religious situation in general. I remain stubbornly liberal. I can see why the proponents of the new theology say that our American Protestantism has been secularized beyond the point of safety. The wise man of Israel said centuries ago, "Thy heart hath gone too far into this world." Hence the constant need to recover man's awareness of the Wholly Other, of which I have spoken. But I cannot understand the cult of irrationality which is much the fashion of the times, or share in the disparagement of the serious work of the modern world, even though the name of God is not always spoken in that connection. Newman once said that nothing is easier than to use the name of God and mean nothing by it. I stand by the prophetic and theocratic interpretation of life and society. I remain unhypnotized by the reckless indictments being meted out to our world, though admitting to the full the tragic occasion for much of the criticism of that world, and apprehension as to its future. Our religious task is to try to persuade serious men and women doing the creative and productive work of our time to follow the lead of their own interests to the point where they can see God, not to divorce from them their tasks and urge upon them an other-worldliness which shall lack all content for them. I know quite well that this is only a religious half-truth, but it is a half-truth which needs today affirmation and interpretation.

JULIAN MORGENSTERN

Never in all my life had I asked myself: Just what am I, and how did I happen to become whatever it is? In fact these questions had never suggested themselves to me. And, to tell the complete truth, the prospect of asking them now, in the period of retirement from much of active life, and of searching, with somewhat painful self-consciousness, for the answers was somewhat repellent to me.

But second thought suggested that there must be some reason for the invitation to contribute to this volume. Obviously some one must have seen, or at least thought that he had seen, in me and in my life and work, something which, correctly or not, warranted my inclusion in this group, with fair expectation that the story of my spiritual unfolding might convey some message worthy of the sympathetic consideration of high-minded and aspiring men and women. And, so I told myself, so long as this possibility existed, and also so long as there was a potential service to be performed, even though the task had little appeal for me, I had no right to refuse.

So here I am, with the story about myself which I have dug up from the dustheap of memory; but, I must add in all honesty, not a little doubtful, confused, and embarrassed. For, as I survey my life, and especially the early and supposedly formative years thereof, it seems to me that I had very little conscious preparation for, and that, rather, I just drifted into, whatever I have done and whatever I have become. I feel myself not a little like Topsy, who was never born, but just grew up.

My parents were immigrants from Western Germany. Each had come to this country while young. My mother had come to relatives. My father had had to make his way unaided from the beginning. I was the second of three children. My sister and I were, I am sure, the only Jewish children ever born in the tiny village of St. Francisville, Illinois, on the bank of the Wabash River. When I was two years old my parents moved to Vincennes, Indiana, just ten miles from my birthplace.

Of course I have only the vaguest recollections of those childhood years. But I do remember that already then Vincennes had a small Jewish congregation, ministered to by a rabbi, and that one of these rabbis, Leon Strauss, who must have served this congregation for approximately two years, lived in my parents' home. I see him still in reverent memory, a tall man, with thin, gray hair, long beard, large spectacles, and a kindly gleam in his eye. He must have taken a fancy to me, for, when I was four years old, he undertook to teach me to read both English and Hebrew. Apparently he succeeded fairly well; for when I was five years old, I was deemed ready to enter public school.

I could read English so fluently that I was immediately placed in the second grade. But it was a not altogether happy situation; for when they put a pen in my hand and told me to write, I had not the slightest idea what the instrument was for or even what writing was. Eventually, however, I did learn to write. And I never forgot how to read Hebrew.

When I was six years old my parents moved to a small town in Western Kansas, where we remained for slightly more than a year. It seems to me, as I look back, that I had relatively little companionship of other children at that time or in the childhood years which followed. I liked playmates and always got along well with them. In fact, I have always found pleasure in friendly companionship and much satisfaction in doing a helpful act whenever I could. But I suppose that I was something of an introvert, especially in my boyhood. I seemed to love books more than people; and I read voraciously.

In Garden City, Kansas, where there was no public library, and where, not at all surprisingly, the family collection of books was exceedingly scanty, I had no wide choice in my reading. In consequence I read over and over again a small Bible History, as it was called, which in some unknown manner had found its way into our family possession. Whether that stimulated in me a love of the Bible and an interest in history, I cannot say; it may have. To some extent I must have inherited my lifelong love of history from my father. I remember that when I was only nine years old he bought for me two volumes, one a history of Greece and the other a history of Rome, both of which I still possess, and which, as a boy, I read repeatedly.

Of course in that little Kansas town there were at that time not enough Jewish families to constitute a congregation. During our thirteen months sojourn there my formal religious education was nil. Both my parents were reverent persons, who attended religious services whenever they could and invariably took their three children with them on those occasions. But in far Western Kansas there were no Jewish religious services anywhere in those days. And in our home, outside of fasting upon the Day of Atonement, eating Matzot during the week of Passover, and kindling the Hanukkah lights at that festival (upon which occasion it was always my privilege to recite the blessings because of my ability to read Hebrew), we observed no religious ceremonies whatever. At the Passover immediately preceding my ordination as rabbi I attended my first Seder service, at the home of a kind and understanding member of the Faculty of the Hebrew Union College, who apparently had compassion upon my Jewish benightedness.

I remember that upon that occasion I thought the Seder a quaint and interesting ceremony, but also that I felt toward it more as a spectator than as a participant. Nor was I alone in this among my classmates at the College, although I was probably extreme among them in this respect. Others of them came also from so-called American Reform Jewish homes, in which at that time Jewish ceremonialism was cultivated but little, and was even looked upon somewhat askance as a survival from a rather remote and now completely outgrown age. I remember, too, that, when we were in the third year of our eight years course of study at the College, my class as a unit suddenly became poignantly aware of its backwardness in Jewish ceremonial matters and so petitioned the Faculty to inaugurate for it a course in Jewish ceremonials. The Faculty, quite startled, I am sure, approved the suggestion heartily. One of the professors undertook to teach us the fundamentals of traditional Jewish religious practice. I fear that I was anything but an apt pupil. At the end of the year, when he asked me what the *Birkat Haminim* (prayer for the extirpation of apostasy) was, I replied, and with complete and self-satisfied assurance and joy in the thought that I had really learned something about Jewish ceremonies, that it was grace after meals.

I have never overcome satisfactorily this initial lack of knowledge and understanding of our ancient and honored ritual and ceremonial institutions. Still today I find myself distinctly ill at ease in an intensely Jewish ceremonial environment, and still to a considerable extent playing the role of spectator rather than of participant. But I feel a certain gratification in having been then one of a group which was instrumental in inaugurating a new course of study in the Hebrew Union College curriculum, a course which is still continued, and, I am sure, much more effectively and for students of background like mine with much more profit than was the case with that initial attempt. Moreover, this experience made me realize that the then curriculum of the College was not entirely adequate for the preparation for the rabbinate of American-born boys who sprang from Reform backgrounds.

But I am running ahead of my story. When I was seven years old my parents moved to Cincinnati, where my mother had close family connections. There my formal Jewish religious instruction began. I entered a Reform Sunday school, as we called it then, attended this for five years, and was confirmed at the traditional age of thirteen. As a part of the confirmation ritual I read from the Torah, a privilege which I valued highly.

Then, at thirteen years, I entered, or, rather, I drifted, into the Hebrew Union College. I had no proper understanding of the rabbinate nor had I ever expressed a desire to become a rabbi. In fact, so far as I can remember, I had never even thought that I might become a rabbi. But for that matter, I had given no thought at all to ever becoming anything, for I was too absorbed in school work, reading, and play. The one thing, however, which I had demonstrated clearly, at least to the satisfaction, or lack of satisfaction, of my parents, was that I was in no way qualified for a business career. And so my father reasoned that it would be timely for me to enter the Hebrew Union College, because students were then admitted at the unripe age of thirteen. Not at all improbably, my ability to read Hebrew fluently played some part in this decision. I was under no compulsion to remain, should I ever wish to leave, or should I develop a desire to follow some other profession. And so I became a student of the Hebrew Union College, and there I continued for the normal eight years, until my graduation and ordination. But during all those years I had no consciousness whatever of a divine call. I fear that I was still drifting and that I remained there chiefly because it was the easiest and simplest thing to do. On the other hand, never once did it occur to me that I might not be qualified for the rabbinate, or that I might prefer some other profession or occupation.

I cannot say that I enjoyed my studies at the Hebrew Union College, or that I was a particularly apt pupil. I cannot say even that I found these studies interesting. The then faculty of the College were all estimable, kindly gentlemen, but, with the exception of Dr. Isaac M. Wise, its founder and first president, and the saintly, beloved Dr. Moses Mielziner, not one impressed me as a stimulating personality or even as a good teacher. My contacts with Dr. Wise, then a man approaching eighty, were too remote to permit me to come under his intimate, personal influence; and my foundation of Jewish knowledge was too inadequate to benefit from advanced work in Talmud under Dr. Mielziner and to acquire for myself any of the stimulation and inspiration which these two noble souls undoubtedly imparted to many others. I became a rabbi at the age of twenty-one with, I am quite sure, the most minimal and abysmal Jewish knowledge of any rabbi ever ordained through all Judaism's history. Whether that was a distinction or not, I leave it to my readers to determine. I was happy when the end came to this period of study, or rather of attendance at classes, an attendance which, I must confess, was not a little irregular; for in those days I was a past master at cutting classes and understood all, and even invented some, of the tricks of studenthood. This knowledge has stood me in good stead not infrequently in subsequent years. I had begun even then to sense the woeful inadequacy of the preparation which the College was giving me for my subsequent career and to become impatient and even somewhat resentful of this condition.

Yet I may not say that those were unhappy years. Quite the contrary. My relations with my classmates and all my fellow students were pleasant and satisfying in every way. I was one, though by no means the only one, of the participants in the endless succession of pranks which we played upon each other and upon our teachers, especially the latter. I always had a merry disposition and an appreciation of humor. I remember that in my junior year at high school, the period of which ran concurrently with my first three years at the College, when, for some strange reason, I was appointed to the board of editors of the school paper, I asked to be put in charge of the department of wit and humor. I confess humbly that under my direction the department manifested little humor and even less wit. But it was an enticing aspiration.

I must have possessed also some capacity of leadership among fellow students. It evolved slowly, for I was always the youngest in my class, not only at the Hebrew Union College but also in high school and university. In my junior year at the University of Cincinnati I was elected treasurer of my class and in my senior year its president; and during both years I was likewise president of the Students' Athletic Association of the University. I even played guard in one football game, against the University of Kentucky, on Thanksgiving Day in my year of graduate study, and emerged therefrom with a badly sprained knee. I might add that we lost the game. In the University, too, my relations with all my fellow students were of the happiest, and, even though I was a Jew, and therefore not a member of any fraternity, I enjoyed intimate friendship with many members of both fraternities and sororities. My years at the University of Cincinnati, four of undergraduate and one of graduate study, the latter coincident with my senior year at the Hebrew Union College, were happy in every way.

And there, at the University of Cincinnati, I came under the influence of two professors, both of whom were exceedingly stimulating, and one truly inspiring. One, Edgar Miles Brown, gave direction to my love for English literature and also the first intimations of what true, creative scholarship meant. The other, P. V. N. Myers, the saintly and scholarly historian, revealed to me, as he did to many others, the full meaning of an ethical interpretation of history as a guide for individual, national, international, and interdenominational relations and aspirations. The spirit, teaching, and example of both men have abided with me through all my years.

At last I was graduated from both University and College, from neither institution with the slightest distinction as a student. I was now an ordained rabbi, but one with no life-program whatever. But that fact did not disturb me in the least. Indeed nothing seems to have then disturbed me much. It had been planned in the family councils that after graduation I should go to Germany, ostensibly to study. But to study what, and for how long a period, and for what particular purpose, no one, and least of all I, had the slightest idea. My father, the only member of his family in America, was eager that his sisters and their children, back in Germany, should get to know at least one member of his family. I was plainly the one most available for this role. So, shortly after ordination off to Germany I went, to meet my father's family, and incidentally to study something.

In Germany I quickly established loving relations with all my many kinsmen of three generations. I spent those first summer months perfecting my knowledge of German. And to my great good fortune and lasting blessing early in September, 1902, I enjoyed a three day visit in Heidelberg with Judah Leon Magnes. I had known him fairly well as a student at the Hebrew Union College. There he had been among his fellow students an outstanding and greatly beloved leader in everything fine and good. He had graduated two years before me. He was now completing his studies for his Doctorate of Philosophy. Learning that I was in Germany, he invited me to visit him. He met me at the railroad station, took me to his room, and immediately asked what I planned to study. I answered frankly that I had not the slightest idea. I knew only that I would not study philosophy. A peculiarly inefficient and to me exceedingly repellent professor of philosophy at the University of Cincinnati had created in me an aversion to philosophy, which has persisted to this day. Magnes suggested that I study Semitic languages; and why not? For me Semitic languages had at that time quite as much appeal as any other scholarly discipline. So Magnes loaned me his Arabic grammar, sat down with me at once and gave me my first lesson. Thus it is that I owe it to Magnes that I became a student of Semitics, and perhaps a student at all.

That experience did even more for me. For the next two months, I worked conscientiously at the Arabic and with such gratifying results that when regular classes at the University began I found myself well prepared. And, of even greater significance, through this discipline I had learned the technique of independent study and the virtues of system and thoroughness. Indirectly this, too, I owe to Magnes. For all this I cherish his memory gratefully.

My two years as a student in Germany, the first in Berlin and the second in Heidelberg, were fruitful in every way. Even in this strange environment I was able to establish pleasant and cooperative relations with fellow students, both Jewish and non-Jewish. I had, undoubtedly because of earlier training in school and upon the playground, no Jewishly self-conscious inhibitions, and all my fellow students accepted me readily for what I was and felt myself to be, an American student of positively Jewish religious convictions and affiliations. In Heidelberg I even enjoyed the unusual and gratifying experience of playing a major role in the public presentation of a German drama by students of the University, all of whom except myself were German and non-Jewish.

In my professors at both universities and in my personal relations with them I was exceedingly fortunate. To two in particular at Berlin, Delitzsch and Meissner, I came very close, so close, in fact, that, at the end of my second semester with him, Delitzsch invited me to accompany him to London during the summer to copy Assyrian inscriptions in the British Museum. Providentially, as I see it now, I could not avail myself of this flattering invitation. For several reasons—chiefly perhaps that I had become engaged to be married shortly before my ordination as rabbi and that my betrothed had borne with me with exceeding patience and generosity, and, secondarily, that I had no right to tax my beloved parents' none too extensive resources unduly—it had become clear to me that I ought to and could remain in Germany only one more year; therefore, if I was to achieve the Doctorate of Philosophy in Semitics in the brief span of two years, I would have to concentrate intensively, and also begin systematic work upon a dissertation during that very summer. So, reluctantly, I declined the invitation. Had I accepted, I would probably be today some conventional worker in the vast and enchanting field of Assyriology. Certainly my life would have been altogether different from what it has been. Plainly, I was still drifting, though not quite so haphazardly as previously.

That year in Berlin was immensely beneficial in many ways. I was fascinated by my field of study. I learned quickly and easily to concentrate, to study patiently and determinedly, and to find joy therein. But I still could work effectively only in fields in which I had a positive and active interest and only under teachers who were stimulating and evinced a personal interest and friendship. Immediately after arrival in Berlin I enrolled at the Hochschule fuer die Wissenschaft des Judentums, the foremost Liberal rabbinical seminary in all Europe at that time. I registered for two courses, hoping that I might acquire there, under the instruction of reputedly eminent scholars, something of what, I now realized clearly, I had missed in my rabbinical preparation at the Hebrew Union College. I attended two lectures by each professor. I found both dull and unrewarding. Despite eminence as scholars, they were, at least so it seemed to me, ineffective teachers. And when I called upon one at his home and presented a letter of introduction, he received me coldly, made a few conventional remarks, and then intimated very plainly that I was staying too long. That terminated my connection with the Hochschule.

During those Berlin days I experienced my first, inner, spiritual struggle; at least I think it was the first. No doubt largely as the result of Semitic studies, particularly in the field of Assyriology, it began to dawn upon me with steadily increasing insistence that not all the statements and narratives of the Bible, not even those of the Torah, the Pentateuch, could be literally true and objectively historic. Particularly was this the case with the traditions and legends about the patriarchs. Actually this was not entirely new to me. I had heard vague mutterings about this in my undergraduate days, but had given to it no more thought than to other aspects of my studies. Now it struck me with insistent force. It left me bewildered, but not too greatly distressed. Daily for some weeks I walked to and from classes at the university with the question constantly pressing me: What is the truth, and what does this mean for the history of Judaism and the Jewish people and what for Jewish doctrine and tradition? I even wondered occasionally whether I could function honestly as rabbi, with these steadily growing doubts and intimations in mind. Gradually, however, confusion was dispelled and doubts vanished. I began to perceive the truth, or what I was then and have ever since been convinced is the truth, clearly and affirmatively. Once again my mind became serene and my faith secure. Principles of study, interpretation, and application to religious belief and practice were integrated within me and have guided me ever since. Above all else, I learned then the important lesson, that science and knowledge in the abstract have little meaning and less value until they are linked closely with life and become guides and impulses to progress in the realm of the human mind and spirit and forces making for richer and happier living.

My year in Heidelberg, that then beautiful and serene city, was the delightful climax of my student days. There my relations with all my teachers, and particularly with Bezold, and with Becker, who was later Minister of Education for Prussia, under whom I did most of my work, were unusually intimate and stimulating. I was like a close, personal friend in the households of both; and I reacted to this influence readily and expansively. My friendship with both men continued until their deaths. To each of them I owe very much. During this year in Heidelberg my ideas and convictions at last began to crystallize. A system of Jewish belief and faith, in positive accord with the results of my studies, and a program of Jewish life and service were now taking definite form. With increasing eagerness, as the days passed, I looked forward to return home and to an active and useful ministry in the rabbinate. At last my studies were completed; my preparation for what I hoped and prayed might be a worthy and useful service to my God, my people, and my fellowmen, was finished. I returned home joyously and to a loving and happy family reunion.

Then followed three years of ministry to the Reform Jewish congregation in Lafayette, Indiana. They, too, were happy years in every way. They witnessed my marriage and the birth of my beloved daughter, my only child. They were years, too, of devoted service to my congregation. I gave to it everything I had, and held nothing back. And its members, in turn, without exception, were responsive and appreciative. They returned friendship for friendship, and affection for affection. I found boundless joy and exhilaration in my ministry to them. Not once did I ask myself whether I had done wisely in becoming a rabbi. I felt now that it was my calling, in the most literal sense, that God had indeed summoned me to His service and had guided me in my preparation for it, that He had steered me somehow in all my drifting, and brought me into the right channel. And I prayed, again and again, that I might prove a worthy servant unto Him and might bring guidance and blessing to all those to whom I was privileged to minister. And before every sermon I would utter a silent but very fervent prayer that the message which I was about to speak might be the true word of God, and might lodge firmly in the minds and hearts of my people.

I enjoyed the teaching and pastoral aspects of my ministry thoroughly. To get close to my people, to enter intimately into their lives, to win their trust and affection, and to admonish them in the true way of God, were my constant ambition and satisfaction. In this I think that I succeeded to some extent, though of course far less than I aspired to. In this service I felt a true sense of consecration. The actual preaching, too, I enjoyed in considerable measure. But the preparation of the sermon, and especially the determination of the theme thereof, were a constant bugbear to me. For the first year and a half I laboriously wrote out and memorized every word which I uttered publicly. But always I had the disquieting feeling that this was a sad waste, that the returns from the preaching did not compensate for the loss of energy and time. Had I only realized then that true preaching was teaching rather than oratory, and that its content and spirit counted for far more than its manner, I am sure that I would have been much happier in this aspect of my service.

In one other phase thereof I experienced great satisfaction, in my relations with the Christian clergy of the city and with the community at large. With one Catholic priest I became fairly intimate through contacts in communal service. And my Protestant colleagues I came to know and gradually to understand well, through membership in the local Ministers' Association. In those days the term, "Fundamentalism," had not yet become current. But I realize now how strong was its spirit in that community and especially in that Association. I was the first non-Protestant admitted to membership. To me it seemed perfectly natural that I should belong to any organization of the local clergy. I could not comprehend at first why no Catholic priest was a member. But I can see now that my admission was a radical, in some respects even a revolutionary, step, and that not a few of my fellow members must have regarded it with misgiving and trepidation.

And I quickly gave substance to their fears. The Association met every Monday morning in the parlors of the First Presbyterian Church. I was welcomed cordially at the first meeting which I attended, and the welcome found a warm response in my heart. I had then been a full year in Lafayette, and some of my colleagues I had already come to know personally. At this meeting the program committee reported the program for the year. Its chairman, as I learned later, was a thorough and sincere Fundamentalist. He stated, as a part of his report, that the Committee was eager to have a paper on "The Virgin Birth," presented from a purely scientific standpoint. There is a certain kind of person who seems to delight to rush in where angels fear to tread. The younger he is, the more readily and rapidly he rushes. I was then only twenty-four. So I leaned forward and whispered to the chairman that I was greatly interested in that theme, and had even investigated it somewhat and would gladly prepare the paper, if desired. He, in turn, arose and announced, without a moment's consideration of my offer, that the rabbi had accepted the assignment. Luckily the historic day was still some months off. During those months I came to know my colleagues and their respective temperaments, and likewise their tempers, better. This knowledge came as a disturbing revelation to me, particularly when I realized that it represented a fair cross-section of Protestant clerical thought of that day.

I prepared the paper with utmost caution and reserve. I was careful to express no opinions of my own or of any Jewish scholar whatsoever. I limited myself strictly to the presentation of views of eminent and responsible Protestant scholars. And I carefully informed my colleagues of this procedure before beginning to read the paper. But my caution and conservatism were of no avail. I could hear a loud and ominous silence as I read; and then the storm broke. Interestingly enough, I was not its chief victim. As one of the members said in his discussion, he could not blame the rabbi. I had said just what should have been expected of a rabbi. He blamed the program committee and most of all its chairman, for assigning this theme to the rabbi. And the poor, innocent, befuddled chairman, who had sat aghast during the reading, could defend himself and his colleagues upon the committee only by pleading that in framing the subject they had contemplated and anticipated a thoroughly scientific presentation of how a woman could bear a child and still remain a virgin. Whether my Protestant colleagues learned aught from my paper I do not know; but I learned much, something from the paper itself, but far more from the discussion.

Yet I can hardly call this an inauspicious beginning of my membership in the Ministers' Association of Lafayette. My colleagues seemed to respect the integrity and the spirit of moderation and reverence for the religious opinions of others with which I had prepared and presented the paper. Our understanding of each other and our mutual regard grew steadily and rapidly, to such an extent, in fact, that before another year had passed I was, despite my youth and my divergent religious views and affiliations, made chairman of a committee appointed to investigate the conduct of a certain Protestant colleague who was suspected of conduct unworthy of a minister.

And when, two years later, I left Lafayette to accept a call to the faculty of my alma mater, many were the expressions of regret, friendship, and brotherhood from fellow members in the Association. I myself had profited in many ways from this fellowship. I had grown especially in understanding of and respect for divergent religious doctrines and rituals. My spiritual preparation was still in process.

Up to this moment the thought of becoming a teacher by profession, and especially a member of the faculty of the Hebrew Union College, had never entered my mind. I was happy and content in my rabbinic ministry. My utmost aspiration in the field of scholarship at that time was perhaps to write something which might in a small way justify the hope and faith which my teachers in Germany had reposed in me. I think that it must have been the burden of finding sermon themes which finally made me impatient and restless. And so when, after three years of a very rewarding ministry in Lafayette, I heard that there was a vacancy upon the faculty of the College, I wrote to Dr. Kaufmann Kohler, then its distinguished president, and made formal application for the post.

I entered upon this new service with enthusiasm and with the firm resolve that, so far as lay within my power, my students should get in their preparation for the rabbinate all that which I had missed. Actually I should have been filled with misgiving and trepidation, for, as I realize now, my preparation for teaching at the College, even with two years abroad and such research as I had been able to pursue in the midst of rabbinic duties, was far from adequate. Fortunately I had learned how to work. Now began a period of intensive study of the very fundamentals of the Hebrew language, of the Bible, and of early Jewish history, the three fields in which my interest centered, and for which such training as I had had fitted me best. Six full years elapsed before I ventured to publish anything of scientific import, and that only hesitantly and with the warm encouragement of a colleague upon the faculty. These six years of earnest study of the essentials of Judaism were also years of spiritual unfolding.

Once again, in this new field of service, my relations with all my associates, faculty and students of the College, and eventually its Board of Governors, were most gratifying. Of the more than four hundred students whom I have taught during my forty-two years at the College exactly three hundred and sixty have become rabbis. Of these I had the great joy of ordaining two hundred and seventy-eight. Many I installed in their pulpits. Thirty I united in wedlock. To all my students, and especially in these latter years, I have felt myself to be more than a mere teacher, even more than a friend. I have felt as a father to them and regarded them in an intimate, spiritual sense as my sons; and I know that many, yes, I venture to think, most, of them have cherished corresponding sentiments toward me. A deep and persistent affection has bound us to each other and has enabled me to enter deeply, I believe, into the lives, thoughts, and aspirations of many of them. This has been the greatest privilege of my teaching and of my administration.

I think that the students of the College felt that I understood them, and so they were drawn to me and I to them. I was the first alumnus to become a regular and permanent member of the faculty. When I came to the College in that capacity my own student days there were only five years behind me. I knew the soul of a student of the College, and especially of one American born and educated, and I sought earnestly to minister to it. Still today, as through all these years, it is my regular and very pleasant duty to umpire the annual baseball game between the upper and the lower classes; and never once has a decision of mine as umpire been challenged. My students have always had faith in me and I in them.

And I think, too, that I have been able to do for the students of the College at least a part of what I had contemplated when I applied for appointment to the faculty. Some of the gravest lacks in their preparation for the rabbinate, which I myself had missed, I have been able to fill. Constantly I have sought to make the life of the students of the College easier, happier, and richer. I hope and pray that I may have succeeded in some measure. If so, I will have achieved one of the main purposes of my life.

I must have been at the College for ten years or more before the thought suggested itself that I might aspire to an even larger and higher service. The then president of the College, Dr. Kaufmann Kohler, an authoritative scholar, particularly in the field of Jewish theology, was growing old. His retirement, after a long and honorable administration, must come at a not too distant day. In the initial years of his presidency he had reorganized both faculty and curriculum in useful manner. But my own experience upon the faculty, as teacher, as its secretary, and also for eight years as secretary of the Central Conference of American Rabbis, had demonstrated to me that there was much more to be done in the way of reconstruction and expansion. And so the ambition was born within me to become the successor of Dr. Kohler, an ambition which, I can say sincerely, was motivated primarily by an urge to render to my alma mater the maximum service within my power and to develop the latent potentialities which I saw so clearly. In this ambition I was encouraged by one member of the faculty to whom I was particularly close.

During the twenty-six years of my presidency I adhered steadfastly to this program. Not all my ambitions for the College have been realized, nor have all its potentialities been developed. But I feel that something has been achieved, and on the whole I am content. The service of the College has been expanded in range and, I trust, also in quality and authority. Above all else, at least in my eyes, it has become a recognized center of creative Jewish scholarship, a service of paramount importance today, when almost all the great centers of Jewish scholarship of the Old World have been ruthlessly destroyed. In this aspect of its expanded service I think that I experience my greatest satisfaction.

Early in my teaching years the monumental work of the eminent anthropologist, Sir James G. Frazer, *The Golden Bough,* came into my hands and fascinated me. This fascination was heightened immeasurably by an evening spent with this modest, genial scholar in his home in London, in which he accorded to me the vastly stimulating honor of listening with sympathetic and helpful criticism to a paper which I was scheduled to present before the International Congress of Orientalists. Almost from the moment of my coming to the College, or perhaps even from my student days in Germany, my studies had turned in the direction of the history of the religions of the Semitic peoples and of their institutions, and, of course, of Judaism in particular. That has been the field of my scholarly passion. And even such studies in biblical exegesis as I have been able to carry on, have been largely in the nature of indispensable preliminaries to a history of Judaism and the Jewish people in the initial period of their unfolding. Many preliminary studies are still to be completed and others perhaps at least to be inaugurated. But eventually I hope to produce a history of Judaism and its institutions during the entire biblical period.

However, even this is not my ultimate goal, but only a stage theretoward. For my studies, especially those of recent years, have disclosed to me something of the nature and importance of what I have come to call peripheral Judaism, the Judaism not only of certain, numerically small Jewish sects, whose centers were in the immediate vicinity of Jerusalem, but also and especially of those many Jewish communities, some of considerable size, which lay beyond the range of direct influence of Jerusalem and the Temple, and the expression and practice of whose Judaism reflected in no small degree their immediate and varying cultural environments.

Among these divergent forms of peripheral Judaism my interest centers most of all in that of Galilee, where, in the midst of a distinctly rural and reactionary Jewish community, many of the traditions, doctrines, and cultural and cultic institutions of early Judaism, which Normative Judaism had long discarded, seem to have persisted and to have contributed much to, and even to have found renewed vitality in, nascent Christianity. As I see it, Christianity was at first only another form of peripheral Judaism, and one much closer in antecedents and content to Normative Judaism than is usually realized or even suspected. To understand both Judaism and Christianity aright, and the latter even more than the former, I am convinced that a thorough study must be made of Galilean Judaism and of its relations, on the one hand, to Normative Judaism, and, on the other hand, to Christianity in its earliest period. It is my further conviction that a right understanding of both Judaism and Christianity in their historic relationship will contribute much, very much, to the constructive coordination of these two intimately related world religions, to the clarification of their true messages and goals, to their indispensable cooperation for the spiritual salvation of mankind, and, for us most immediately, to the spiritual enrichment of American life and culture.

For earnest study through the years has made clear to me that what is fundamental and eternal in Christianity is what it has derived from Judaism, its parent. What Hellenism and other cultures have superimposed upon it seems to me largely secondary and non-essential. Furthermore, in one fundamental respect Christianity is the indispensable complement of Judaism. Judaism is in basic principle and in spirit definitely a universalistic religion: a universalistic religion, however, upon the practical program of which the circumstances of history have imposed the limitations and inhibitions of a firmly rooted and persistent nationalism. Christianity, on the other hand, is in every respect a universalistic religion which transcends in character, organization, and program all the implications, restrictions, and compulsions of nationalism.

In principle it has been Judaism's task, from the time of Deutero-Isaiah, to bring to the world the knowledge of the one universal God, to win all mankind to His way of life, to promote democracy, justice, peace, and brotherhood, and thus to enable men and nations to find the salvation which then and at all times the world has been so eagerly, so desperately, seeking. This principle, this truth, this way of life and faith, Judaism has been proclaiming in doctrine and prayer for twenty-five hundred years. But upon a positive and aggressive program of realization of it by Judaism, Jewish religious nationalism, revived and enforced by Ezra and Nehemiah about the middle of the fifth century B.C.E., rigidly particularistic and isolationist in principle and application, has imposed a positive and compelling limitation and inhibition. Viewed from one angle this was indeed a fortunate, perhaps even a providential, circumstance of history; for it, far more than aught else, has kept the Jewish people alive, preserved its integrity, and, with the Jewish people as its bearer, has enabled Judaism, too, to persist, to live vitally and creatively and to continue to utter its message of life and to bear testimony by its very existence and by its word to the one, universal, eternal God.

But at the same time it has made it totally impossible for Judaism to become an actively propagandistic, and still less a conversionist religion, to formulate and determinedly pursue a program of winning all nations and all mankind to positive and concrete acceptance of its teaching and its faith, and to living in conformity with God's way of life, revealed through Israel's prophets. Even with the eventual and not too long delayed partial modification of the program of Ezra and Nehemiah and the inevitable softening of its extreme particularism and isolationism, the other nations and peoples could not, in principle and doctrine, attain to a position in the sight of God and in the actual life of the world on a par with Israel, the "kingdom of priests and the holy nation." Working from such a premise, Israel could not possibly win the world to the way and worship of the one, true God and bring to it that salvation which Israel had been the first to proclaim.

And so, I believe, still through the workings of providence, this task of converting the world devolved upon Christianity. Judaism's mission is still to proclaim in unfaltering tones the eternal truth of the one, living God in all its far reaching implications. Christianity's mission is to enforce this truth, to win the entire world to it. Christianity's *raison d'être,* its historic vocation, is to bring the message of Judaism to actual realization. Whatever is essential and eternal in Christianity is Jewish through and through. Christianity is still, in inner truth, naught but a-normative, peripheral Judaism, precisely as it was at the beginning. Divested of the external trappings of its own Hellenistic mythology and ritual, it is essentially Judaism, Judaism stripped of nationalist, isolationist wrappings, reverting in very large measure to its form and expression of the pre-Ezranic period, and seeking to make real and vital the vision and the message of the one, universal God and the world encompassing democratic life, which Judaism first proclaimed. The mission of Christianity is the complement of the mission of Judaism. Each without the other is incomplete, unreal, and unrealizable. Each is indispensable to the other. Alone, by itself, neither can fulfil its God-appointed destiny and save the world. Together, understanding each other, trusting each other, working together as partners in destiny, as loving mother and devoted daughter, they can and must bring to fulfilment the all embracing beneficent purpose of the one God of all the world.

This is my conviction, growing out of a half-century of earnest and sincere thought and study. This is my faith. And to the systematic formulation of this faith and to its dissemination I have set myself for the remainder of my days. This I conceive to be my ultimate life work. To this, I believe sincerely, God has called me. And though outwardly I seem to have drifted into it, even as I have indicated, now that, from the vantage point of advancing years and with steadily expanding perspective, I can look backward and view my life and my preparation for service as a whole, I cannot but be convinced that God's hand has been in it, that He has guided my preparation and has made me whatever I am today.

And even today I stand only on the threshold of my service. I pray that I may be granted to carry it on a little further. But I know that the goal is far too vast for me to reach alone. I pray also therefore, that there may be others to carry on after me, a few disciples of the word perhaps and many more disciples of the spirit, day by day, year by year, bringing the goal a little nearer to realization. One God, one world, one humanity, and Judaism, in both its Jewish and its Christian forms, its herald and its guide. This is the service of God. In this service I have sought to be an earnest and a humble worker. I trust and I pray that in this service I have kept faith with God, with Israel, with my colleagues and my students, and with mankind.

BIOGRAPHICAL SKETCHES

CLARENCE E. PICKETT

Born Cissna Park, Illinois, 1884; studied at Penn College, Hartford Theological Seminary, and the Harvard Divinity School; married and has two daughters; ordained to ministry of Society of Friends, 1913, he was pastor of the Friends Meeting, Toronto, Canada, 1913–1917, and in Oskaloosa, Iowa, 1917–1919; then secretary, Young Friends Organization of America, 1919–1922; he was professor of Biblical literature, Earlham College, 1923–1929; and executive secretary, American Friends Service Committee, 1929–1950; is now honorary secretary; he is director, United States Committee for Care of European Children and of the Pendle Hill Graduate School; he was recipient in 1939, with Dr. Rufus M. Jones, of the Philadelphia award for services advancing the best interests of the community; appointed a member of the President's Commission on Immigration and Naturalization, 1952.

ORDWAY TEAD

Born in Somerville, Massachusetts, in 1891; graduated from Amherst College; married and has a daughter; Amherst College Fellow, 1912–1914; a member of firm of industrial consultants, 1915–1917; with Bureau of Industrial Research, New York, 1917–1919; in charge of war emergency employment management courses of War Department at Columbia University, 1917–1918; lecturer in personnel administration, Columbia, since 1920; member, department of industry, New York School of Social Work, 1920–1929; editor, business books, McGraw-Hill Book Company, 1920–1925; editor, social and economic books, Harper & Brothers; chairman, Board of Higher Education of New York City; chairman, board of trustees, Briarcliff

Junior College; member, American Economic Association, American Management Association, American Psychology Association, Society for the Advancement of Management; author and editor.

HENRY NORRIS RUSSELL

Born in Oyster Bay, New York, in 1877; studied at Princeton University, King's College, Cambridge University; married and has a son and three daughters; was research assistant with Carnegie Institution, Washington, stationed at Cambridge, England, 1903–1905; went to Princeton in 1905 and until 1908 was an instructor in astronomy, assistant professor, 1908–1911, professor, 1911–1947, director of observatory, 1912–1947, research professor, 1927–1947, emeritus, 1947; research associate, Harvard College observatory since 1947; served as Engineer, Aircraft Service, United States Army, 1918; member, National Academy of Sciences, American Philosophical Society (president, 1931–1932), American Academy of Arts and Sciences American Astronomical Society (president, 1934–1937), American Physical Society; fellow, American Association for the Advancement of Science (president, 1933); member of several foreign scientific academies; recipient of many medals from scientific associations; author and contributor on astronomical and physical topics to scientific journals.

EDWIN GRANT CONKLIN

Born in Waldo, Ohio, in 1863; studied at Ohio Wesleyan University, and The Johns Hopkins University; holds honorary degrees from there and from Yale University, Western Reserve University, University of Pennsylvania, Princeton University; widower; had one son and two daughters; was professor of biology at Ohio Wesleyan, professor of zoology at Northwestern University and University of Pennsylvania; professor of biology at Princeton from 1908–1933, emeritus since 1933, and special lecturer in biology; trustee, Woods Hole Laboratory and Woods Hole Oceanographic Institution; former president, Bermuda Biological Station; to mention only American societies—member, National Academy of Sciences; fellow, American Association for the Advancement of Science (president, 1936), American Academy of Arts and Sciences; member, American Society of Zoologists (president, 1899), Association of American Anatomists, American Society of Naturalists (president, 1912); held position as secretary, vice president, executive officer, American Philosophical Society, was president from 1942–1945 and 1948–1952; vice president (1901–1950), Philadelphia Academy of Natural Sciences; recipient of John J. Carty gold medal and award, National Academy of Sciences, 1943, National Institute of Social Science gold medal, 1943; co-editor, *Biological Bulletin, Journal of Experimental Zoology, Genetics;* author of over two hundred works on heredity, development, education, evolution, etc.

RICHARD McKEON

Born in Union Hill, New Jersey, in 1900; studied at Columbia University, University of Paris, École des Hautes Études; married and has two sons and a daughter; served as apprentice seaman in the United States Navy, 1918; taught philosophy, Greek, and Latin at Columbia University, 1925–1935; has been associated with The University of Chicago since 1934 as visiting professor of history, professor of Greek, professor of philosophy, dean of the Division of Humanities, and in 1937 became distinguished service professor of Greek and philosophy; was a member of the United States delegation to the General Conference of Unesco in Paris, 1946, Mexico City, 1947, Beirut, 1948; United States counselor on Unesco Affairs, American Embassy, Paris, 1947; chairman United Nations Association of Chicago, 1949–1950; member, United States National Commission for Unesco; fellow, Mediaeval Academy of America, American Academy of Arts and Sciences; member, American Philosophical Association (president, Western Division, 1951–1952), American As-

sociation for the Advancement of Science, American Philological
Association, History of Science Society, American Council of Learned
Societies (vice chairman, 1939), member, Board of Directors, Con-
ference on Science, Philosophy and Religion; author and co-author of
books on history, philosophy, etc., *i.e., Freedom and History,* 1952;
member, board of editors, *Classical Philology* and *Journal of the
History of Ideas;* contributor to the *Encyclopedia of the Social
Sciences* and various journals.

ERWIN D. CANHAM

Born in Auburn, Maine, in 1904; studied at Bates College, and
was a Rhodes Scholar at Oxford University; married and has two
daughters; reporter, *Christian Science Monitor,* 1925; covered annual
sessions of the League of Nations Assembly, 1926, 1927, and 1928,
and Ramsay MacDonald's tour in the United States, 1929; was chief
correspondent for the *Christian Science Monitor* at the London
Naval Conference in 1930; correspondent at Geneva, Switzerland,
1930–1932; head of the Washington Bureau, *Christian Science
Monitor,* 1932–1939; general news editor, 1939–1941; managing editor,
1941–1944; since 1945 has been editor of the publication; radio com-
mentator, 1938–1939, 1945–; vice president, American Society of
Newspaper Editors; president, American Society of Newspaper
Editors, 1948–1949; deputy chief, American delegation to the United
Nations Conference on Freedom of Information at Geneva, 1948;
United States delegate to the United Nations General Assembly,
1949; member United States Advisory Commission on Information;
vice-chairman of the United States National Commission for
Unesco; author (with others), *The World at Mid-Century,* 1951.

ELBERT D. THOMAS

Born in Salt Lake City, Utah, in 1883, studied at the University of
Utah (A.B.), University of California (Ph.D.), received honorary
degrees from University of Southern California and University of

Hawaii (LL.D.) and National University (Litt.D.), married and has three daughters; served as missionary for the Church of Jesus Christ of Latter-Day Saints in Japan, 1907–1912; traveled and studied in Asia and Europe, 1912–1913; taught Latin and Greek at the University of Utah from 1914–1916, secretary-registrar from 1917–1921; fellow, political science at the University of California, 1922–1924; professor of political science at the University of Utah, 1924–1933; Oberlaender Award for study in Germany, 1934; member of the United States Senate, 1933–1951; United States High Commissioner Trust Territory of the Pacific Islands, with rank of Ambassador, since 1951; served as Major in the Inspector General's Department, Utah National Guard and the United States Reserves, 1917–1926; member, General Board, Deseret S.S. Union; delegate, United States Senate Interparliamentary Union, Budapest, 1936, Paris, 1937; chairman, Thomas Jefferson Memorial Commission; director, Columbia Institute for the Deaf; appointed United States delegate, International Labor Organization, United Nations, Philadelphia, 1944, Paris, 1945, Montreal, 1946, Geneva, 1947, San Francisco, 1948; member, American Association of University Professors, American Society of International Law (honorary vice president), American Political Science Association (vice president, 1940–1941), Chinese Political and Social Science Association; Council of American Learned Societies, American Oriental Society, Carnegie International Conference of American Professors (1926), Conference of Teachers of International Law, Washington, D.C. (1925–1928), Board of Advisers, Institute of World Affairs; author of *Sukui No Michi* (in Japanese) (1911), *Chinese Political Thought* (1927), *World Unity Through Study of History* (1933), *Thomas Jefferson, World Citizen* (1942), *The Four Fears* (1944), and *This Nation Under God* (1950).

JUDITH BERLIN LIEBERMAN

The daughter of the outstanding Jewish leader, Rabbi Meir Berlin, and wife of Professor Saul Lieberman, was born in Lithuania in 1905. She received her elementary education at a Berlin elementary school, her secondary and college education in New York City. After receiving her B.A. from Hunter College, she did post-graduate work at Columbia University, and the Universities of Berlin and Zurich, where she received the Ph.D. She is the author of *Robert Browning and Hebraism*. Active in educational and social fields, she taught from 1932–1940 at the Mizrachi Teachers' College for Women, Jerusalem, and organized various social projects for the rehabilitation of children under Mizrachi auspices. Returning to the United States in 1940, she has been principal of the Shulamith School for Girls—an institution that pursues a bi-lingual program—English and Hebrew. She has served as National Political Chairman of the Mizrachi Women's Organization of America, and has contributed articles on political and educational issues to *The Mizrachi Woman* and other publications.

CHANNING H. TOBIAS

Born in Augusta, Georgia, in 1882; studied at Paine College, Drew University, Morehouse College; holds honorary degrees from Gammon Theological Seminary, Jewish Institute of Religion, Morehouse College, New School for Social Research, New York University; widower, had two daughters; professor of biblical literature at Paine College, 1905–1911; secretary, student department, National Council, Young Men's Christian Association, 1911–1923; senior secretary, Interracial Services of Y.M.C.A.s, 1923–1946; member, executive committee, Commission on Churches and Race Relations, Field Department, and Committee on Worship of the Federal Council of Churches of Christ in America; director and trustee, Phelps-Stokes Fund; member, board of trustees, Howard University; member, American Section of the Universal Christian Council for Life and Work, Pan-African Congress, Paris, 1921; student deputation that visited European relief areas, 1921; delegate and speaker at the World Conference of Y.M.C.A.'s, Finland, 1926; lectured in Latvia, 1926; associate director, Commission on Interracial Cooperation, 1935–1942; delegate and chairman of the commission on race relations, World Conference of Y.M.C.A.'s, India, 1937; appointed member, National Advisory

Committee on Selective Service, 1940; Joint Army and Navy Committee on Welfare and Recreation, 1941; chairman, board of trustees, Hampton Institute, 1946; trustee, New School for Social Research, 1946; member, President's Committee on Civil Rights, 1946; member, Civilian Committee of the United States Navy, 1946; member, executive committee, World's Committee of Y.M.C.A.; alternate delegate from the United States to the Sixth General Assembly of the United Nations, 1951; member, Board of Managers, American Bible Society; received Harmon award for religious service, 1928; Spingarn Medal, National Association for the Advancement of Colored People, 1948; author of numerous articles.

DAVID de SOLA POOL

Born in London, England, in 1885; studied at Jews' College (London), University of London, University of Berlin, University of Heidelberg, Rabbinerseminar (Berlin); married Tamar Hirshenson, and has a son, Professor Ithiel, and a daughter, Dr. Naomi; minister of the Spanish and Portuguese Synagogue, Shearith Israel, New York City, since 1907; one of the three Jewish representatives appointed to serve on Herbert Hoover's food conservation staff, 1917; vice president, Jewish Welfare Board, field organizer of its welfare work, 1917–1918, and chairman, Committee on Army and Navy Religious Activities and representative of Jewish Army and Navy chaplains to Chief of Chaplains, 1940–1947; appointed one of three American representatives on Zionist Commission to Palestine, 1919; regional director for Palestine and Syria of the Joint Distribution Committee of American Funds for Jewish War Sufferers, 1919–1921; director, Jewish Education Association; president, Young Judea of America, 1915–1919, 1924, 1925; president, New York Board of Jewish Ministers, 1916–1917; president, Union of Sephardic Congregations since 1928; president, Synagogue Council of America, 1938–1940; member, Advisory Committee, National Youth Administration, 1935–1943; author of various volumes and editor and translator of volumes on Hebrew liturgy.

BASIL O'CONNOR

Born in Taunton, Massachusetts, in 1892; graduate, Dartmouth College, Harvard Law School; married and has two daughters; formed law partnership with Franklin D. Roosevelt as Roosevelt & O'Connor in 1925, continuing until Mr. Roosevelt assumed the office of President of the United States in 1933; now senior partner in O'Connor & Farber; chairman, Board of Governors, League of Red Cross Societies, 1946–1950; president, American Red Cross, 1944–1949; president, National Foundation for Infantile Paralysis, Inc.; president, Georgia Warm Springs Foundation; chairman, Board of Trustees, Tuskegee Institute; vice president, National Health Council; officer, director and trustee of numerous other educational, humanitarian and legal institutions.

WILLARD L. SPERRY

Born in Peabody, Massachusetts, in 1882; received B.A. at Olivet College (Michigan); B.A. and M.A. at Oxford University (Rhodes Scholar); M.A. at Yale University; D.D. from Yale University, Amherst College, Brown University, Williams College; S.T.D. Harvard University; Litt.D. Boston University; married and has a daughter; ordained a Congregational minister in 1908 and was pastor of churches in Fall River and Boston until 1922; lecturer and professor of practical theology at Andover Theological Seminary, 1917–1925; dean of the Harvard Divinity School and professor of practical theology since 1922; member, board of preachers, Harvard, since 1921; chairman, board of preachers, and Plummer professor of Christian morals since 1929; dean of National Council on Religion in Higher Education, 1927–1931; has lectured extensively at educational institutions here and abroad; trustee, Vassar College, 1942–1946; fellow, American Academy of Arts and Sciences, 1927; author and frequent contributor to magazines and religious journals.

JULIAN MORGENSTERN

Born in St. Francisville, Illinois, in 1881; studied at University of Cincinnati, Hebrew Union College, University of Berlin, University of Heidelberg; married and has one daughter; ordained as rabbi in 1902; served as rabbi in Lafayette, Indiana, 1904–1907; has been professor of Bible and Semitic languages at Hebrew Union College since 1907, also serving in the capacities of acting-president (1921–1922), and president (1922–1947), and has been president emeritus since 1947; member, Central Conference of American Rabbis (secretary, 1907–1915), American Oriental Society (president, Western branch, 1919–1920, and of general society, 1927–1928), Society of Biblical Literature and Exegesis (president, Midwest branch, 1938–1939, and of general society, 1940–1941), Alumni Association of Hebrew Union College (president, 1916–1918); American vice president, World Union for Progressive Judaism; honorary member, British Society for Old Testament Studies, 1951; author of numerous books on the Bible and Semitics, and contributor to magazines.

INDEX

Abbot, Lyman, 56
Abelard, Peter, 87
Abrahams, Israel, 207
Abramson, Dr. Harold A., 124
Adams, William Wisner, 240-242, 243
Adkinson, Reverend L. G., 53
Administration as moral responsibility, 28-29
Africa, South, 195, 197
Aggression of mass man, 250
Agnostics, 35
Alexander, Will W., 185
Alger, Horatio, pattern of American life, 20
Allegories, 42
American Friends Service Committee, 11, 275
American life, unity from diversity, 176
American National Red Cross, 221
Amherst College, 16
Anabaptism, 234
Andover Creed, 244
Andover Seminary, 231
Anglo-Catholics, 34
Animal development, 47-48
Anthropocentric humanism, 24
Apologia Pro Vita Sua, Cardinal Newman, 247-248
Arabs, 171
Aristotle, 88, 89
Arizona Temple (Mormon), 139
Arnold, Matthew, 75

Assyriology, 260, 261
Atlanta University, 178, 179
Augusta Chronicle, 179
Augusta, Georgia, 177ff.
Autobiography, 78-79

Bacon, Francis, 73, 85
Bacon, Leonard, 36
Baeck, Rabbi Leo, 12
Bakewell, Professor, 238
Balfour Declaration, 215
Barkley, Alben W., 140
Barnett, Lincoln, 124
Bashford, James W., 55
Bates College, 120, 121
Beauty, through arts and in nature, 29
Behavior, trial and error, 69
Bell, William Y., 190
Bennett, Charles, 238
Bergson, Henri, 85
Berlin, Rabbi Meir, 162
Berlin, Rabbi Naphtali-Zvi Yehuda, 160-162
Berry, William, 8
Bethune, Mary McLeod, 185, 187
Bible:
    reading of, 16
        in home, 3-4
    study of, 8
Bismarck, 136
Bloom, Sol, 133
Bowles, Gilbert, 4-5

Boys' clubs, 16
Brandeis, Mr. Justice, 153
Briarcliff Junior College, 24
Brooks, W. K., 54, 73
Brotherhood of Man, 220-221, 222, 229
Brown, Edgar Miles, 259
Brown, John, 52
Brown University, 181
Browning, Robert, 45, 169, 206
Brunschvicg, Léon, 85, 87
Bryan, William Jennings, 56, 140
  Scopes trial, 66
Buber, Martin, 12
Buchenwald, 12
Buddhism and Buddhists, 152, 158
Buddhist temples, 138
Butler, Bishop, 73
Buttz, Dr. Henry Anson, 190

Calculating machines, 70
Calvinism, 231, 244
Cambridge University, 33, 34
  academic degrees, 45
Campbell, Robert L., 180
Canham, Erwin D., 115-127
  biographical sketch, 278
  education of, 120
  family background, 115-118
  illness of mother, 119-120, 121
  religious practices in home, 115-123
  Rhodes scholar, 121
Carey, James B., 188
Carleton College, 15
Carlyle, Thomas, 59-60
Carnegie Institution, 35
Carpetbaggism, 152
Carter, Randall A., 190
Cause and effect, chain of, 65-66
Character, definition of, 48
Chayyim, Rabbi, 160
Chicago, University of, 89-101
Chicago World's Fair, 133, 134, 136
Chinese proverb, 13
Christian Endeavor Society, 6-7
Christian Science, 115-127
  abstinence of members, 117
  Sunday School, 121-122
Christian Science Monitor, 126

Christian theology, Trinitarian creeds, 40
Christianity:
  and nobility of labor, 224
  as peripheral Judaism, 269-272
  future of, 250-251
Christianity and the Social Crisis, Walter
    Raushenbush, 16
Christians and Jews, National Con-
    ference of, 221
Christians, race, and human relations,
    17-18
"Christmas Eve," Robert Browning, 45
Church:
  and state, separation of, 142-143
  case for, 250
  "shopping around for," 249
Churches of Christ in America, National
    Council of, 185
Cicero, on old age, 139
Cincinnati, University of, 258, 259, 260
Civil Rights, President's Committee on,
    186, 187, 188, 189
  Report, 183
Clark, Dr. W. B., 54
Clemens, Samuel, 49
Cleveland, Grover, 140
  on role of U.S. government, 145
Coleridge, Samuel Taylor, 248
Columbia University, 23, 80, 87
  War Emergency Employment Manage-
    ment Courses, 22
Commission on Human Rights, 109
Communist propaganda, 49
Conference of Allied Ministers of Educa-
    tion (CAME), 107
Confession, 78
Confucianism, 142-143
Congregationalism, 231, 239, 240, 243
Congressional committees, 49
Conklin, Belle Adkinson, 53-54
Conklin, Edwin Grant, 47-76
  at Woods Hole, Massachusetts, 54-55
  biographical sketch, 276-277
  books by:
    Direction of Human Evolution, The,
      57
    *Heredity and Environment in the
      Development of Man,* 48

Conklin, Edwin Grant (*cont.*):
  Man: Real and Ideal, 75
  confession of faith, 74-76
  early years, 49-50
  education of, 50-55
  on evolution and creation, 59-64
  on freedom and responsibility, 64-67
  on mechanism and finalism, 67-72
  on nature and the supernatural, 72-74
  professor, 52-57
    Johns Hopkins University, 54-55
    Northwestern University, 55-56
    Rust University, 53-54
    University of Pennsylvania, 56
  religion and church relations, 57-59
Conscientious objectors, 249
Creation, evolution and, 59-64
Creative synthesis, 62, 63
Creeds, Trinitarian, 40, 41
Crime, Clarence Darrow, 65
Cry, the Beloved Country, 27
Cultures:
  humanistic aspects of, 110
  interrelations of, 102-106
Cybernetics, 70

Dalai Lama priests, 152
Daniels, Jonathan, 187
Darrow, Clarence, 65
  Scopes trial, 66
Darwin, Charles, 59, 60, 71, 72, 73
  theory of natural selection, 60, 68
Darwinism, 135
Davis, John D., 66-67
Declaration of Independence, 136, 142
Dedication, triumphant, 30
Delaware, Ohio, 49, 50
Democracy, 141, 222
  and moral responsibility, 29
  meanings of, 109-110
  merit system and, 222-223
Democracy in a World of Tensions, 109
Democritus, 89, 111
Descartes, René, 85, 87
Determinism, absolute, theory of, 65-67
Dewey, John, 20, 82, 83, 89, 92, 111
Dickinson, G. Lowes, 20

Dinwoody, Henry, 144
Divine call, 257
Dixon, W. MacNeill, 25
Dooley, Mr., 49
Drama, religious, 250
Drew Theological Seminary, 181, 190
Dreyfus case, 208
Dunbar, Helen Flanders, 124

Earlham College, 11
Ecclesiasticism, 250
Eclecticism, theological, 248
Ecumenical movement, 248
Eddington, Sir Arthur, 63
Eddy, Mary Baker, 121, 122, 125, 126
Edinburgh Conference on Faith and Order, 248
Education:
  and moral responsibility, 29
  from biological viewpoint, 48
  general, new forms of, 97-101, 102
  in Georgia, 178
  knowledge through, 225
  Negro, 191-192
Education, Conference of Allied Ministers of, 107
Eisenhower, Dwight David, 155
Electron, behavior of, 42
Eliot, Charles W., 140, 246, 247
Embree, Edwin R., 185
Emerson, Ralph Waldo, 206
Emotions and Bodily Changes, Helen F. Dunbar, 124
Environment, heredity and, 48
Eppstein, Rabbi Michael, 162
Error, probability of, 66
Ether, elastic solid, 44
Evangelization of world, 8-9
Evansville College, 53
Evil:
  breaking the cycle of, 14
  goodness and, 25
  Quakers' views of, 12-13
Evolution:
  and creation, 59-64
  religion and, 55
Extremes, avoiding, 65

Fabian socialism, 209
Farming, 2-3, 9
Faulkner, Alfred, 190
Field, Marshall, Foundation, 185
Final Faith, The, W. D. McKenzie, 10
Finalism, mechanism and, 67-72
Finkelstein, Louis, 219
Fitch, Albert Parker, 244
Floyd, Silas X., 177
Force, use of, 14
Foss, Martin M., 22
Fox, George, 13
Frazer, Sir James G., 268
Freedom, and responsibility, 64-67
Freud, Sigmund, 92
Friedlaender, Michael, 207
Friend, The, 7
Friends Service Committee, American, 11, 275
Fundamentalism, 246, 264

Galilee, peripheral Judaism in, 269
Galsworthy, John, 20
Gandhi, Mahatma, 30, 141, 192-195
Georgia, occupational patterns in, 179
Georgia State College for Negroes, 178
German Jews, 172
Germans in Illinois, 2
Germany, and Versailles Treaty, 14
Gettysburg Address, 49
Ghetto, London, 210
Gilbert, John Wesley, 181
Gilson, Étienne, 87
God, 75
    "absolute" knowledge of, 42
    and racial segregation, 183
    as personal being, 43
    Christian Science view of, 122, 123, 124-126
    idea of, 242
    Jewish-Christian, 142, 270-272
    Spinoza's view of, 84
    Tead's view of, 25-27
    use of word, 12, 251
    various names for, 76
    Whitehead's view of, 63-64
Golden Bough, The, Sir James G. Frazer, 268

Golden Rule, 192
Goodwill, self-giving, 14
Gossip, 175-176
Gracious living, 30
Grant, Heber J., 144, 148
Green Pastures, The, 27

Habits, establishment of, 48
Hadley, Dr. Stephen, 7
Haggadic literature, 176
Hamlett, J. Arthur, 190
Hankey, Donald, 43
Hankinson, Mrs. M. Z., 180-181
Happiness, labor and, 224
Hartford Theological Seminary, 10
Hawaiian Temple (Mormon), 139
Health of mankind, 226-228
Hebrew, study of, 8
Hebrew Union College, 255-258, 266-268
Heidelberg University, 260, 262
Hellenism, 270
Henderson, Lawrence J., 71
    Order of Nature, The, 72
Heredity, 64-65
    and environment, 48
Herzl, Theodor, 208
Hinduism, 157
Hinks, Arthur, 35
Hirai, Kinza, 133
History, 77
    research, 78
    study of, 93
    transformed into fiction, 77
Hitler, Adolf, 14
Hodges, Dean, 239
Holidays, Jewish, 205, 255
Holland, J. G., 224
Holsey, Bishop Lucius H., 190
Hope, John, 179
Hudson, Thomson Jay, 17
Human being, definition of, 47
Human relations, Christians and, 17-18
Human Rights:
    Commission on, 109
    Universal Declaration of, 109
Human Situation, The, W. M. Dixon, 25
Humanism, 247
    scientific, 24

Humanities:
  and social sciences, 92-96
  shift from science to, 197
Hume, David, 92
Humor, sense of, 49
Hunton, William A., 185
Hutchins, Robert Maynard, 89
Huxley, on teleology, 71-72
Hyde, Orson, 138
Hypnosis, 124

Ibsen, Henrik, 20
Ideas, American attitudes toward, 85-86
Imagination, repeated forcible expansion
  of, 39
India, 192-195
Individual:
  freedom and, 64-67
  vs. aggression of mass man, 250
Individualism, rugged, 20
Industrial counseling, 21
Industrial Revolution, 134
Infantile Paralysis, National Foundation
  for, 221
Infinite numbers, 41
Infinity, philosophy of, 40-41
Instincts in Industry, Ordway Tead, 17
Insurance, unemployment, 21
Intelligence, a moral obligation, 19
Intolerance, racial, 17-18, 183
Irrationality, cult of, 251
Israel (*see also* Palestine):
  Land of, return to, 162

James, William, 20, 248
Japan, 134, 135, 147, 157
  baseball in, 148-149
  conference of religious sects, 149-150
  Friends' Girls School, Tokyo, 4, 5
  women's suffrage in, 144
Jeans, Sir James, 39
Jefferson, Wilson, 177-178
Jeremiah, 176
Jerusalem, 138, 169
  Wailing Wall, 197, 216
Jesus, 241
  and problems of everyday life, 242

Jesus (*cont.*):
  sacrifice of, 14
  use of word in religious talk, 12
Jesus Christ and the Social Question,
  Francis Greenwood Peabody, 17
Jewish Agency, 170
Jewish ceremonials, 255-256
Jewish-Christian ethic, 250
Jewish-Christian God, 142, 270-272
Jewish Education Association, New York
  City, 216
Jewish holidays, 205, 255
Jews:
  and Torah, 172-174
  contemptuous remarks against, 203-
    204
  English, 201
  German, 172
Jews' College, London, 207, 211
Johnson, James Weldon, 186
Joint Distribution Committee in Syria
  and Palestine, 215
Jones, Rufus M., 275
Jones, Sam, 180
Judaism, 12
  history of, 268
  peripheral, 269-272

Kellogg-Briand Peace Pact, 214
Kingdom of God, 29
Kohler, Dr. Kaufmann, 266, 267-268

Labor audits, 17, 21
Labor, concepts of, 222-224
LaGuardia, Fiorella, 23
Land Grant College Act, 155
Language:
  challenge of words, 251
  study of, 92-93
  teaching of, 102-106
Lanier, Sidney, 177
Law of Psychic Phenomena, The, Thom-
  son Jay Hudson, 17
Layman's Movement, 250
League of Nations, 214
League to Enforce Peace, 140
Lewis, Rosa, 8

Liberalism, tradition of, in United States, 86
Lieberman, Judith Berlin, 159-176
  and Mizrachi Women's Organization, 174-175
  biographical sketch, 279-280
  education of, 168-170
  father of, 164-167, 168
  grandfather of, 159-162
  grandmother of, 162-164
  in Jerusalem, 169-171
  mother of, 166-167
  on study of Torah, 172-174
  principal, Shulamith School for Girls, 175
  return to United States, 171
Life, elemental properties of, 62-63
Light-waves, theory of, 44
Lippmann, Walter, 40
Loeb, Jacques, 65
London ghetto, 210-211
Lost in the Stars, 27
Love, and human relations, 29
Lowell, Lawrence, 245
Lyons, Judson W., 178

Magnes, Judah Leon, 259-260
Man, mass, aggression of, 250
Martin, H. Newell, 54
Marxism, 135
Massachusetts Committee on Unemployment, 21
Mayan monuments, 137
McKenzie, Dr. William Douglas, 10, 12
McKeon, Richard, 77-114
  and Unesco, 107-109
  biographical sketch, 277-278
  education of, 80-87
  on educational problems, 89-101, 113, 114
  on philosophic problems, 80-89, 113, 114
  on political problems, 102-110, 113, 114
  professor:
    Columbia University, 87-88
    University of Chicago, 89-101
McKinley, William, 178

Measurability, limited, theory of, 66
Mechanism, and finalism, 67-72
Meditation, 29
Meiklejohn, Alexander, 246
Meldola, Raphael, 201
Mendes, Frederick de Sola, 202
Mendes, H. Pereira, 202, 212
Merit system, 222-223
  and democracy, 222-223
Metcalf, Henry C., 22
Methodist Book of Discipline, The, 57
Methodist Church, 52, 53, 55, 56, 57, 115-118
  Colored, 189-190
  "Report of Southeastern Jurisdiction of Women's Society of Christian Service," 183-184
Michelson, Albert, 61
Mielziner, Dr. Moses, 257
Militarism, 244
Milton, John, 64
Ministry:
  as profession, 9, 17-20
  "call" to, 52
  lay, 18
Missionary movement, 8-9
Mizrachi communities, Palestine, 170, 171
Mizrachi Organization, 174
  Women's membership, 174-175
Mizrachi Teachers' Training School for Girls, 171
Mohammedanism, 157
Moore, Bishop Arthur J., 181
Moore's Hill College, 53
Moorland, Jesse E., 185
Moral responsibility, key words of, 28-29
Morehouse College, 179
Morgenstern, Julian, 253-272
  as college president, 268
  as college professor, 266-268
  becomes rabbi, 257
  biographical sketch, 283
  childhood of, 254-257
  education of, 256-259
  family background, 254
  in Lafayette, Indiana, 263-266
  marriage of, 263

Morgenstern, Julian (*cont.*):
    Ministers' Association, member of, 264-266
    paper on "The Virgin Birth," 264-265
    student in Germany, 259-263
Morley, Christopher, 30
Mormons, 129-158
    amnesty gained by, 144
    care for children and youths, 153
    chaplains, in World War I, 150
    cooperatives, 144
    home missions, 146
    Meeting House, 131
    missionaries, 148
    Patriarchial blessing, 143
    Pioneers, 131
    Relief Society Sisters, 144-146
    Salt Lake Temple, 136-139
    storage of wheat by, 144-145
Moton, Robert R., 185
Mott, John R., 185
Mourner's bench, 58
Mueller, Johannes Peter, 84
Myers, P. V. N., 259
Mysteries, 42
    artificial, 43-44

National Association for the Advancement of Colored People, 185, 187, 188
National Conference of Christians and Jews, 221
National self-interest, 136
National Urban League, 185
Natural selection, theory of, 60, 68
Nature, and the supernatural, 72-74
Negroes:
    classes of, 184
    education of:
        in Georgia, 178
        Rust University, 53-54
Neighborhood idea, 20
New York School of Social Work, 23
Newman, Cardinal, 247-248
Newman, Henry Stanley, 7
Niebuhr, Reinhold, 19
Nietzsche, Friedrich, 241
Niles, David K., 189

Nisei, 147
Non-resistance, Tolstoi's doctrine of, 243
Non-violence, and peace, 29
Northland College, 15
Northwestern University, 55-56
Noyes, Jesse Smith, Foundation, 185
Numbers, transfinite, 40-41

Ockham, William of, 87
O'Connor, Basil, 219-229
    biographical sketch, 282
    home background of, 220
    on education, 225
    on health of mankind, 226-228
    on merit system and labor, 222-224
    work in humanitarian organizations, 221
Ohio Wesleyan University, 50, 55
Olivet College, 231, 234
Ordination, validity of, 45
Organized religion, 17-19, 26
    of tomorrow, 27
Origin of Species, Charles Darwin, 59
Orlando, Florida, 183
"Overbeliefs," 24, 27
Over-simplification, vice of, 233
Oxford University, 143, 236-239
    academic degrees, 45

Pacifism, 30, 244
Paine College, 181
Paine Institute, 180
Palestine, 138, 169-171, 192-193, 215-217
Panic of 1893, 134
Parker, Carleton H., 17
Passover, 255
Pastoral care, psychological interpretation of, 250
Paton, J. L., 293
Peabody, Francis Greenwood, 17
Pearl Harbor, 135
Penn College, Iowa, 7, 9, 10
Pennsylvania, University of, 56
Perry, James DeWolfe, 239
Perry, Leslie, 188
Personnel Administration: Its Principles and Practice, Metcalf and Tead, 22

Phelps-Stokes Fund, 185
Phenomena:
  incompletely understood, 42
  physicists and, 61
Philadelphia, Declaration of, 134
Phillips, Charles H., 190
Philosophic scholarship, problems of, 79
Philosophy, 79-89
  French, 85-87
  literature and courses of 1920's, 82-85
Physical phenomena, knowledge of, 39
Physical reality, 38
Physicists, and phenomena, 61
Physics, and ultimate reality, 39
Pickett, Clarence E., 1-14
  abroad, 11-12
  American Friends Service Committee,
    11
  as college professor, 11
  as minister, 10-11
  biographical sketch, 275
  brothers and sisters, 1-2, 4-5
  education of, 5, 7-10
  father of, 2-4
  leader in Young Friends' Movement,
    11
  mother of, 1-2
  vocations available to, 9
Pickett, Minnie, 1-2, 4-5
Pilgrims, descendants of, 36
Pitts, James, 6
Plato, 88, 89
Pompey, 137
Pool, David de Sola, 201-217
  biographical sketch, 281
  books that influenced, 206
  education of, 206-207, 208-209, 211-
    212
  home background of, 201ff.
  in New York City, 212
  in Palestine, 215-217
  influence of arts on, 207-208
  ministry of, 212
  persons who influenced, 207
  religious views of, 213-217
  World Wars I and II, 214-215
  writings of, 213-214
  Zionist interests of, 208-209

Pool, Tamar Hirshenson de Sola, 212
Porter, Frank, 239
Prayer in the home, 3-4
Presbyterian Church, Confession of Faith,
    32
Probability of error, 66
Psychodynamics and the Allergic Patient,
    Dr. Harold Abramson, 124
Psychosomatic medicine, 124
Punishment, crusades of, 13
Purdy, Alexander, 8
Purdy, Ellison R., 9-10

Quakers (*see also* Society of Friends):
  concerned, 7
  "sense of the meeting," 247
Quanta, 38
Quest of the Historical Jesus, Albert
    Schweitzer, 142

Race Relations, American Council on, 185
Race relations, Channing Tobias on,
    182ff.
Racial intolerance, 17-18
Racial segregation, 182-183
Randall, James Rider, 177
Raushenbush, Walter, 16
Realism:
  of Quakers, 14
  social, 20
Red Cross, American National, 221
Reform Judaism, 255-256, 263
Reissig, Dr. Frederick E., 188
Relativity, and absolute simultaneity, 40
Religion:
  and evolution, 55
  "high," and social responsibility, 29
  ideal personal, 76
  organized, 17-19, 26
  orthodoxy of, 250
  public profession of, 58
  science and, 58
Religionists, professional, 18-19
Religious Education Movement, 250
Responsibility:
  freedom and, 64-67
  heredity and, 65, 66
  relative, principle of, 66

Retaliation, effects of, 14
Revival meetings, 6, 57-58
Rhodes Scholarship, 121, 143, 236-239
Robin, Léon, 87
Rodgers, Henry Wade, 55
Rogers, Robert W., 190
Roosevelt, Eleanor, 118
Roosevelt, Franklin D., 140, 186-187
Roosevelt, Franklin D., Jr., 187-188
Roosevelt, Theodore, 34
Rosenwald, Julius, 191-192
Ruskin, John, 206
Russell, Henry Norris, 31-45
  at Princeton, 35, 37
  biographical sketch, 276
  children of, 35, 36
  church membership, 35-38
  education of, 33-34
  family background, 31-32
  religious background, 32-33
  religious convictions, 38-45
Russell, Mrs. Henry Norris, 34, 35
Rust, Reverend R. S., 53
Rust University, 53-54

Salt Lake City, 131
Salt Lake Temple, 136-139
Salvation Army, 205
Sanday, Canon, 247
Schieffelin, William Jay, 185
Schiller, on religion, 26
Scholarship:
  and teaching, 112
  fellowship of, 45
Scholasticism, 89, 292
Schweitzer, Albert, 242
Science:
  and religion, 58
  and the absolute, 65-67
  concerns of, 67
  ethics of, 74
  shift from, to humanities, 197
  social uses of, 29
Science and Health with Key to the Scriptures, Mary Baker Eddy, 121, 125

Science and Theology, History of the Warfare of, Andrew White, 32
Scientific humanism, 24
Scopes, John T., 66
Seder service, 255
Segregation, Channing Tobias on, 182-183
Segregation in the Nation's Capital, National Committee on, 185
Semitic languages, 260
Sephardic Jews, 201
Sermons, 250-251
Shaw, G. B., 20
Shinto, 133, 157
  priests, 152
  shrine, 137
Shishkin, Boris, 188
Shulamith School for Girls, 175
Sin, as fact, 19
Sinnott, Edmund W., quoted, 123-124
Smith, George Albert, 148
Smith, Joseph, 138, 142, 157
Smythe, Dr. Newman, 240
Social realism, 20
Socialism, Fabian, 209
Society of Friends, 2ff., 18
  American Friends Service Committee, 11
  development of, 6
  in England, 7
  ministry, 10-11
  views on evil, 12-13
  Young Friends' Movement, 11
Socrates, 89
  on excess, 30
Sola, Abraham de, 201
Sola, Samuel de, 201
Soldier Education Bill, 155
Sophocles, on labor, 222
South Africa, 195, 197
South End House, Boston, 20
Southern Regional Council, 185
Speer, Robert E., 235
Sperry, Willard L., 231-251
  and doctrine of non-resistance, 243-244
  at Andover Theological Seminary, 244

Sperry, Willard L. (*cont.*):
  before Association of Congregational
    Ministers, 239-240
  biographical sketch, 282
  books that influenced, 234
  Dean of Harvard Divinity School, 245-
    247
  death of friend, 235
  education of, 234-240
  father of, 231, 236
  in Boston, Massachusetts, 243-244
  in Fall River, Massachusetts, 240-243
  mother of, 231
  religious background, 231, 232-234
  religious ideas of, 248-251
  Rhodes Scholar, 236-239
  Y.M.C.A. traveling student secretary,
    235-236
Sperry, Mrs. Willard L., 238
Spinoza, 82, 83, 84, 87, 111, 113
Spiritual, meaning of term, 48
Spy scares, 49
State, church and, separation of, 142-143
Stokes, Anson Phelps, 185
Strauss, Rabbi Leon, 254
Streeter, Canon, 237, 238
Student Volunteer Movement, 8-9
Sun Yat-Sen, 141
Supernatural, nature and, 72-74
Survival, universal goal, 69
Swastika sign, 138

Taft, William Howard, 140
Talmud, 161
  new edition of, 166
Talmudic Encyclopedia, 166
Taoism, 158
Teaching:
  profession, 9
  scholarship and, 112
Tead, Ordway, 15-30
  author, *Instincts in Industry,* 17
  biographical sketch, 275-276
  Board of Higher Education, New York
    City, 23-24
  books that influenced, 16-17
  co-author, *Personnel Administration:
    Its Principles and Practice,* 22

Tead, Ordway (*cont.*):
  editor, 22-23
  education of, 16-17
  family of, 15-16
  industrial counselor, 21-22
  labor relations training for War De-
    partment, 22
  leader of boys' clubs, 16
  on moral responsibility, 28-29
  reasons for withdrawing from minis-
    try, 17-20
  secretary of Massachusetts Committee
    on Unemployment, 21
  teacher:
    Columbia University, 23
    New York School of Social Work,
      23
  theistic view of, 24-27
  trustee, Briarcliff Junior College, 24
Tead, Mrs. Ordway, 24
Technical assistance, 3
Teleology, Huxley on, 71-72
Temples, religious, 136-140
Terminology, and religion, 11-12
Terry, General, 186-187
Theological eclecticism, 248
Theological orthodoxy, 250
Theology:
  contributions by physics to, 39
  new, 251
Thomas, Edna Harker, 134, 148
Thomas, Elbert D., 129-158
  author:
    Thomas Jefferson, World Citizen,
      141, 143
    *World Unity Through Study of His-
      tory,* 138, 154
  biographical sketch, 278-279
  childhood memories, 143-147
  during World Wars, 135, 146-147, 150,
    155
  education of, 132, 135, 140-141
  home and family, 132*ff.*
  in Germany, 151, 155
  in Japan, 134, 135, 141
  in Senate, 154-155
  influence of great men on, 140
  instructor at University of Utah, 154

Thomas, Elbert D. (*cont.*):
  messages to Japanese people, 135
  missionary to Japan, 134
  Mormon background, 131*ff.*
  Oberleander award, 151
  on experience vs. book training, 153-154
  on international relations, 141
  Oriental courses, 155
  temple experiences, 136-140
  travels after World War II, 155-156
Thomas Jefferson, World Citizen, Elbert D. Thomas, 141, 143
Thomson, J. J., 33
Thucydides, on history, 77
Tobias, Channing H., 177-199
  as teacher, 181
  background in Georgia, 177-181
  biographical sketch, 280-281
  daughters of, 199
  education of, 180-181
  family background, 179-180
  meeting with Gandhi, 192-195
  on classes of Negroes, 185
  on race relationships, 182*ff.*
  organizations associated with, 185
  persons who have influenced, 185-189
  religious influences on, 189-199
  Y.M.C.A. work, 192
Tobias, Mrs. Channing H., 199
Tokyo, Friends' Girls School in, 4
Tolstoi, Count Leo, 241, 243
Torah, 160, 161, 162, 164, 165, 172-174
Tories, 35
Tradition, validity of, 45
Transfinite numbers, 40-41
Trial and error behavior, 69
Trinitarian creeds, 40, 41
Trotsky, Leon, 141
Truman, Harry S., 155, 156, 188-189
  and civil rights, 183
Tuskegee Institute, 191, 221
Twain, Mark (*see* Clemens, Samuel)
Tyrrell, Father, 249

Uncertainty principle, 38, 66
Unemployment:
  insurance, 21

Unemployment (*cont.*):
  Massachusetts Committee on, 21
Unesco, 107, 277
  Committee on Human Rights, 109
  General Conferences of, 107-108
United Nations, Charter of, 107
United Nations Educational, Scientific and Cultural Organization (Unesco), 107-109 (*see also* Unesco)
Universal Declaration of Human Rights, 109
Universe and Dr. Einstein, The, Lincoln Barnett, 124
Utah:
  coal mining industry in, 150
  memories of, 143-147
  University of, 140-141, 146

Valentine, Robert G., 21
Versailles Treaty, 14
Virgin Birth, 232, 264-265

Walker Brothers, Salt Lake City, 132
Walker, Charles T., 178-179
Walker, Dr. George Williams, 180-181, 182
Walker, Williston, 239
Wallace, Alfred Russell, 60
Wallas, Graham, 20
Walton, George, 177
War, moral dilemmas presented by, 244
Warsaw, Jews in, 173
Washington, Booker T., 191, 194
Washington, D.C., 129-130
Watson, William, 43
Webb, Beatrice and Sidney, 20
Wells, Emaline B., 145
Wells, H. G., 20, 206
Welsh miners, in Utah, 150
Whewell, William, 73
White, Andrew, 32
White, Walter, 187, 188-189
Whitehead, Alfred North, 25, 63-64, 233
Whittaker, Sir Edmund, 64
Williams, Albert Rhys, 16
Williams, Robert S., 190

Willkie, Wendell L., 185
Wilson, Charles E., 185, 189
Wilson, T. Woodrow, 140, 145, 146
Wise, Dr. Isaac M., 257
Wise, Rabbi Stephen S., 186
Women, role of, 29
Women's suffrage, 143-144
Woodbridge, Frederick J. E., 82-83
Woodman, Charles M., 10
Woods Hole, Massachusetts, biological
    center at, 54, 55, 277
Woods, Robert A., 20
Words:
    challenge of, 251
    key, of moral responsibility, 28-29
Work relations, 28
World dominion, 105
World War I, conflicts during, 80, 111
World War II, and cultural interrelations,
    102, 106
World wars, and the Jews, 167

Worship, enriching of, 250
Wright, Richard R., 178

Yale Divinity School, 239-240
Yeshiva of Volozhin, 160
Young, Brigham, 144, 145
Young Friends' Movement, 11
Young Judea, 212
Young Men's Christian Association, 185,
    235
Young Women's Christian Association,
    185

Zion, Lovers of, 161
Zionism, 208-209
    ancient Biblical, 216
    orthodox branch of movement, 174
    Religious, 165
Zionist Commission, 215
Zionist Congress, Zurich (1937), 213
Zoroastrianism, 158